The  Guide to

1001 PLACES TO GO
TO IN THE
SCHOOL HOLIDAYS

The **Wall's** Guide to

1001 PLACES TO GO
TO IN THE
SCHOOL HOLIDAYS

Selected by
George Thaw

Good Books

Published in association with Birds Eye Wall's Limited
by Good Books (GB Publications Limited)
Lagard Farm, Whitley, Melksham, Wilts SN12 8RL

A CIP catalogue record for the book is available from the British Library.

ISBN 0 946555 32 X

Illustrations by Jack Pennington
Designed by Design/Section, Frome
Printed and bound in England by Cox & Wyman, Reading

The publishers wish to thank all the venues featured for their cooperation in supplying
details of their attractions and facilities.

Contents

A few words from Wall's...

We are delighted to be sponsoring this invaluable guide which, for parents and children alike, will open up a world of activities and attractions you would never have thought possible. We are sure that many of the surprising activities selected in this guide will mean that school holidays will be better than ever.

Wall's ice cream has always been a family favourite - adding pleasure to many an occasion. In the same way, we hope that this guide will become a source of many pleasurable activities for you and your family.

John Sharpe
Chairman
Birds Eye Wall's Limited

Introduction

The school holidays children remember are the active ones when pleasures are shared with all the family. And there are lots of pleasurable experiences awaiting you in this guide, whether it is out and out fun you are after, or a little enjoyable learning.

Those attractions in each region which seem to me particularly unusual or interesting, or especially good value for money, are indicated by the Cornetto cone symbol. You will no doubt discover your own favourites.

The details of the 1001 places listed were bang up to date as the book rolled hot off the press, but life is a moveable feast so remember that perhaps the most important item is the telephone number of each venue. A quick call can give you up-to-the-minute information about what's on special offer that very day, or if something has happened to alter the opening times, prices or access. If, for instance, you're expecting to see the sea lions being fed and they've gone off to the seaside for the day, you'll be told and can make your visit another time.

The call ahead is a sensible precaution too if one of your party is disabled. The degree of access is important for their enjoyment, and much depends on the extent or nature of the disability. In many of the places listed the folk running the attractions will make sure there is someone on hand to help, if warned in advance. And there are often price concessions for the disabled.

Similarly, if you are heading out on a railway trip, check the timetable to make sure you don't miss the train. If you are venturing into woodland or rough heathland, see that you wear solid shoes. If you are going down into caves or up mountains, wrap up for it can be cool and damp underground or on high.

Conditions vary too at the turnstiles. In some places Family Ticket means two adults and two children, in others it might be one adult and up to four children. Again, it's best to get it straight before you go.

Then there is only one thing left to do...have fun.

Guide to Symbols and Explanatory Notes

♟	Author's choice of special venue
⊙	Opening times
£	Admission price
SC	Senior citizen/concessions
f/t	Special-rate family ticket available
✳	Special facilities/features
/A\	Nearest main road or general direction
▦	Nearest railway station
⊖	Nearest Underground or metro station
BH	Bank Holiday
BHM	Bank Holiday Monday
♿	Access for disabled
♿(res)	Restricted access for disabled
⛺	Picnic site
☕	Beverages and snacks or cafeteria
¶◎¶	Restaurant
🛍	Shop
℗	Parking (free or at a nominal rate)
NT	National Trust Property
NTS	National Trust for Scotland property
EH	English Heritage site

- The attractions are listed alphabetically within each of the 17 regions. The general index will help you locate a venue if you cannot find it in a particular region.

- It is advisable to confirm opening times, prices, directions and any special requirements (such as access for the disabled) before setting out.

- Months shown for opening times are inclusive: eg Apr-Oct = 1 April to 31 October.

- Most venues are closed for Christmas Day, Boxing Day and New Year's Day, even if they are open at other times during the Christmas/New Year period.

- Closing times and last admissions can vary, especially in the winter season, depending on weather conditions and on how busy the venue is on any given day.

- Boat trips, flying demonstrations (birds or aircraft), pony trekking and most other outdoor activities are 'weather permitting'.

- Dogs, other than guide dogs, are not allowed at most venues, whether the attractions are indoors or out. Telephone first if you are thinking of taking your dog.

- Along with details of the nearest railway station is an indication of the distance or average walking time. Some minor stations have an infrequent service, particularly at weekends.

- Where the admission price for children specifies a particular age level (eg 5+), those under the limit are usually admitted free.

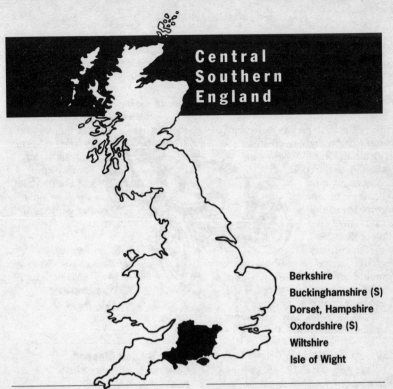

Central Southern England

Berkshire
Buckinghamshire (S)
Dorset, Hampshire
Oxfordshire (S)
Wiltshire
Isle of Wight

Abbotsbury Swannery

New Barn Rd, Abbotsbury,
Weymouth DT3 4JG
☎ 0305 871684

The world's only managed
gathering of mute swans, where
you can see them nest in a colony.
Walks through ancient reed beds,
the oldest duck decoy in the country
and Ugly Duckling activity trail for
children. Sub-tropical gardens and
rural museum in nearby tithe barn.

🕐 Apr–Oct, daily. Swannery/Barn:
   9.30–6. Gdn: 10–5. Winter/phone
💷 Swannery: Ad £3.50, Chd £1,
   SC £3. Gdn/Barn extra (chd free)
🅰 B3157
☕ 🎁 🅿

Bear Museum

38 Dragon St, Petersfield, Hants GU31 4JJ
☎ 0730 265108

Said to be the very first bear
museum in the country, with a
huge, lovingly presented display,
from classic German and early
American bears to Paddington,
Rupert et al.

🕐 All year, Mon–Sat 10–5
💷 Adm free
🅰 Nr town centre
🚉 Petersfield 10 min
🎁 🅿

Beaulieu & National Motor Museum

John Montagu Building, Beaulieu,
Hants SO42 7ZN
☎ 0590 612345/612123 info

The Palace House has its treasures and a charmingly re-created Victorian kitchen where you can talk to the cook, kitchen maid or bootboy, but most come to see the cars. There are more than 250 vehicles: luxury models, world record-breakers, mould-breakers. Viewing is from a monorail entering the roof of the museum. You can try driving experience rides, play with super radio-controlled cars...the list goes on.

🕐 Daily: May–Sep 10–6; Oct–Apr 10–5
💷 Ad £7.50, Chd £5, SC £6, f/t
🛈 B3056, 7 miles from Lyndhurst
♿ ⛺ 🍴 🍽 🍴 🅿

Bekonscot Model Village

Warwick Rd, Beaconsfield, Bucks HP9 2PL
☎ 0494 672919

The oldest model village in the world, with 160 houses, railway and harbours, gardens, and a road network buzzing with busy small vehicles. Model makers will be fascinated and envious. Children just think it is great.

🕐 Mid Feb–Oct, daily 10–5
💷 Ad £3, Chd £1.50, SC £2, f/t
🛈 M40 jnct 2
🚻 Beaconsfield 5 min
⛺ 🍽 🍴 🅿

Blackgang Chine

Nr Ventnor, Isle of Wight PO38 2HN
☎ 0983 730330

One of the longest-established theme parks, with a basket-load of themes and (quieter) rides in Dinosaurland, Fantasy-land and Frontierland, as well as a maze, water gardens and more.

🕐 Daily: Jun–Sep 10–10;
Apr/May/Oct 10–5.30
💷 Ad £4.99, Chd (3–13) £3.99
🛈 A3055 at Blackgang
♿(res) ⛺ 🍴 🍽 🅿

Blake's Lock Museum

Gasworks Rd, off Kenavon Drive,
Reading RG1 3DH
☎ 0734 390918

On the Kennet & Avon Canal, Blake's Lock is now an industrial museum recalling Reading's commercial past. The waterway meant thriving wharfs bringing goods for the printers, brick makers and ironfounders, all trades displayed here.

🕐 All Year, Tue–Fri 10–5, Sat/Sun/BH 2–5
💷 Adm free
🛈 NE of town centre
🚻 Reading 10 min
♿ 🍽 🅿

Bowood House

Calne, Wilts SN11 0LZ
☎ 0249 812102

Scientist Joseph Priestley discovered oxygen in one of the rooms here. You can discover the chair Queen Victoria used at her marriage, an impressive costume collection and a stunning display of jewels. The grounds contain a lake, temple, hermit's cave, and a fine adventure playground complete with pirate ship.

🕒 Easter–Oct, daily 11–6/dusk
💷 Ad £4.50, Chd £2.30, SC £4
🚗 A4 btwn Chippenham/Calne
♿ (res) 🍵 🍴 🎁 Ⓟ

Breamore Manor House Museums & Village

Breamore House, Fordingbridge, Hants SP6 2DF
☎ 0725 512468/512233

The 400-year-old family house has fine furniture and paintings, and a great, restored kitchen. Down in the thatched country village, they have full-sized furnished replicas of a farmer's cottage, a brewery, dairy, cooperage and more. There is a carriage collection, maze and adventure playground.

🕒 Mus: Apr–Sep 1–5.30. Hse 2–5.30:
   Apr, Tue/Wed/Sun; May–Jul/Sep,
   Tue–Thu/Sat/Sun; Aug, daily
💷 Ad £4, Chd £2.50, SC £3.50
🚗 A338, N of Fordingbridge
♿ (res) 🍵 🎁 Ⓟ

Bucklebury Farm Park

Bucklebury Estate,
Bucklebury, Berks RG7 6RR
☎ 0743 714187

Everybody gets a free tractor-trailer ride around the 60-acre estate, which has red deer roaming free as well as cattle and sheep. You can get close to the piglets and lambs in season, and see sheep sheared. Then pick your own strawberries.

🕒 Easter–Sep, Fri–Sun/BH/sch hols 10–6
💷 Ad £1.80, Chd £1.20
🚗 A4, signs at Woolhampton
♿ 🍴 🍵 🎁 Ⓟ

▼ Buckler's Hard Maritime Museum

Buckler's Hard, Beaulieu, Hants SO42 7XB
☎ 0590 616203

The museum records the history of the village where Nelson's fleet was built, with models of many of the actual ships. In the village itself, cottage interiors re-create life in the 1790s. You can visit The New Inn, look at the homes of a shipwright and of a poor labourer, while down the street Master Shipbuilder Henry Adams' home and lifestyle are there to see.

🕒 Daily: Easter–Spr BH 10–6;
   Spr BH–Sep 10–9; Oct–Mar 10–4.30
💷 Ad £2.50, Chd £1.70, SC £2.05, f/t
🚗 B3056 to Beaulieu, signs
🍵 🎁 Ⓟ

Cerne Giant
Cerne Abbas, Dorset

The famous chalk figure cut in the hillside is 55m long, and his club stretches 37m. The body (believed to be a fertility symbol) is outlined by trenches up to 61cm wide. Known of in Roman-British times and perhaps a lot older than that.

🕐 All year, all day
£ Adm free
🄰 A352, N of Dorchester

Cholderton Rare Breeds Farm Park
Amesbury Rd, Cholderton, Salisbury SP4 0EW
☎ 0980 64438

Jersey Giants and Sicilian Buttercups are not football teams, but rare breeds of poultry. They live here alongside other threatened animals. Young visitors like the 50 different kinds of bunnies in Rabbit World, and the racing pigs.

🕐 End Mar–Oct, daily
10–6; last adm 4.45
£ Ad £3.20,
Chd £1.60, SC £2.80
🄰 Signs at jnct
A303/A338
♿ ⛲ 🍴 🎁 🅿

Compton Acres Gardens
Canford Cliffs, Poole, Dorset BH13 7ES
☎ 0202 700778

An impressive layout of international gardens spread over 9 acres, with matching and modern statues, overlooking the busy sailing harbour of Poole. The fountains delight young visitors.

🕐 Mar–Oct, daily 10.30–6.30/dusk;
last adm 5.45
£ Ad £3.70, Chd £1, SC £2.70, f/t
🄰 Head for harbour, signs
♿ ⛲ 🍴 🅿

Coral Reef Waterworld
Nine Mile Ride, Bracknell, Berks RG12 7JQ
☎ 0344 862525/862484 info

Forget swimming baths, what Coral Reef offers is froth and flumes, water cannon pirate ships, bubble loungers and something called the White Volcano. There is also a toddlers' pool and the Lazy River.

🕐 All year. Mon–Fri 10.30–3.30
(9.45pm sch hols), Sat/Sun 9–5.45
£ Ad £4.50, Chd £3.10, f/t;
off–peak cheaper
🄰 Signs from town centre
♿ ⛲ 🍴 🎁 🅿

Crown Jewels of the World

47–50 Peascod St, Windsor,
Berks SL4 1DE
☎ 0753 833773

The jewels on show here make our
Royals look positively modest.
Reproductions, 150 or so, of crowns,
sceptres, orbs and state jewels
from 12 countries and the Vatican.
Dazzling.

🕐 All year, daily 11–5; Nov–Mar/phone
💷 Ad £3.50, Chd/SC £2, f/t
🅰 Town centre
🚇 Windsor 5 min

Deep Sea Adventure & Titanic Story

9 Custom House Quay, Old Harbour,
Weymouth DT4 8BG
☎ 0305 760690

Live diving displays combine with
videos to tell the story of deep-sea
diving. Find out how modern
diving techniques salvaged millions
in Russian gold from HMS
Edinburgh, and monitor the distress
signals from the *Titanic*.

🕐 Daily: Mar–Jun/Sep/Oct 10–5.30;
   Jul/Aug 10–10; Nov–Feb 10–4.30;
   last adm 1hr before
💷 Ad £3.35, Chd (5–15) £2.35, SC £2.80
🅰 Harbour front
🚇 Weymouth 20 min
♿ 🎁 🅿

Didcot Railway Centre

Didcot, Oxfordshire OX11 7NJ
☎ 0235 817200

They have reproduced a section of
Isambard Kingdom Brunel's
original broad gauge, and are
restoring a collection of steam locos.

You can see this and many relics in
the engine shed and at the country
station, look at the signal box built
by buffs...and ride on steam trains.

🕐 Apr–Sep, daily 11–5; Oct–Mar Sat/Sun
💷 Ad £4.50, Chd £3, SC £3.50, f/t
🅰 On concourse of Didcot Parkway Stn
🚇 Didcot Parkway
♿ (prior notice)
🍴 🚉 🎁 🅿

Dinosaurland

Coombe St, Lyme Regis, Dorset DT7 3NY
☎ 0297 443541

Specialised exhibits from the
Jurassic period. Ammonites,
trilobites and sea creatures much in
evidence, and should be noted for
spotting on guided beach walks.
Good graphic displays.

🕐 Easter–Nov, daily 10–5; winter/phone
💷 Ad £2.90, Chd (4–16) £1.90, SC £2.10
🅰 Town centre
♿ 🎁

Dinosaur Museum

Icen Way, Dorchester, Dorset DT1 1EW
☎ 0305 269880

Clever use of audio-visuals and
computer graphics, mixed with
reconstructed skeletons and
models as well as actual
fossils. They all
come together
to amuse and
inform.

🕐 All year, daily 9.30–5.30
£ Ad £3.50, Chd £2.25, SC £2.75, f/t
🅰 Town centre
🚉 Dorchester S or W, 15 min
♿ 🏛

Dorset Heavy Horse Centre

Edmondsham Rd, Verwood,
Dorset BH21 5RJ
☎ 0202 824040

No fewer than 6 different breeds of
huge horse on show. You appreciate
their size and power when you see
them in harness and as they
stand beside the Shetland
ponies which live here too.
Visitors can also mingle
with goats, sheep and
rabbits.

🕐 Daily: summer 10–5; winter 11–4
£ Sum/Win: Ad £3.50/£2.75,
   Chd £2/£1.75, SC £3/£2.25, f/t
🅰 B3081, W of Ringwood
♿ 🍽 🏛 🅿

Farmer Giles Farmstead

Teffont Magna, Salisbury, Wilts SP3 5QY
☎ 0722 716338

A 'hands-on' experience in farming,
with special paddocks holding
Highland cattle, belted Galloways
and other breeds which are very
approachable. Nature trail, adventure playground and an exhibition
of farming life in the old days.

🕐 End Mar–beg Nov, daily 10.30–6;
   winter Sat/Sun
£ Ad £3, Chd £2, SC £2.50
🅰 A303, B3089, W of Wilton
♿ 🚻 🍽 🏛 🅿

Golden Cap

Nr Bridport, Dorset
☎ 0297 89628 (Warden)

Two thousand acres of cliff, beach,
hill and farm land. Golden Cap,
blue clay topped by yellow
limestone, is the highest cliff in
southern England. Walk the 7½-mile
coastal path and see the fossil-
studded cliffs along the beach.

🕐 All year, dawn–dusk
£ Adm free
🅰 Signs from A35, W of Bridport
🅿 NT

16

Highclere Castle

Highclere Park, Highclere,
Newbury RG15 9RN
☎ 0635 253210

The architect Sir Charles Barry also designed the Houses of Parliament, but Highclere is thought to be his best building. Inside, there are treasures like Napoleon's desk and chair and the Egyptian collection by the Carnarvon who found Tutankhamen's tomb. The grounds have a lovely little secret garden and a selection of American wildflowers.

🕐 Jul–Sep, Wed/Thu/Sat/Sun/BHM 11–6; last adm 5
💷 Ad £5, Chd £3, SC £4, f/t
✳ Special events
🅰 A34, 4½ miles S of Newbury
♿ ☕ 🎁 🅿

Hollycombe Steam Collection

Iron Hill, Midhurst Rd, Liphook,
Hants GU30 7LP
☎ 0420 474740

Fairground steam and it runs Gallopers and a Big Wheel and a Razzle Dazzle - plus the oldest steam engine in the world. Lots of fairground fun.

🕐 Easter–beg Oct, Sun/BH 1–6
💷 Ad £4.50, Chd (2–15) £3.50, SC £4, f/t
🅰 A3, SE of Liphook
🍴 ☕ 🎁 🅿

Isle of Wight Steam Railway

Railway Station, Havenstreet,
Isle of Wight PO33 4DS
☎ 0983 882204/884343 timetable

A serious railway, with some engines more than 100 years old, 4 stations - Wootton, Havenstreet, Ashey, Smallbrook Junction - a bright green livery and much polished brass. Tickets can be combined with a 'go as you please' day on the island's railways, including the Ryde-Shanklin line.

🕐 Phone for details
💷 3rd Class rtn: Ad £4.50, Chd(5+) £3.50, f/t
🅰 Signs from Ryde
🚉 Ryde Pier Head
♿ 🍴 ☕ 🎁

Kennet Horse Boat Company

32 West Mills, Newbury RG14 5HU
☎ 0635 44154

Queenie and Hannah are just waiting to take you for a ride. They are barge horses on the Kennet & Avon Canal, pulling the 20m narrowboat and 70 passengers for about 90 minutes a time. There are also motor-barge trips from Newbury which last 3 hours, but somehow it doesn't seem the same. Horse-drawn times vary, and trips must be pre-booked.

🕐 Apr–Sep, daily 10–6.30
💷 Horse–drawn: Ad £3.50, Chd/SC £2.50. Motor: £4.50/£3.50
🅰 Kintbury or Newbury Wharf
🚉 Kintbury or Newbury
♿ (res) ☕ 🎁 🅿

Littlecote

Hungerford, Berks RG17 0SS
☎ 0488 684000

The world's finest collection of Civil War armour meets a Roman villa, a classic car museum, an adventure playground and Alice in Wonderland, at this Tudor mansion set in 100 acres. If that is not enough, they joust from May to September.

🕐 Apr–Sep, daily
   10.30–5
💷 Ad £5.50, Chd
   £4, SC £4.50
🅰 M4 jnct 14
♿ ⛲ ☕ 🍴 🛍
🅿

Longdown Dairy Farm

Deerleap Lane, Longdown, Ashurst,
Southampton SO4 4UH
☎ 0703 293326/293313 info

Combines an English farm with the exotic world of butterflies. You can cuddle a calf, watch milking, take a wagon ride...then go on to peer at strange foreign insects and walk through a cloud of butterflies to see dragonfly ponds.

🕐 End Mar–Oct, daily 11–5
💷 Ad £3.50, Chd (3–14) £2.50,
   SC £3.20, f/t
🅰 A35
♿ ⛲ 🛍 🅿

Longleat House

Warminster, Wilts BA12 7NW
☎ 0985 844400

Packed with paintings and other treasures. The Victorian kitchens show another side of the life of the rich. The Marquess of Bath's contemporary murals carry a PG warning. Outside, apart from the narrow gauge railway, there is the world's biggest maze, Postman Pat's village, and a simulator to imitate the thrills of skiing, motorcycling or flying a plane. And much more.
   Drive through the **Safari Park** among the rhinos, lions, giraffes, zebras and elephants. The famous white tiger roams free, too. Safari boats circle Gorilla Island, the sea lions and the hippos.

🕐 Easter–Sep (Safari Park to Oct),
   daily 10–6; winter/phone
💷 Hse: Ad £4, Chd £2, SC £3.
   Saf Park: £5.50/£3.50/£4.50.
   Cmbd tkt: £10/£8/£8
🅰 A362
♿ ⛲ ☕ 🍴 🛍 🅿

Maiden Castle

Cranborne, Dorchester, Dorset

The word 'maiden' is from early Celtic, and means 'stronghold by the plain'. This stronghold, a huge Iron Age hill fort, was a winner till the Romans stormed it in AD43.

🕐 All year, dawn–dusk
💷 Adm free
🅰 A354, 2 miles S of Dorchester
♿ 🅿 EH

Marwell Zoological Park

Colden Common, Winchester,
Hants SO21 1JH
☎ 0962 777406

One thousand animals in 100 acres.
The most antelope and zebra
species in Britain. A road train takes
visitors around the park to see
special attractions like the tigers or
lemurs. An 'encounter village' lets
youngsters get close to domestic
animals.

🕐 Daily: summer 10–6; winter 10–5
£ Ad £6, Chd (3–14) £4.50, SC £5.50
🅰 B2177, 6 miles SE of Winchester
⧟ Eastleigh (bus link)
♿ 🍴 ♨ 🍽 🛍 🅿

Merley House & Model Museum

Merley, Wimborne, Dorset BH21 3AA
☎ 0202 886533

Toy cars, boats, planes...there are
5,000 of them, all ages and sizes,
along with the working layouts of
N-gauge railway sets. The house
itself is an 18th-century mansion,
with exhibitions ranging from
miniature paintings to embroidery
and textiles.

🕐 Mar–Sep, daily 10.30–5
£ Ad £1.65, Chd 95p, SC £1.40
🅰 A31, S of Wimborne Minster
♿ ♨ 🛍 🅿

Needles Pleasure Park

Alum Bay, Isle of Wight PO39 0JD
☎ 0983 752401

Seaside fun. Crazy golf, Super X
flight simulator, children's play area
and chairlift to beach. Boat trips to
the Needles and Alum Bay
glassworks, for the sand in bottles.

🕐 Apr–Oct, daily 10–5 (6pm Aug)
£ Adm free. Attractions: pay as you go
🅰 Signs from Freshwater
♿ 🍴 ♨ 🛍 🅿

New Forest Butterfly Farm

Longdown, Ashurst,
Southampton SO4 4UH
☎ 0703 292166/293367 info

The best place for miles for seeing
the Mexican red-kneed tarantula. To
do that you have to walk through
exotic tropical butterflies at the
entrance, and see honeybees and
ants at work in the colonies. The
tarantula is in the insectarium along
with scorpions. Then there is the
fire-bellied toad!

🕐 End Mar–Oct, daily 10–5
£ Ad £3.50, Chd £2.50, SC £3.20, f/t
🅰 A35
♿ 🍴 ♨ 🛍 🅿

19

New Forest Museum & Visitor Centre

High St, Lyndhurst, Hants SO43 7NY
☎ 0703 283914

Oldest forest in England. The Centre tells you about the trees and wildlife (including the ponies) and the ancient laws of the forest. Good audio-visual about the forest year. Did you know that Alice in Wonderland is buried in the churchyard at Lyndhurst?

🕐 All year, daily 10–5
(longer in summer)
£ Ad £2.50, Chd
£1.50, SC £2, f/t
⟁ Town centre
♿ 📷 🅿

Paulton's Park

Ower, Romsey, Hants SO51 6AL
☎ 0703 814455

Over 40 different attractions, including a magic forest where nursery rhymes come to life, lots of rides, and a 3-acre adventure playground. Exotic birds, a watermill and 140 acres of parkland add to the enjoyment.

🕐 Mid Mar–Oct,
daily 10–6.30;
last adm 4.30
£ Ad £6.50, Chd/SC
£5.50, f/t.
Chd under 1m free
⟁ M27 jnct 2
♿ ⛲ 🍽 📷 🅿

Osborne House

York Avenue, East Cowes,
Isle of Wight PO32 6TY
☎ 0983 200022

Prince Albert designed the house, so Queen Victoria loved it dearly. The private apartments have been left exactly as they were when she died in 1901. Amazingly over-furnished and stuffed with presents given to the queen by princes, potentates and loyal subjects. Take a carriage ride in the grounds to the Swiss Cottage Albert designed for the children.

🕐 Apr–Oct, daily 10–6
£ Ad £5.50, Chd £2.75, SC £4, ♿ free
⟁ 1 mile SE of East Cowes
♿(prior notice) ⛲ 🍽 📷 🅿 EH

Poole Pottery

The Quay, Poole, Dorset BH15 1RF
☎ 0202 666200

A commercial concern that lets visitors have a bash at throwing a pot, or at painting and colouring ware. It will certainly produce some very individual souvenirs.

🕐 Daily: summer 9.30–9; winter 9.30–5
£ Tour: Ad £1.95, Chd/SC £1.50, f/t
⟁ Quayside
▦ Poole 10 min
♿ 🍽 📷

20

Portsmouth Historic Ships
HM Naval Base, College Rd,
Portsmouth PO1 3LJ
☎ 0705 861533

Three of England's most famous
historic ships are berthed here,
along with the extensive Royal
Navy Museum. The ticket price
depends on whether you see one, 2
or all 3 ships, or just the museum, or
go on a harbour trip. Or do the lot.

🕓 Daily: Mar–Oct 10–5.30; Nov–Feb 10–5
💷 Ad £2.50–£12.50, Chd £1.50–£8.75,
   SC £2–£11, f/t
🅰 M27, M275
🚉 Portsmouth Harbour
♿ (res) ☕ 🍽 🛍 🅿

The Mary Rose
On a sunny day in 1545, Henry VIII
watched in horror as his favourite
warship and the 700 men aboard
sank in a calm sea. The ship was
raised from the sea bed 400 years
later, with a surprising
amount of her
contents intact.

HMS Victory
Nelson's 104-gun
flagship at
Trafalgar. You
will be
surprised at
how cramped
it must have
been, and
how
dangerous
those guns
were - to both
sides. Where
was Nelson
when he was
shot?

HMS Warrior
Built in 1860, she was Britain's first
iron-clad, iron-hulled warship. The
tables are laid just as if the crew had
stepped off for shore leave. Don't
miss the captain's posh cabin, or the
cat o' nine tails.

Royal Naval Museum
Not about the ships but about the
men. Heroes and villains, drunken
sailors who became sober admirals,
pressed men who died far from
home. How they lived, what they
were paid. How they spent their
spare time and why more of
Nelson's sailors died in accidents
than in battle.

Portsmouth Sea Life Centre
Clarence Esplanade, Southsea,
Portsmouth PO5 3PB
☎ 0705 734461

There is just a 14m-high window
between you and a shark. And you
can pick up a lobster or crab and
realise you are not afraid. Deep sea
thrills.

🕓 All year, daily 10–6 (9pm summer hols)
💷 Ad £4.25, Chd £3.25, SC £3.50,
   ♿ £2.50
🅰 M275, signs
🚉 Southsea 20 min
☕ 🍽 🛍 🅿

Regimental Badges
Fovant, Wilts

The regimental badges lining the scarp slope of Fovant Down were carved by regiments stationed nearby during World War I. Many regard them as a memorial to those who later died in Flanders. Near Chiselbury Hill Fort.

🕒 All year, all day
💷 Adm free
🅰 A30, W of Wilton

Royal Navy Submarine Museum
Haslar Jetty Rd, Gosport PO12 2AS
☎ 0705 529217

This is the show that allows you to scan the waterways of Portsmouth Harbour through the Search and Attack periscope of Falklands veteran HMS *Conqueror*. Touring the 1947-built HMS *Alliance* is much more the real thing: hot, sweaty and worrying. The 'Submarine Experience' simulates the under-water sailor's life.

🕒 Daily: Apr–Oct 10–5.30;
    Nov–Mar 10–4.30
💷 Ad £3.50, Chd/SC £2.50, f/t
🅰 M27 jnct 11, A32
🍴 🎁 🅿

Splashdown & Icetrax
Tower Park, Poole, Dorset BH12 4NU
☎ 0202 716000

Where to go if it gets too hot, or too cold. Icetrax is a split-level rink, part of which runs outside the building. Splashdown runs at a steady 29°C for water lovers, with things like Torpedo Run, a 122m-flume starting 15m up. There's a total darkness splash, too. Toddlers have a fun paddling pool.

🕒 Splash: Mon–Fri 2–9, Sat/Sun 10–7,
    sch hols/BH 10–9 (Sat/Sun 10–7).
    Ice: daily 9.30am–10.30pm
💷 Splash: £4.50 per head, f/t.
    Ice: £3.50 (under 5s £1), f/t.
    Cmbd tkt: £7, f/t
✳ Skate hire £1
🅰 A3049, 2 miles from town centre
🍴 🎁 🅿

SS Shieldhall
Ocean Village, Canute Rd,
Southampton SO1 1JS
☎ 0703 230405

The *Shieldhall* is the largest working steamship preserved in Britain, and the work goes on. The wheelhouse and the saloon are on the way, and what about those 21 steam engines, all different, on board?

🕒 All year, daily 11–5
💷 Adm free (donations)
🅰 Nr city centre/Ocean Village signs
🚉 Southampton Central (bus link)
🍴 🅿

Stonehenge

Nr Amesbury, Wilts
☎ 0980 624715

Built 5,000 years ago but no one knows exactly why, or how. A remarkable feat of prehistoric engineering and an enduring mystery.

🕐 Daily: Apr–Oct 10–6; Nov–Mar 10–4
💷 Ad £2.85, Chd £1.40, SC £2.15
🅰 Jnct A303/A344
🚌 Salisbury (bus link)
♿ ☕ 🎁 🅿 EH

Stratfield Saye House

Stratfield Saye, Reading RG7 2BT
☎ 0256 882882

The Duke of Wellington bought Stratfield with his winnings at Waterloo. It is stuffed with Wellington memorabilia, both as General and PM. A stone marks the grave of his charger, Copenhagen, and you can see the Iron Duke's funeral carriage, all 18 tons of it, made from captured French cannon.

🕐 May–Sep, Sat–Thu 11.30–4
💷 Ad £4.50, Chd £2.25
🅰 A33, S of Reading
♿ ☕ 🎁 🅿

Studland Beach & Nature Reserve

1 Marine Tce, Studland,
Swanage BH19 3AX
☎ 0929 44259

The parking fee gets you on to 3 miles of one of the finest unspoiled sandy beaches in England. Behind lies the nature reserve with mile-long way-marked trails, which take you through woodland or over the sand dunes.

🕐 All year, daily.
Car parks 9–8pm
💷 Pkg (high/low) £3/£1.70
✳ Boat hire
🅰 A351, B3351
☕ 🅿 NT

Tank Museum

Bovington, Wareham, Dorset BH20 6JG
☎ 0929 403329

Never mind that driving-test simulator, have you tried the Challenger tank one? You will look on these tanks and armoured vehicles, 270 or so, with even more respect. You can examine World War I tanks, find out what Lawrence was up to in Arabia, and see the battleplan for El Alamein.

🕐 All year, daily 10–5
💷 Ad £5, Chd £3, SC/♿ £3.50, f/t
🅰 A352 at Wool
🚌 Wool 5 min
♿ 🍴 🎁 🅿

Underground Quarry

Park Lane, Corsham, Wilts SN13 0QR
☎ 0249 716288

Unusual underground quarry
where generations of quarrymen
have cut and shaped the distinctive
'Bath stone', used for buildings not
just in Bath but around the world.

🕐 Apr–Jun, Sun/BHM+h/term;
   Jul–Sep, Sat–Thu; Oct, Sun.
   Tour times/phone
💷 Ad £3.20, Chd(5+) £1.90, f/t
🅰 A4
🔦 💼 🅿

Watercress Line: Alresford to Alton

Railway Station, Alresford, Hants
SO24 9JG
☎ 0962 733810/734866
timetable

Volunteers rescued this
1860s-built line in 1977, and
now trains chug cheerfully
along the 10½ miles of
cuttings, embankments and
stiff climbs through a
'conservation corridor' of
plants and wildlife.

🕐 All year exc Nov. Phone for details
💷 Rtn: Ad £6.50, Chd/SC £4.50, f/t
✳ Ropley Stn for loco shed/picnics
🅰 Signs on A31 Guildford/Winchester
🚻 Alton, platform 3
♿(prior notice) 🍵 🍴 💼 🅿

Waterfront & Scaplen's Court Museum

4 High St, Poole, Dorset BH15 1BW
☎ 0202 749094

Waterfront is about the sea and how
it has coloured the life of the town.
On 5 floors are imaginative stagings
of the days of merchant princes and
desperate smugglers, and the
underwater archaeology on the
Studland Bay wreck of a 15th-
century merchant ship.

Waterfront starts with a
Victorian street scene, **Scaplen's
Court** goes 'indoors' with displays
of domestic life through the ages, all
with that whiff of authenticity.

🕐 All year, Mon–Sat 10–5, Sun 2–5
💷 W'front: Ad £2.95, Chd £1.50,
   SC £2.25, f/t.
   Scaplen's Ct: 75p/30p
🅰 On Poole Quay
🚻 Poole 10 min
♿ 🍵 💼 🅿

Westbury White Horse

Bratton, Wiltshire

One of six white hillside horses in
Wiltshire, it was cut in 1778 on the
site of a much earlier horse believed
to have been carved in AD878 to
celebrate the Battle of Ethandun.
Views of 3 counties: Avon, Wiltshire
and Somerset.

🕐 All year, all day
💷 Adm free
🅰 B3098 Westbury road
🅿 EH

24

Weymouth Sea Life Park

Lodmoor Country Park,
Weymouth DT4 7SX
☎ 0305 788255

Series of
themed aquaria
with sharks
in one tank,
rays in
another, a
fish nursery,
fish you can
feed, and between
all these things you can play
shipwrecks, lay hands on crabs or
nip along to the adventure
playground where they have a pets'
corner. Don't forget the iguanas in
the rainforest.

🕐 All year, daily 10–6
💷 Ad £4.75, Chd (4–14) £3.25, SC £3.75
🛣 A353
🚉 Weymouth 10 min
♿ ⛺ ☕ 🎁 ℗

Whitchurch Silk Mill

28 Winchester St, Whitchurch,
Hants RG28 7AL
☎ 0256 893882

The winding machinery is powered
by a waterwheel, and they use
original looms to weave the silk.
Reminder of simpler days, but the
video on silk production is bang
up to date.

🕐 All year, Tue–Sun 10.30–5
💷 Ad £2.50, Chd 60p, SC £1.90, f/t
🛣 Town centre
🚉 Whitchurch 15 min
☕ 🎁 ℗

White Horse & Castle

Uffington, Oxfordshire

The castle is actually an Iron Age
fort on the ancient Ridgeway path.
Underneath, etched in chalk, is the
huge white horse galloping
on into time.

🕐 All year, all day
💷 Adm free
🛣 B4507 Wantage road
℗ EH

Wilton House

Wilton, Salisbury, Wilts SP2 0BJ
☎ 0722 743115

They have 7,000 toy soldiers on
display, and The Pembroke Palace
dolls' house, reckoned to be one of
the most lavish and intricate in the
world. Downstairs in the real house,
the Tudor Kitchen and Victorian
Laundry are 'staffed' with life-size
figures. Good paintings, great
garden, huge adventure playground.

🕐 Easter–Oct, daily 11–6; last adm 5
💷 Ad £5.50, Chd (5–15) £3.50,
SC £4.50, f/t
🛣 A30, 3 miles W of
Salisbury
♿ ⛺ ☕ 🎁
℗

Windsor Castle

Windsor, Berks SL4 1NJ
☎ 0753 868286/831118 info

Less to see than before the fire.
There is an art gallery made from a
cloistered area, 2 chapels and the
state rooms. Top attraction is Queen
Mary's Dolls' House, 3 years in the
making, every bit to scale with
working lifts, plumbing and electric
light. Almost worth the entry price
on its own.

🕐 Daily: Mar–Oct 10–4 (last adm);
   Nov–Feb 10–3
£ Ad £8, Chd £4, SC £5.50, f/t;
   Sun/cheaper
🅰 Town centre
�># Windsor 5 min
♿ 🛍 Ⓟ

Woodland Park & Heritage Museum

Brokerswood, nr Westbury,
Wilts BA13 4EH
☎ 0373 822238/823880

The wood is recorded in the
Domesday Book and at least one
tree has been standing for a lot
longer than that. The nature trail
leads around a lake and through 80
acres of woodland laced with
wildflowers. Narrow gauge railway,
adventure playground, wildfowl
and peacocks, and displays of flora
and fauna in the log cabin museum.
Special events include a 4am Dawn
Chorus Bird Walk.

🕐 Daily: Easter-Oct 10-6, Nov-Mar 10-4
£ Ad £2, SC £1.75, Chd free with adult.
   Rlwy: 50p
✳ Holiday events; fishing; BBQ sites
🅰 A36, A361
♿ 🍴 🚂 🛍 Ⓟ

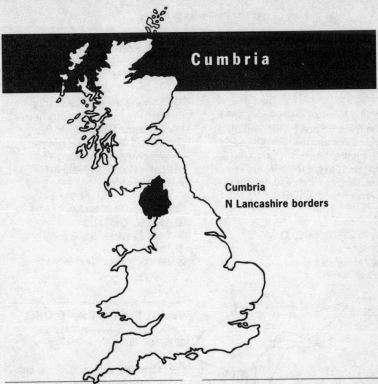

Cumbria

Cumbria

N Lancashire borders

Adrian Sankey Glass

Rydal Rd, Ambleside LA22 9AN
☎ 05394 33039

All the glass-blowing is done as you
watch. Using techniques first
perfected in the Middle Ages, the
glassworkers produce items ranging
from perfume bottles to
contemporary lighting.

🕐 All year, daily 9–5.30
💷 Ad 30p, Chd free
🅰 Behind Bridge House
♿ 🎁 🅿

Alston & Killhope Riding Centre

Low Cornriggs Farm, Cows Hill,
Wearhead, Co Durham
☎ 0388 537600

Something here for everyone, from
the first-aboard rider to real
keenies. The riders travel on old
packhorse routes in the Pennines.

🕐 All year, daily 9–6.30
💷 From £6.50 per
   hour/£32 per day.
   Chd/Sun £20
✳ Minimum age 8 yrs
🅰 A689 Alston/Stanhope
   ☕ 🍽 🅿

Appleby Castle Conservation Centre

Appleby–in–Westmorland CA16 6XH
☎ 07683 51402

A fine Norman castle sits guarding the river, helped by wakeful owls, pheasants, finches, parakeets and rare animal breeds. Those who do not want to see the porcelain from the *Nanking* cargo will delight in the Tarzan woodland trail.

🕐 Late Mar–Oct, daily 10–5
💷 Ad £3.50, Chd/SC £1.50
🅰 A66
🚉 Appleby 15 min
♿ 🚻 🏛 Ⓟ

Armathwaite Hall Equestrian Centre

Coalbeck Farm,
Bassenthwaite Lake, Keswick
☎ 07687 76239

Qualified instructors to escort or teach on horse-riding treks along woodland trails or open bridlepaths.

🕐 All year, daily 10–4
💷 From £9 per hour
✳ Minimum age 8 yrs
🅰 Signs off A591
Ⓟ

Beatrix Potter Gallery

Main St, Hawkshead LA22 0NS
☎ 05394 36355

The pictures are the beautifully detailed originals of the much-loved tales: Jemima Puddleduck, Peter Rabbit and the rest. The stories chosen change every year. The gallery was once her solicitor husband's office.

🕐 Apr–Oct, Mon–Fri/BH Sun 10.30–4.30
💷 Ad £2.50, Chd £1.30
✳ Timed tkt system; Braille guide
🅰 Town centre
🏛 NT

Beatrix Potter's Lake District

Packhorse Court, Keswick CA12 5JB
☎ 07687 75173

Less about the rabbits than the lady herself. Although there is a very impressive audio-visual show on her life and work, the centre commemorates her buying and conservation of 6,000 lovely acres of the Lake District.

🕐 Apr–Oct, daily 10.30–5.30;
   Nov–Mar, Sat/Sun 12–4
💷 Ad £2.50, Chd £1.30, f/t
✳ Deaf loop
🅰 Town centre
♿ 🏛 NT

Birdoswald Roman Fort

Nr Gilsland, Brampton CA6 7DD
☎ 06977 47602

Stand on the wall at the fort and
imagine it is the year AD121; it is
winter, and you would rather be in
Italy. Hadrian's great barrier against
the northern invaders
has lasted well.
Visitor centre
displays the
Roman
soldier's
lifestyle.

🕓 Apr–Oct,
   daily 10–5
💷 Ad £1.75, Chd £1, SC £1.25
🅰 B6318
♿ ☕ 🛍 🅿

🌟 Cars of the Stars
Motor Museum

Standish St, Keswick CA12 5LS
☎ 07687 73757

FAB 1, Batmobile, Chitty Chitty
Bang Bang, Knightrider's Kitt, a
Delorean from *Back To The
Future* and the James
Bond cars...even
Del Boy's Robin
Reliant made it.
Take yourself for a
dream ride.

🕓 Mar–Dec, daily 10–5
💷 £2.50 per head
🅰 Town centre
♿

Colony Country Store

Lindal Business Park, Lindal–in–Furness,
Ulverston LA12 0LL
☎ 0229 465099

Not the place you would expect to
find the largest makers of scented
candles in Europe. Factory tours
show the techniques and tricks.

🕓 All year, Mon–Sat 9–5, Sun 12–5
💷 Adm free
🅰 Signs from Ulverston
🚻 Ulverston 2 miles
♿ 🍴 🛍 🅿

🌟 Cumberland Pencil
Museum

Southey Works, Keswick CA12 5NG
☎ 07687 73626

From the moment around AD1500
when they discovered the special
graphite here in Cumbria, the
writing was on the wall. You can
see the biggest pencil in the world,
and pencils you can use to draw
watercolours.

🕓 All year, daily 9.30–4
💷 Ad £2, Chd/SC £1, f/t
🅰 W of town centre
♿ 🛍 🅿

Cumberland Toy & Model Museum

Banks Court, Market Pl,
Cockermouth CA13 9NG
☎ 0900 827606

Almost 100 years of mainly British toys, from tinplate trains to Scalextric. Re-created toyshop and a railway shed starring Hornby trains.

🕐 Feb–Nov,
   daily 10–5
£ Ad £1.60,
   Chd(5+) 80p, SC
   £1.40
🅰 Town centre
🅿

Cumbria Crystal

Lightburn Rd, Ulverston LA12 0DA
☎ 0229 584400

Starting with molten glass, you see craftsmen turn, shape, cut and polish to produce bowls, vases, glasses and more. Monday to Thursday displays of engraving. Video of specially intricate creations.

🕐 All year, Mon–Thu 9–4, Fri 9–3
£ Ad £1, Chd/SC 50p, f/t
🅰 A590
🚏 Ulverston 15 min
♿ 🍴 🅿

Dock Museum

North Rd, Barrow–in–Furness LA14 2PW
☎ 0229 870871

Museum in the town's Victorian graving dock shows how they build steel ships. Active display of how the ship grows and is launched. Also a reconstruction of a dock worker's cottage in 1900.

🕐 End Apr–Oct, Tue–Fri
   10–5, Sat/Sun 10–6
£ Adm free
🅰 A590
🚏 Barrow–in–Furness 15 min
♿ 🍴 🅿

Dolls House Man

Furness Galleries, Theatre St,
Ulverston LA12 7AQ
☎ 0229 587657

Very special dolls' houses made to order, often for adults. The models on display change because they are sold fast.

🕐 All year, Tue/Wed/Fri 10.30–4,
   Thu/Sat 9.30–5
£ Adm free
🅰 Town centre
🚏 Ulverston 10 min
🅿

Flying Buzzard, The
Elizabeth Dock,
Maryport Harbour CA15 8AB
☎ 0900 815954

You can inspect *The Flying Buzzard*, a Clyde-built, steam tugboat, from the wheelhouse to the gleaming brass of the engines. Alongside, the *VIC 96*, a 1945 naval supply ship, has a hands-on show of sea-going exhibits.

🕐 Easter–Oct, daily 10–5
£ Ad £1.60, Chd/SC £1.10, f/t
🅰 A594/A596
🚉 Maryport 10 min
♨ Ⓟ

Four Seasons Farm Experience
Sceugh Mire, Southwaite, Carlisle CA4 0LS
☎ 06974 73309/73753

This family farm offers bread and butter - which you can help make there. Usual farm animals, plus deer and ornamental birds, way-marked woodland walks and playground.

🕐 Apr–beg Oct, daily 10.30–5;
   Oct–Dec, Sun 10.30–5
£ Ad £2.50, Chd/SC £1.65
🅰 M6 jnct 41/42
♿ ♨ ☕ Ⓟ

Gosforth Pottery
Seascale CA20 1AH
☎ 09467 25296

Cheery, busy country pottery where they find time to demonstrate their skills and, in summer, invite visitors to have a go at throwing their own pots.

🕐 Jan–Mar, Tue–Sun 10–5;
   Apr–Dec, daily 10–5.30
£ Adm free
🅰 A595
🚉 Seascale 2 miles
♿ 🛍 Ⓟ

Grizedale Forest Park & Theatre In The Forest
Hawkshead, Ambleside LA22 0QJ
☎ 0229 860373 (Pk)/860291 (Th)

Between the visitor centre and the theatre lie 9 way-marked walks, 4 way-marked bike trails, orienteering courses and a Sculpture Way showing natural materials in a natural setting. Beautiful country.

🕐 All year. Info: 10–5.30 (not Jan)
£ Forest: free. Theatre/events: vary
✳ Art gallery
🅰 Signs from Hawkshead
♿ ☕ 🛍 Ⓟ

Heron Corn Mill & Museum of Papermaking

Beetham, Milnthorpe LA7 7AR
☎ 05395 63363

A waterwheel powers the corn mill and the museum tells about early experiments to produce paper, and shows modern techniques. Hand-making of paper some days.

🕐 Apr–Sep, Tue–Sun 11–5
💷 Ad £1.25, Chd/SC 80p
🅰 A6, S of Milnthorpe
♿ ☕ Ⓟ

Holker Hall/Gardens & Lakeland Motor Museum

Cark–in–Cartmel, Grange–over–Sands LA11 7PL
☎ 05395 58328 (Hall)/58509 (Mus)

The motor museum is in the Hall grounds, but before that there is the house, gardens, 125 acres of deer forest, an adventure playground, a collection of timeless toys and Teddies, and the world's largest slate sundial to see.

The Motor Museum has over 100 classic cars, motorcycles, bikes and tractors, and a re-creation of a 1920s garage.

🕐 Apr–Oct Sun–Fri. Hall: 10.30–4.30. Mus: 10.30–5
💷 All–in: Ad £5.75, Chd(6+) £3.25. Hall or Mus: £4.75/£2.85. Grnds: £3/£1.70
🅰 A590, B5278
♿ ⛟ ☕ 🛍 Ⓟ

Lake District National Park Visitor Centre

Brockhole, Windermere LA23 1LJ
☎ 05394 46601

Exhibitions and events cover what is happening in this scenic treasure area. In the grounds are activity trails, an adventure playground and lake cruises off the jetty.

🕐 Late Mar–beg Nov, daily 10–5
💷 Adm free; pkg £2.20
🅰 A591 W'mere/Ambleside
♿ ☕ 🍴 Ⓟ

Lakeland Bird of Prey Centre

Old Walled Garden, Lowther,
Penrith CA10 2HH
☎ 0931 712746

The 5-acre garden is home to a large collection of birds. Many are trained hunters, and you can see them display their soaring and swooping skills at 12.30, 2 and 4 every day.

🕐 Easter–Oct, 10–5.30
💷 Ad £3, Chd £2, SC £2.50
🅰 A6, S of Penrith
♿ ☕ 🛍 Ⓟ

Lakeland Wildlife Oasis
Hale, Milnthorpe LA7 7BW
☎ 05395 63027

Amid animals from around the
world, hands-on activities to weigh
a whale or try to 'design' a
mammal. An involving approach to
natural history with a tropical zone,
butterfly house and aquarium.

🕒 All year, daily 10–4
💷 Ad £2.85, Chd £1.50, SC £1.75, f/t
🅰 A6, S of Milnthorpe
♿ 🍴 🅿

 Laurel & Hardy Museum
4c Upper Brook St,
Ulverston LA12 7BQ
☎ 0229 582292/861614

Stan Laurel was born in Ulverston,
and this amazing collection of
Laurel and Hardy memorabilia
includes letters, personal
items, life-size statues,
topped off with clips from
the films.

🕒 All year, daily 10–4.30
💷 Ad £2, Chd/SC £1, f/t
🅰 Town centre
🚉 Ulverston 5 min
♿ 🅿

Levens Hall
Nr Kendal LA8 0PD
☎ 05395 60321

They have been cutting the hedges
at Levens Hall for 300 years, and
you probably won't see a more
impressive display of topiary
anywhere in the world. The
Elizabethan house and steam
collection make it a full day.

🕒 Apr–Sep, Sun–Thu 11–5 (Steam Coll 2–5)
💷 Hse/Gdn: Ad £3.90, Chd £2.30,
   SC £3.40. Gdn: £2.60/£1.60/£2.40
🅰 A6, 5 miles S of Kendal
♿ 🎠 🍴 🛍 🅿

Lowther Leisure Park
Hackthorpe, Penrith CA10 2HG
☎ 0931 712523

A Big Top circus is just one of 40-
odd attractions. One ticket lets you
on them all, from the junior ferris
wheel to the Rio Grande Train ride,
from the miniature train to the
Tarzan trail. Set in 150 acres of
parkland.

🕒 Easter+w/ends to end May;
   Jun–mid Sep, daily 10–5 (6pm sum hols)
💷 Ad/Chd £5.50, SC £3.75
🅰 A6, 4 miles S of Penrith
♿ 🎠 🍴 🍽 🅿

Michael Moon's Bookshop

41–43 Roper St, Whitehaven CA28 7BS
☎ 0946 62936

A mile of shelves, 100,000 books
and room for 100 browsers of all
ages. Watch your time, you will stay
longer than you planned.

🕐 All year, Mon–Sat 9.30–5
💷 Adm free
🅰 Town centre
♿

Mirehouse

Underskiddaw, Keswick CA12 4QE
☎ 07687 72287

The fascinating contents of a family
house that has only been sold once,
in 1688. Outside a choice of 4
adventure playgrounds, and forest
and lakeside walks.

🕐 Apr–Oct. Grnds: daily 10.30–5.30.
  Hse: Sun/Wed (+Fri/Aug) 2–4.30
💷 Hse/Grnds: Ad £3, Chd £1.50, f/t.
  Grnds: £1/80p
🅰 A591, 3 miles N of Keswick
♿ ☕ 🅿

Muncaster Castle Gardens & Owl Centre

Ravenglass CA18 1RQ
☎ 0229 717614 / 717203

The castle has been here since the
13th century, and parts of it stand
on Roman foundations. But the big
thrill comes every day at 2.30, when
you can meet the birds at the owl
centre and, weather permitting, see
them fly.

🕐 Gdn/Centre: all year, daily 11–5.
  Castle: late Mar–Oct, Tue–Sun 1–4
💷 All–in: Ad £4.90, Chd £2.50, f/t.
  Gdn/Centre: £3/£1.60
🅰 A595, S of Seascale
♿ ☕ 🛍 🅿

Museum of Lakeland Life & Industry

Abbot Hall, Kirkland, Kendal LA9 5AL
☎ 0539 722464

Any museum which devotes
displays to local heroes like
Postman Pat and the Swallows and
the Amazons has to be worth
looking at. In a series of rooms you
can see rebuilt shops, find out about
local mining and wool, and about
Cumberland wrestling.

🕐 Summer, Mon–Sat 10.30–5,
  Sun 2–5. Winter/phone
💷 Ad £2.50, Chd/SC £1.25, f/t
🅰 Signs in town centre
🚉 Oxenholme 2 miles
♿ ☕ 🅿

Ponsonby Farm Park

Cumrey Kitchen, Ponsonby,
Calder Bridge CA20 1BX
☎ 0946 841426

Working farm, but for young
visitors most of the action is around
the donkeys and llamas. Pets'
corner, farm walks and play area.

🕓 Easter/May–Sep, Tue–Sun 10.30–5
💷 Ad £2.20, Chd £1.10
🄰 A595, signs from Calder Bridge
▦ Seascale 2 miles
♿ 🛝 ☕ 🛍 🅿

Printing House Museum

102 Main St, Cockermouth CA13 9LX
☎ 0900 824984

Printing changed the medieval
world the way electronics is
changing it today. This display of
printing presses from all over
Britain shows how printing grew
from carved wood blocks to million
circulation tabloids.

🕓 Easter–Oct, Mon–Sat 10–4
💷 Ad £1.50, Chd 75p, SC £1, f/t
🄰 Town centre
♿ 🅿

Ravenglass & Eskdale Railway

Ravenglass CA18 1SW
☎ 0229 717171

One of England's oldest narrow
gauge railways, on a beautiful 7-
mile route. A little museum tells the
story of it all.

🕓 Late Mar–late Oct, daily.
Phone re times/winter
💷 Rtn: Ad £5.60, Chd £2.80,
SC £5.10, f/t
🄰 Follow rlwy signs
♿ ☕ 🅿

Senhouse Roman Museum

The Battery, Sea Brows,
Maryport CA15 6JD
☎ 0900 816168

New museum housed imaginatively
in a Victorian fort has the history of
Romans living here written by
themselves. The writing is on stone
- monuments, tombstones, mile-
stones and altars. Reconstructions of
Roman arms and armour and mock-
ups of living conditions.

🕓 Jul–Sep, daily 10–5; Apr–Jun/Oct
(not Mon/Wed) 10–5; Nov–Mar,
Fri–Sun 10.30–4
💷 Ad £1.50, Chd 75p
🄰 Signs from town centre
▦ Maryport 15 min
♿ 🛍 🅿

South Lakes Wild Animal Park

Crossgates, Dalton–in–Furness LA15 8JR
☎ 0229 466086

Some 100 species of animals and
birds including wallabies, raccoons
and exotic pheasants, spread over
16 acres of parkland.

🕐 End May–Aug, daily 10–6;
   Sep–end May, daily 10–4
£ Ad £2.75, Chd/SC £1.80, f/t
🚗 A590
♯ Dalton–in–Furness 15 min
♿ ☕ Ⓟ

South Tynedale Railway

Railway Station, Alston CA9 3JB
☎ 0434 381696

Not just British steam, but foreign
engines too, on this little line which
runs along the beautiful South Tyne
valley. The restored Victorian
station still has the original
ticket office.

🕐 Easter–Oct; phone for details
£ Rtn from: Ad £2, Chd £1
🚗 A686, A689
♿ ⛽ ☕ Ⓟ

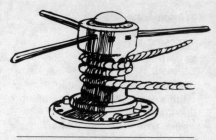

 ## Steam Yacht Gondola

Gondola Bookings, Pier Cottage,
Coniston LA21 8AJ
☎ 05394 41288

The National Trust has lovingly
renovated this steam yacht, first
launched in 1859. You can travel in
style, lolling on rich upholstery. A
grand way to see the lake.

🕐 Mar–Oct, daily; phone for details
£ Vary
🚗 Signs from town
Ⓟ NT

Stott Park Bobbin Mill

Finsthwaite, Ulverston LA12 8AX
☎ 05395 31087

The Victorians and Edwardians
used bobbins for spinning,
twisting, weaving, sewing,
making lace. You can see, still
using the same steam power,
how they made them.

🕐 Apr–Oct, daily
   10–5/dusk
£ Ad £2.20, Chd £1.10,
   SC £1.65
🚗 Signs from Ulverston
♿ Ⓟ

Talkin Tarn Country Park

Brampton CA8 1HN
☎ 06977 3129

Around 183 acres of wood, water
and fresh air with facilities for
sailing, fishing, rowing, canoeing
and more. Mountain bikes for hire,
and nature trails.

🕐 Easter–Oct, daily 10–6
£ Adm free; hire rates for bikes/boats vary
✱ No swimming or power boats
⚐ B6413
♿ 🚵 ☕ Ⓟ

Tobilane Designs

Newton Holme Farm, Whittington,
Carnforth, Lancs LA6 2NZ
☎ 05242 72662

They invented the Woolly Rockers,
rocking sheep you could cuddle as
well as ride. Imaginative toys
produced by craftsmen.

🕐 All year, daily 10–5
£ Adm free
⚐ B6254, S of Kirkby Lonsdale
♿ 🛍 Ⓟ

Trotters & Friends Animal Farm

Coalbeck Farm, Bassenthwaite Lake,
Keswick CA12 4RE
☎ 07687 76239

Lots of animals you can get close to,
including rare breeds and
traditional farm stock.

🕐 Apr–Oct, daily 10–5
£ Ad £2.25, Chd £1.50, SC £2.25
⚐ A591
♿ ☕ Ⓟ

Tullie House Museum

Castle St, Carlisle CA3 8TP
☎ 0228 34781

A vivid history of the borders in some
of the galleries, targeting 3 exciting
periods: the Romans, the Reivers
(border raiders) and Railways.

🕐 All year, Mon–Sat 10–5, Sun 12–4
£ Galleries: Ad £3.30, Chd/SC £1.70, f/t.
   Other areas: free
⚐ Town centre
🚋 Carlisle 10 min
♿ ☕ 🛍

Ullswater Navigation & Transit Co Ltd

13 Maude St, Kendal LA9 4QD
☎ 07684 82229/0539 721626

One- and 2-hour cruises give you a
chance to sit back and enjoy the
wonderful lakeland scenery.

🕐 Apr–Oct, daily; phone for details
£ Vary
⚐ Piers at Glenridding, Pooley, Howtown
♿ ☕ Ⓟ

Whinlatter Visitor Centre

Braithwaite, Keswick CA12 5TW
☎ 07687 78469

The heart of England's only
mountain forest. You can learn all
about it, and an indoor playroom
has conservation games. Or you can
just walk the way-marked trails.

🕐 Feb–Dec, daily 10–5.30
💷 Adm free; pkg £1
🅰 B5292, W of Keswick
♿ ☕ 🅿

Windermere Iron Steamboat Co Ltd

Lakeside, Newby Bridge,
Ulverston LA12 8AS
☎ 05395 31188

Three boats, *Swan, Teal* and *Tern*,
ply Lake Windermere picking
people up and dropping them off at
handy jetties. Some people connect
with a steam train, others stay on
and sail the company's Ten Miles of
Magic cruise. You could try both.

🕐 All year, daily 10–5 (later in summer)
💷 Boat: Ad £4.95–£7.95.
   Train: Ad from £3. Chd ½ price; f/t
🅰 A590, Lakeside Steamer signs
♿ ☕ 🅿

Windermere Steamboat Museum

Rayrigg Rd, Bowness–on–Windermere
LA23 1BN
☎ 05394 45565

The collection of craft (many
afloat, all still working) includes
classic motor boats and the steam
launch *Dolly* as she was built in
1850, which makes her the oldest
mechanically-powered boat in
the world.

🕐 Late Mar–beg Nov, 10–5
💷 Ad £2.80, Chd £1.40, SC £2.50, f/t
🅰 A592, signs from Windermere
🚆 Windermere 1½ miles
♿ 🦽 ☕ 🎁 🅿

World of Beatrix Potter Exhibition

The Old Laundry, Bowness–on–Windermere
LA23 3BT
☎ 05394 88444

Models, animation and a 9-screen
Video Wall join forces with Peter
Rabbit & Co. There is also a film on
Beatrix Potter's life.

🕐 Apr–Sep, daily 10–6.30; Oct–Mar 10–4
💷 Ad £2.85, Chd £1.65
🅰 Town centre
♿ ☕ 🅿

Cambridgeshire
Essex
Norfolk
Suffolk

Abberton Reservoir Wildlife Centre

Church Rd, Layer-de-la-Haye,
Colchester CO2 0EU
☎ 0206 738172

One of the largest reservoirs in the
country and a Special Protection
Area for birds. It has nesting
cormorants and swans,
terns and geese in
thousands. There
are hides and an
observation room.

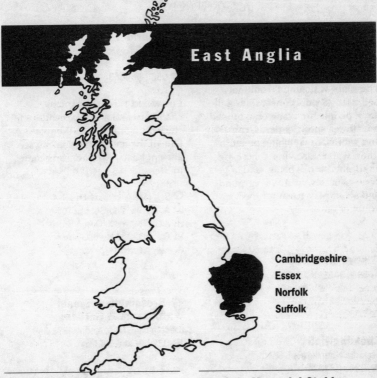

🕓 All year,
  Tue–Sun 9–5 (later
  in summer)
💷 Adm free (donations)
🛣 B1026, S of Colchester
♿ (res) ☕ 🎁 Ⓟ

Ada Cole Memorial Stables

Broadlands, Broadley Common, Roydon,
Essex EN9 2DH
☎ 0992 892133

Visitors are welcome to walk round
the paddocks and meet rescued
horses, ponies, mules and
donkeys. Showing affection
is encouraged.

🕓 All year, daily 2–5
💷 Adm free
🛣 B181 Epping road
♿ ☕ 🎁 Ⓟ

39

Banham Zoo

The Grove, Banham, Norfolk NR16 2HE
☎ 0953 887771

When not watching the animals being fed (8 public mealtimes a day), people are going on a guided tour to see snow leopards, camels and zebras, or watching penguins underwater. Elsewhere, there are children's stories being read, a pets' corner, an adventure playground, and a soft play room for the younger ones.

🕐 All year, daily 10–4 (last adm)
💷 Ad £5.50, Chd (4–14) £3.50, SC £4, f/t
🅰 B1113, SE of Attleborough
♿ ⚐ 🍴 🍽 🛍 🅿

Blickling Hall

Blickling, Norfolk NR11 6NF
☎ 0263 733084

A beautiful 17th–century house and gardens, with a lake and parkland walks. Children have a guide, a special menu and scribble sheets to make notes.

🕐 End Mar–Oct, Tue/Wed/Fri–Sun/BH:
Hse 1–5; Gdn 12–5 (daily Jul/Aug)
Park: all year, daily
💷 Hse/Gdn: Ad £4.50, Chd £1.75 (Sun/BH £5.50/£2.25).
Gdn: £2.50/£1.25
🅰 B1354, 1½ miles NW of Aylsham
♿ ⚐ 🍴 🍽 🛍 🅿 NT

Boatworld

Sea Lake Rd, Oulton Broad,
Lowestoft NR32 3LQ
☎ 0502 569663

Boatworld is part yard, part chandlery and a big part college for students from all over the world. One of the few places you can see ancient boat–building crafts come to life.

🕐 Beg May–Sep, Mon–Fri 10–4
💷 Ad £1.95, Chd/SC £1.60, f/t
🅰 A1117, signs in Oulton Broad
🚉 Oulton Broad North 3 min
♿ ⚐ 🛍 🅿

Bressingham Steam Museum & Gardens

Bressingham, Diss, Norfolk IP22 2AB
☎ 037988 386/382 info

Four different railway gauges run through the gardens, and the 40–odd locos on display (including *The Royal Scot*) are joined by a Victorian steam roundabout on which you can ride. There is a collection of fire engines, too. Gardens often seen on TV.

🕐 Apr–Sep: Tue–Sun 10–5.30,
Mon gdn only. Oct: Sun/half–term
💷 Ad £3.30, Chd £2.30, SC £2.60, f/t.
Rides extra
🅰 A1066, 2 miles W of Diss
🚉 Diss 2½ miles
♿ ⚐ 🍴 🛍 🅿

Bure Valley Railway

Aylsham Station, Norwich Rd, Aylsham,
Norfolk NR11 6BW
☎ 0263 733858

Nine miles of narrow gauge time
travel. Passengers can combine it
with a visit to the lovely Blickling
Hall [qv], or take a boat trip on the
Broads from Wroxham.

🕒 Easter/May–Nov, daily 10–5
💷 Single Pk/Off Pk: Ad £5.50/£5,
   Chd £3/£2.50, SC £4.50/£4; f/t
✱ Museum
🛈 Off A140, N of Norwich
♿(prior notice) 🚻 🎁 🅿

Bygone Heritage Village

Burgh St Margaret, Fleggburgh,
Gt Yarmouth NR29 3AF
☎ 0493 369770

Effective re–creation of a Victorian
village, plus steam and traction
engines, wild animals, pets' corner, a
whole fairground and small railway.

🕒 Easter–Oct, daily 10–6;
   Nov–Mar, Sun–Thu 10–5
💷 Ad £4.80, Chd (4–15) £3.60, SC £4.30
🛈 A1064, NE of Acle
♿ ⛴ 🚻 🎁 🅿

Colchester Zoo

Maldon Rd, Colchester CO3 5SL
☎ 0206 331292/330253 info

Active audience
participation
with close–ups
of snake
handling, penguin
parades, elephant
encounters, parrot
displays and
falconry, not to
mention tigers, snow leopards,
rhinos and other exotic species.

🕒 Daily: summer 9.30–5.30;
   winter 9.30–1hr before dusk
💷 Ad £6, Chd (3–13) £4,
   SC £4.50, ♿£2.50
🛈 A12 jnct A604
♿ ⛴ 🍴 🎁 🅿

Colne Valley Railway

Castle Hedingham, Halstead,
Essex CO9 3DZ
☎ 0787 461174

This collection of station buildings,
signal box, bridges and rolling stock
was carefully re–erected and
restored. Regular steam rides are
supplemented by specials for
children (free ride if carrying teddy
bear) and adults (dining in a
Pullman car).

🕒 Mar–Dec, daily 11–5. Phone for details
💷 Steam days/inc rides: Ad £4,
   Chd £2, f/t; Non–steam: £2/£1
🛈 A604, 5 miles NW of Halstead
♿(res) ⛴ 🚻 🎁 🅿

Cromer Lifeboat & Museum

Cromer Pier, Cromer NR27 0HY
☎ 0263 512503

One of the crucial lifeboat stations
on the North Sea. The lifeboat
itself is very impressive, and the
museum in the old lifeboat house
records many famous rescues...and
brave deaths.

🕐 May–Sep, daily 10–4
💷 Adm free
/i\ On sea front
♿ ☕ 🛍 Ⓟ

Curiosity Street Experience

Reepham Station, Station Rd,
Reepham, Norfolk NR10 4LJ
☎ 0603 871187

A curious mix. Thousands of ads for
things found in shops which closed
years ago, a railway display,
tape–recorded tours, old–fashioned
sweets and giant games of draughts
and snakes & ladders. Curiouser
and curiouser.

🕐 Apr–Oct, daily 10–4
💷 Ad £2, Chd (10–17) £1, SC £1.50, f/t
/i\ A1067, NW of Norwich
♿ ☕ 🛍 Ⓟ

Dedham Rare Breeds Farm

Mill St, Dedham, Essex
☎ 0206 322176

The animals are clearly identified
and all are approachable from wide,
grass walkways.
There are a lot
of breeds:
Norfolk
Horns, British
Lops and
Irish Moiled
are all waiting
to meet you.

🕐 Daily: Mar 10–4.30; Apr–Sep 10–5.30;
Oct–mid Jan 10–dusk
💷 Ad £2.75, Chd £1.75, SC £2.25
/i\ A12, signs in Dedham
♿ ⛲ 🛍 Ⓟ

Discoverig

East Point Pavilion, Royal Plain,
Lowestoft NR33 0AP
☎ 0502 523000

Imaginatively based on the
off–shore oil–rigs, this playground
has scramble nets, crawl–through
tubes, tanks filled with balls, a giant
slide, and more. Children have an
hour to see how much fun they can
get out of it. Special 'play pad' for
under 4s.

🕐 Apr–Sep, daily 10–6; winter/phone
💷 Chd (3–12) £1.95;
   Toddlers play pad £1.50
/i\ On Royal Plain
▦ Lowestoft 10 min
♿ ☕ 🍴 🛍

Docwras Rock Factory

23 Regent Rd, Gt Yarmouth NR30 2AF
☎ 0493 844676

The largest rock shop in the whole
world, selling more than 1,000 lines
of confectionery. After the rock
show, you can see them make
hand–dipped chocs.

🕒 Easter–Oct, daily 10–5
£ Adm free
⚠ Btwn town centre & sea front
⧉ Gt Yarmouth 15 min
♿ ▥

Duxford Airfield

Duxford, Cambridge CB2 4QR
☎ 0223 835000

Duxford, a Battle of Britain airfield,
is now part of the Imperial War
Museum with class exhibits like the
test–flight Concorde, an American
U–2 spyplane, and the only F111
swing–wing bomber on show in
Europe. Among a host of star
attractions a re-staged World
War II raid on Duxford and the
latest in simulator rides which lets
you 'fly' in a Spitfire–Messerschmitt
dogfight.

🕒 Daily: end Mar–mid Oct 10–6;
   mid Oct–end Mar 10–4; last adm
   45 min before
£ Ad £5.95, Chd £2.95, SC £3.95, f/t
✳ Special events, pleasure flights
⚠ Next to M11 jnct 10
⧉ Whittlesford 1 mile
♿ ⚐ ▤ ▯ ▥ Ⓟ

East Anglian Falconry Centre

Kelling Park Aviaries, Weybourne Rd, Holt,
Norfolk NR25 7ER
☎ 0263 712235

Over 350 birds, some of which can
be handled, take part in flying
displays. Star turns are peregrine
falcons which dive at 150 mph, and
pet owls which like to show off.
Three flying displays every day in
summer.

🕒 Apr–Sep, daily 10–5; Oct–Mar,
   Tue–Sun 10–3
£ Ad £3, Chd/SC £2.50
⚠ A149, W of Sheringham
♿ ▤ ▯ ▥ Ⓟ

East Anglian Railway Museum

Chappel & Wakes Colne Station,
Colchester CO6 2DS
☎ 0206 242524

The huge viaduct (7 million bricks)
points to the station. They restore
old engines here, and you can have
a go pulling levers in the signal box.
On steam days, visitors can have
unlimited rides on a variety of
engines and trains.

🕒 All year, Mon–Sat 10–5, Sun 10–5.30
£ Ad £2, Chd/SC £1.
   Steam days: £4/£2; f/t
⚠ A604
⧉ Chappel & Wakes Colne
♿(res) ⚐ ▥ Ⓟ

Easton Farm Park

Easton, Wickham Market, Suffolk IP13 0EQ
☎ 0728 746475

Visitors feed the goats and other animals in the pets' paddock. There is lots to see and enjoy, whether it is a working blacksmith, turkeys being reared, a Victorian dairy, old farm equipment or the adventure playpit.

🕐 Mid Mar–beg
Oct, daily 10.30–6
💷 Ad £3.85, Chd £2.10, SC £3
🅰 B1116, 3 miles N of Wickham Mkt
♿ ⛺ ☕ 🏠 Ⓟ

Great Bircham Windmill

Great Bircham, Norfolk PE31 6SJ
☎ 048 523 393

One of many windmills you can visit in East Anglia. Five floors to the top to see how it all works. The mill also has a coal–fired oven where they bake fresh bread and rolls daily. Pony rides, bikes for hire and a playground.

🕐 Easter–Sep,
daily 10–6
💷 Ad £2, Chd £1.25,
SC £1.75
🅰 B1153, NE of
King's Lynn
⛺ ☕ 🏠 Ⓟ

Grime's Graves

Lynford, Thetford, Norfolk IP26 5PE
☎ 0842 810656

Neolithic flint mines. It was here that early man dug out flints to shape into spears, axes and short daggers. The 300 pits and shafts are littered with broken flints. There is nothing else like it in the country.

🕐 Apr–Oct, daily 10–6;
Nov–Mar, Wed–Sun 10–4
💷 Ad £1.25, Chd 60p, SC 95p
🅰 A134, 7 miles NW of Thetford
🏠 Ⓟ EH

Guildhall of Corpus Christi

Market Place, Lavenham,
Suffolk CO10 9QZ
☎ 0787 247646

At one time pretty Lavenham was the 12th largest town in England. The Tudor Guildhall tells you how wool made the whole area rich, and how that wool was made into cloth for export. The curious can see the lock–up and mortuary. Wander round the town and see the Crooked House.

🕐 End Mar–Oct, daily 11–5
💷 Ad £2.40, Chd: 2 free, then 60p
🅰 Town centre
☕ 🏠 NT

House on the Hill Toy Museum

Stansted Mountfitchet, Stansted,
Essex CM24 8SP
☎ 0279 813237

The emphasis is on animated toys,
and the collection here is one of the
biggest in the country. Shop sells
new and antique toys.

🕐 All year, daily 10–5
💷 Ad £2.80, Chd £1.80, SC £2.30
🅰 By Mountfitchet Castle [qv]
🚉 Stansted M'fitchet 2 min
♿ (res) 📷 🅿

Kentwell Historical Re–Creations

Kentwell Hall, Long Melford,
Suffolk CO10 9BA
☎ 0787 310207

On re–creation days the manor is
bustling with Tudor life; folk are not
just dressed the part, they speak the
part, act the part and work at the
kind of jobs you might expect,
whether writing with quill pens or
making arrows for their longbows.
Startlingly authentic.

Other times the moated Tudor
mansion is open to the public in the
normal way, and visitors can see
around the house, tackle the Tudor
Rose–shaped maze and wander
round the farm gardens looking at
rare breeds.

🕐 Mar–Oct; phone re times
💷 Ad £4, Chd £2.50, SC £3.50.
Re–creation Days extra
🅰 A134, 4 miles N of Sudbury
🚉 Sudbury (bus link)
♿ (res) 🍴 🥤 📷 🅿

Kingdom of the Sea

Marine Parade, Gt Yarmouth NR30 3AH
☎ 0493 330631

The big item in this display is the
tropical sharks, seen above and
around you as you walk through a
transparent tunnel. Then, from the
Green Submarine, you can see a
coral reef full of exotic fish. There
are 25 themed displays in this
underwater world.

🕐 All year, daily 10–5 (later in summer)
💷 Ad £4.25, Chd (4–15) £2.99,
SC £3.25, f/t
🅰 On sea front
🚉 Gt Yarmouth 15 min
♿ 🍴 📷

Langham Glass

Nr Holt, Norfolk NR25 7DG
☎ 0328 830511

There is someone to explain what is
happening when the glassblower is
doing his stuff. Or you can see the
video, and slope off to the
adventure playground.

🕐 Easter–Oct, daily 10–5;
Nov–Mar, Mon–Fri
💷 Ad £3, Chd £1.50, SC £2
🅰 B1388; Langham village
♿ 🥤 🍴 📷 🅿

Layer Marney Tower

Layer Marney, Colchester CO5 9US
☎ 0206 330784

The tallest Tudor gatehouse in the country – all 8 storeys of it. Once you have your breath back, there are the farm animals to feed, rare ones who will probably let you stroke them, and the deer park.

🕐 Apr–beg Oct, Sun–Fri 2–6
💷 Ad £3, Chd £1.50, f/t
🅰 B1022, SW of Colchester
♿(res) ⛟ ☕ 🎁 🅿

Linton Zoo

Hadstock Rd, Linton, Cambs CB1 6NT
☎ 0223 891308

The boa constrictor is called Blossom, just one of a comprehensive gathering of exotic and interesting creatures, including snow leopards, Sumatran tigers, zebras and tarantulas. Set in 16 acres, the zoo runs special interactive trails for young visitors to follow.

🕐 All year, daily 10–6/dusk
💷 Ad £3.75, Chd (under 14) £2.75, SC £3.50
🅰 B1052, 10 miles SE of Cambridge
♿ ⛟ ☕
🎁 🅿

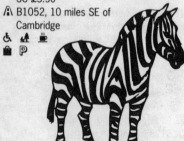

Long Shop Museum

Main St, Leiston, Suffolk IP16 4ES
☎ 0728 832189/830550

The inventor of the production line was not Henry Ford but Richard Garrett, and this is where it all happened. The Long Shop was the name given to the building Garrett needed to produce portable steam engines after a rush of orders at the 1851 Great Exhibition. On display are all sorts of steam engines, brass highly polished, back where they started.

🕐 Apr–Oct, Mon–Sat 10–5, Sun 11–5
💷 Ad £1.50, Chd/SC 75p
🅰 Town centre
♿ 🎁 🅿

Mangapps Farm Railway Museum

Southminster Rd, Burnham–on–Crouch, Essex CM0 8QQ
☎ 0621 784898

An amazing range of railway memorabilia: everything from GWR teaspoons to complete signalling systems. Among the locos, some vintage diesel engines – you can ride behind one.

🕐 All year, Sat/Sun+BH (daily in sch hols)
💷 Ad £3, Chd £2, SC £2.50 (extra on steam days)
🅰 1 mile N of rlwy stn
🚉 Burnham–on–Crouch 20 min
☕ 🎁 🅿

Mechanical Music Museum

Blacksmith Rd, Cotton, Stowmarket,
Suffolk
☎ 0449 613876/781988

It takes real enthusiasm to buy a
mighty Wurlitzer Theatre pipe
organ and then reconstruct a
cinema to house it. The Wurlitzer
joins other organs, gramophones,
polyphons, musical dolls, a musical
bowl and, yes, a genuine musical
chair.

🕐 Jun–Sep, Sun 2.30–5.30
£ Ad £2.50, Chd 50p
🚗 B1113, N of Stowmarket
♿ ☕ Ⓟ

Mill Farm Rare Breeds

Hindringham, Norfolk NR21 0PR
☎ 0328 878149

More than 50 rare farm breeds, plus
fallow deer, a pets' corner, butterfly
garden and flower meadow, nature
trail and adventure playground.

🕐 Easter–Sep, Tue–Sun/BH 10–5
£ Ad £2.50, Chd £1.50,
  SC £2
🚗 A148 Fakenham/Holt
♿ 🔦 ☕ 📷 Ⓟ

Minsmere RSPB Nature Reserve

Westleton, Saxmundham, Suffolk IP17 3BY
☎ 072 873 281

Great wildlife in
1,560 acres of
woods, heath
and reeds.
Casual gazers
suddenly
realise they
have seen an
avocet (the one
with the bendy bill used as a symbol
by the RSPB) or a marsh harrier.
There are rabbits galore, and that
might be a fox over there...

🕐 All year, Wed–Mon 9–9/dusk
£ Ad £3, Chd 50p, SC £2
✳ Battery car for ♿(prior notice)
🚗 B1125
♿ 🔦 📷 Ⓟ

Mountfitchet Castle & Norman Village of 1066

Stansted Mountfitchet, Essex CM24 8SP
☎ 0279 813237

The castle was built by a relative of
William the Conqueror. This clever
reconstruction shows how houses
were built then and how the
peasant community was organised
in the feudal system. Animals
popping in and out of the houses
are an authentic touch.

🕐 Mid Mar–mid Nov, daily 10–5
£ Ad £3.50, Chd £2.50, SC £3
✳ Next to House on the Hill Toy
  Museum [qv]
🚗 M11 jnct 8
🚆 Stansted M'fitchet 2 min
♿(res) ☕ 📷 Ⓟ

Museum of East Anglian Life

Stowmarket, Suffolk IP14 1DL
☎ 0449 612229

A 13th–century barn, watermill,
wind pump, smithy...plus steam
engines and farm stock. You might
see people making corn dollies, or
barrels, or lace. Sometimes butter is
churned, sometimes horses plough
the field. Real country matters.

🕓 Easter–Oct, Tue–Sun 10–5
(BH/Jul/Aug, daily 10–5)
💷 Ad £3.70, Chd £1.60, SC £3, f/t
🅰 Town centre
🚉 Stowmarket 10 min
♿ 🚻 ☕ 🎁

Mustard Shop

3 Bridewell Alley, Norwich NR2 1AQ
☎ 0603 627889

The shop, run by Colman's
Mustard, is a fascinating look at the
history of mustard, how it is made
and how many types and flavours
can be produced.

Just round the corner is **The
Castle Museum** (☎ 0603 223624),
where you can see an amazing
flying dragon used in medieval
town celebrations, and manuscripts
written by Rider Haggard,
author of *King Solomon's
Mines*.

🕓 All year, Mon–Sat 9.30–5
💷 Adm free
🅰 City centre
🚉 Norwich 15 min
♿ 🎁 🅿

National Horseracing Museum

99 High St, Newmarket, Suffolk CB8 8JL
☎ 0638 667333

Every thoroughbred racing horse in
the world is descended from 3
famous runners. The museum
traces that and the sport's
glamorous history, boosted by
Charles II's love of a canter on
Newmarket Heath. He moved the
court to Newmarket twice a year,
and is the only British monarch to
have ridden a winner on the flat.

🕓 End Mar–beg Dec, Tue–Sat 10–5,
Sun 12–4; Jul/Aug, Mon–Sat 10–5,
Sun 12–4
💷 Ad £3.30, Chd £1, SC £2
🅰 Town centre
🚉 Newmarket 5 min
♿ ☕ 🎁 🅿

National Motor Boat Museum

Pitsea Hall Country Park, Pitsea,
Essex SS16 4UW
☎ 0268 550088

An impressive selection of boats:
pleasure, sporting and working.
Good displays of motor boat origins
and development.

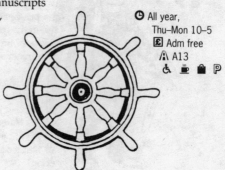

🕓 All year,
Thu–Mon 10–5
💷 Adm free
🅰 A13
♿ ☕ 🎁 🅿

National Stud
Newmarket, Suffolk CB8 0XE
☎ 0638 663464

The 75–minute tour takes in
top–class racehorses, the stables
where great horses like Mill Reef
stayed, and the foaling unit where
future champions are born.

🕐 Late Mar–Sep (+Oct race days).
  Tours: 11.15/2.30 w/days; Sat
  11.15/Sun 2.30
💷 Ad £3.50, Chd(5+)/SC £2.50
🅰 Beside July Racecourse
🚉 Newmarket 3 miles
♿ 🍵 🛍 🅿

Norfolk Lavender
Caley Mill, Heacham, King's Lynn PE31 7JE
☎ 0485 570384

The lavender starts blossoming from
June, and the main harvest is mid
July to mid August. During that
time you can take a guided minibus
tour of the lavender, and perhaps
see the distillery.

🕐 All year, daily 10–5
💷 Adm free
🅰 A149, 10 miles N of
  King's Lynn
♿ 🍵 🛍 🅿

Norfolk Rural Life Museum & Union Farm
Beech House, Gressenhall,
East Dereham, Norfolk NR20 4DR
☎ 0362 860563

Edwardian–furnished cottages, a
smithy, village shop and hardware
store. Across the road the farm still
uses horses to plough and haul, and
the fields are worked as if it was
still the 1920s, with the breeds
raised then.

🕐 Easter–Oct, Tue–Sat/BH 10–5,
  Sun 12–5.30
💷 Ad £3.50, Chd £1.50, SC £2.50, f/t
✳ Nature trail, special events
🅰 B1146, 2 miles N of E Dereham
♿ 🧒 🍵 🛍 🅿

Norfolk Shire Horse Centre
West Runton, Cromer, Norfolk NR27 9QH
☎ 0263 837339

The horses are at work every day,
demonstrating at 11.15 and 3. There
are free cart rides for children,
ponies and foals to see being fed,
plus a collection of bygones
including gypsy caravans.

🕐 Easter–Oct, Sun–Fri 10–5 (+BH Sat)
💷 Ad £3.50, Chd(4+)/SC £2
🅰 A149
🚉 West Runton 5 min
♿ 🧒 🍵 🍴 🛍 🅿

49

Norfolk Wildlife Centre & Country Park

Great Witchingham, Norwich NR9 5QS
☎ 0603 872274

Philip Wayre, who pioneered otter conservation, runs this 40–acre park, where there are reindeer and badgers, waterfowl and rare trees. There is a model farm area with tame animals, 2 play areas, a pets' corner and rides on a little steam railway.

🕐 April–Oct, daily 10.30–6/dusk
£ Ad £3.80, Chd (4–15) £2.30, SC £3.30
✶ Free rides with Santa's reindeer
🅰 A1067, NW of Norwich
🕭 ⚒ ☕ 🎒 ℗

Old Gaol House

Saturday Market Place,
King's Lynn PE30 5DQ
☎ 0553 763044

A personal stereo guide takes you through the 1930s police station, and there in the gaol you hear true tales of highwaymen, witches, robbers and worse. You can try the stocks or the fetters and manacles for yourself.

🕐 Easter–Oct, daily 10–5;
Nov–Mar, Fri–Tue 10–5; last adm 4.15
£ Ad £2, Chd/SC £1.50
🅰 In TIC in town centre
🚌 King's Lynn 10 min
🕭 ℗

Otter Trust

Earsham, Bungay, Suffolk NR35 2AF
☎ 0986 893470

The world's largest collection of otters in natural enclosures. The Trust also has splashing clouds of water birds, including the night heron, and a herd of the little muntjac deer.

🕐 Apr–Oct, daily 10.30–6/dusk
£ Ad £3.50, Chd (5–16) £2.50, SC £3
🅰 A143, W of Bungay
🕭 ⚒ ☕ 🎒 ℗

Park Farm

Snettisham, King's Lynn PE31 7NQ
☎ 0485 542425

The safari–style tour of the red deer park gives close–ups of the large resident herd. Indoors, you can see chickens hatching, visit the pets, pigs and play barn, or look at craft shops or the art gallery. Outside, the choice is pony rides, sheep centre, nature trails, a children's farmyard or the big adventure playground.

🕐 All year, daily 10.30–5
£ Ad £3.50, Chd (3–16) £2.50, SC £3.
Inc Safari: £6/£4/£5; f/t
🅰 A149, in Snettisham
🕭 ⚒ ☕ 🎒 ℗

Pensthorpe Waterfowl Park

Fakenham, Norfolk NR21 OLN
☎ 0328 851465

The park keeps an exotic collection,
as well as attracting both native and
migratory fowl. In
the indoor viewing
gallery, bird
spotting can
be enjoyed
in comfort.
You can
hire
binoculars.

🕒 Mid Mar–Dec,
   daily 11–5; Jan–beg Mar, Sat/Sun
💷 Ad £3.95, Chd £1.80, SC £3.40, f/t
✱ Adv playgnd, exhib centre
🅰 A1067, SE of Fakenham
♿ ⛺ ☕ 🍴 🛍 Ⓟ

Pleasurewood Hills American Theme Park

Corton Rd, Lowestoft NR32 5DZ
☎ 0502 513627/508200 info

Once through the turnstile, every
attraction is free (except the slot
machines, of course), so those who
want to go round and round on
the chairoplane can do it all day.
Some might prefer to look at all 6
special shows.

🕒 Easter/BH/mid May–mid Sep,
   daily 10–5 (6pm summer)
💷 £9 per head
✱ BBQ
🅰 A12, 2 miles N of Lowestoft
▦ Lowestoft (bus link)
♿ ☕ 🍴 🛍 Ⓟ

Redwings Horse Sanctuary

Hill Top Farm, Hall Lane, Frettenham,
Norwich NR12 7LT
☎ 0603 737432

Caring for 1,500 horses, ponies,
donkeys and mules, and some
goats. Has an Adopt A Rescued
Pony or Donkey scheme.

🕒 Easter–mid Dec, Sun/BH 1–5
   (Mon Jul/Aug)
💷 Ad £2, Chd/SC £1
🅰 B1150, N of Norwich
♿ ☕ 🛍 Ⓟ

Ripley's Believe It Or Not!

The Windmill, 9 Marine Parade,
Gt Yarmouth NR30 3AH
☎ 0493 332217

Come in and watch the NINE
moving videos! There are TEN
themed galleries! A LEPRECHAUN
has been found in Paris! Top exhibit
is the ACTUAL Berlin Wall...a LOT
of harmless fun!

🕒 Apr–Oct, daily from 10am;
   Nov–Mar, Sat/Sun/sch hols
💷 Ad £2.99, Chd £1.99, SC £2.20,
   ♿ free
🅰 On sea front
▦ Gt Yarmouth 3 miles
♿(res) 🛍

River Lee Country Park
Waltham Abbey, Essex EN9 1XQ
☎ 0992 713838

The park sometimes has otter in its
streams and rare over–wintering
wildfowl on its lakes. Bats,
kingfishers, great–crested grebes
and bittern also call it home. Bird
hides at weekends, and nature
trails.

🕐 All year, dawn–dusk
💷 Adm free
🅰 M25 jnct 26, A121
♿ 🅿

Roydon Mill Leisure Park
Roydon, Harlow, Essex CM19 5EJ
☎ 0279 792777

Water skiing off a man–made beach,
plus speedboats, canoes, pedaloes.
A 58–acre water pleasure area.

🕐 All year, daily 8–dusk
💷 £1 per head; pkg £2
✳ Water ski instruction
🅰 B181 Epping road
♿ 🍴 🖼 🛍 🅿

Sandringham House
Sandringham, Norfolk PE35 6EN
☎ 0553 772675

As you go in the front door there is
a weighing machine which Edward
VII installed to make sure his guests
put on weight when they came to
visit. A chance to see a royal house
that is lived in. The gardens are
spacious, the park rolling, and the
collection of cars in the garage
impressive.

🕐 Apr–beg Oct, daily. Hse: 11–4.45
   (Sun 12–4.45). Grnds: 10.30–5 (Sun
   11.30–5). Closed mid Jul–beg Aug
💷 Hse: Ad £3.50, Chd £2, SC £2.50.
   Grnds/Mus: £2.50/£1.50/£2.
   Park: free
🅰 A148/A149
♿ 🚻 🖼 🍴 🛍 🅿

Scott Polar Research Institute
Lensfield Rd, Cambridge CB2 1ER
☎ 0223 336540

Set up as a place to house the
papers and details of Captain Scott's
trips to the South Pole, the institute
now has the most impressive
collection of memorabilia of polar
expeditions, including tents, sledges
and equipment.

🕐 All year, Mon–Sat 2.30–4
💷 Adm free
🅰 City centre
🚉 Cambridge 10 min
♿ 🛍 🅿

Seal Trips & Blakeney Point

John Bean Boat Trips (☎ 0263 740038)
Graham Bean Boat Trips (☎ 0263 740505)
Temple's Ferry Service (☎ 0263 740791)

A popular trip out to see, close up, the North Sea seal colony off Blakeney Point (NT). The Point was Norfolk's first–ever nature reserve, and is home to Common and Grey seals as well as a host of birds.

🕒 All year; phone for details
£ From: Ad £3, Chd (under 12) £2

/ⁱ\ Morston/Blakeney, off A149

Sedgwick Museum

Department of Earth Sciences, Downing St, Cambridge CB2 3EQ
☎ 0223 333456

The museum has one of the best collections of fossils anywhere in the world. Experts and scientists study here, but casual visitors can share the delights of the Jurassic, the Permian and the Triassic, and all the rest.

🕒 All year (not Xmas/Easter),
Mon–Fri 9–1 & 2–5, Sat 10–1
£ Adm free
/ⁱ\ City centre
✧ Cambridge 20 min
♿(res) ▪

Southend Planetarium

Central Museum, Victoria Ave,
Southend–on–Sea SS2 6EW
0702 330214

The planetarium, where you can see the skies move, is the only one in the South East outside London – and a lot easier to get into.

🕒 All year, Wed–Sat 10–5
£ Ad £2, Chd/SC £1.50, f/t
/ⁱ\ Town centre
✧ Southend Victoria (next to)
▪ Ⓟ

Station 146

Toad Lane, Seething, Norfolk
☎ 0508 550787

Lovingly preserved World War II control tower used by 448th Bomber Group USAAF. Collection of memorabilia, reminiscences of air crews and personal diaries, all in a tower maintained as it was while in service.

🕒 May–Oct, 1st Sun every month
only, 10–5
£ Adm free
/ⁱ\ B1332, S of Norwich
♿(res) ☕ ▪ Ⓟ

Thrigby Hall Wildlife Gardens

Thrigby Hall, Filby, Gt Yarmouth NR29 3DR
☎ 0493 369477

Asia and the Orient arrive in the
landscaped gardens via
tigers (seen from a rope
walk in the trees above),
snow leopards and
crocodiles, and a
re–creation of the
garden you see on
Willow Pattern china,
complete with the temple and
12 bridges.

🕐 All year, daily 10–dusk
£ Ad £4, Chd £2.50, SC £3.50
🚗 A1064, S of Filby
♿ ⛪ ☕ 🎁 🅿

Welney Wildfowl & Wetlands Centre

Hundred Foot Bank, Welney,
Wisbech,
Cambs PE14 9TN
☎ 0353 860711

Welney is 900 acres
of fenland. There is a
planned route with 21
bird hides and, in
season, the place
attracts 40,000–odd wild duck
and 5,000 Bewick's and
Whooper Swans. You can hire
binoculars, but take wellies.

🕐 All year, daily 10–5
£ Ad £2.95, Chd £1.50, f/t
🚗 A10, 12 miles N of Ely
♿ ⛪ ☕ 🎁 🅿

Thursford Collection

Thursford, Fakenham, Norfolk NR21 0AS
☎ 0328 878477

There are great, gleaming
steamrollers and steam ploughs
here but youngsters head for the
steam fairground roundabouts and
the waltzer. Nine mechanical
organs, a giant Wurlitzer and
musical shows every day.

🕐 Daily: Apr/May/Sep/Oct 1–5;
   Jun–Aug 11–5
£ Ad £4.35, Chd £1.95, SC £3.95
🚗 A148
♿ ☕ 🍴 🎁 🅿

West Stow Country Park & Anglo–Saxon Village

Icklingham Rd, West Stow,
Bury St Edmunds IP28 6HG
☎ 0284 728718

Heathland reserve (125 acres) with
nature trails, wildfowl, woods, river
and lake, and in the middle,
Anglo–Saxon England. Craftsmen
and volunteers have tried to build
and live in Anglo–Saxon style,
farming, weaving, keeping animals.
Impressive results, and taped
guides with imaginary voices of
early inhabitants shed some light on
the Dark Ages.

🕐 All year: daily 10–5, last adm 4.15
£ Park: adm free. Village: £2.50
🚗 A1101, N of Bury St Edmunds
♿ ⛪ ☕ 🅿

Wildlife Water Trail
How Hill, Ludham, Norfolk Broads
☎ 0692 678763

Moving silently along the dykes of
How Hill Nature Reserve, the
electric boat, plus guide, takes you
to see things like cormorants, rare
marsh harriers and dragonflies. The
tiny, canopied boat holds only 8
people, so book the 50–minute trip
in advance.

🕒 Jun–Sep, daily 10–5; other times/phone
💷 Ad £2.50, Chd £1.50, f/t
🅰 A1062, E of Hoveton
🅿

Wood Green Animal Shelter
Kings Bush Farm, London Rd,
Godmanchester, Huntingdon PE18 8LJ
☎ 0480 830757

Not just cats and dogs. This
progressive centre also cares for
horses, donkeys, swans, llamas and
pot–bellied pigs. A place for animal
lovers.

🕒 All year, daily 9–3
💷 Adm free (donations)
✳ Special events arena
🅰 A1198
🔺 🍴 🎁 🅿

Wimpole Hall & Home Farm
Arrington, Royston, Cambs SG8 0BW
☎ 0223 207257

The Hall: elegant, designed by
famous architects and gardeners, a
revealing behind–the–scenes look at
the servants' quarters. Home Farm:
designed to be a Model Farm and
now filled with rare breeds, big
horses working the land, horse and
cart rides, and an adventure
playground. Pick which you prefer,
or try both.

🕒 Late Mar–Oct. Days/times vary,
   phone first
💷 Hall/Gdn: £4.50. Farm: Ad £3.50,
   Chd £1.75. Cmbd tkt £6
🅰 A603, 8 miles SW of Cambridge
♿ 🍴 🍽 🎁 🅿 NT

Working Silk Museum
New Mills, South St, Braintree CM7 6GB
☎ 0376 553393

The handlooms have been weaving
silk for the last 150 years. See the
whole process from original design
to finished product, from men's ties
to drapes for royal palaces.

🕒 All year, Mon–Fri 10–12.30/1.30–5.
   Tours: Sat at 2/3/4pm
💷 Ad £2.75, Chd £1.50, f/t
🅰 Signs from town centre
🚉 Braintree 5 min
♿ 🎁 🅿

55

Greater London

Bank of England Museum
Threadneedle St, London EC2R 8AH
☎ 071 601 5545/5792 info

It is pretty impressive to see a stack
of gold bars as you walk in. That is
before you see the £1,000 notes or
sneak a look at George
Washington's bank balance. Later,
you find what connects the Bank of
England with *Wind in the Willows,*
and can ask a computer for the
latest prices on stocks and securities.

🕑 All year, Mon–Fri 10–5,
   Sun/pub hols 11–5
£ Adm free
🚉 Liverpool St/Fenchurch
   St/Cannon St
⊖ Bank
♿ 🛍

Battersea Park Children's Zoo
Battersea Park, London SW11
☎ 081 871 7540

Not the most obvious place to meet
otters and flamingoes, or to shake
hands with a monkey. There are
farmyard animals too, and after that
you can have a picnic in the park.

🕑 Easter–Sep, daily 11–6
£ Ad 90p, Chd 30p,
   SC 25p, ♿free
🚉 Battersea Park 5 min
♿ 🛍 🅿

Bethnal Green Museum of Childhood

Cambridge Heath Rd, London E2 9PA
☎ 081 980 3204/2415 info

More and better historical toys, dolls, dolls' houses and costumes than you will see anywhere else. The stuff, particularly mechanical toys and jigsaws, is so good you wish there were more hands-on exhibits.

🕐 All year, Mon–Thu/Sat 10–6,
    Sun 2.30–6
🅴 Adm free
🛆 Signs from Underground
Cambridge Heath 5 min
⊖ Bethnal Green
🛍

British Museum

Great Russell St, London WC1B 3DG
☎ 071 636 1555

Britain's most important museum offers everything from Egyptian mummies to the Elgin Marbles, from Shakespeare's writing to mechanical man-eating tigers. Buy a simple guidebook and pick your targets.

🕐 All year, Mon–Sat 10–5, Sun 2.30–6
🅴 Adm free
⊖ Tottenham Ct Rd/Russell Sq/Holborn
🛆 🚼 🍴 🛍

Buckingham Palace

Buckingham Palace Rd, London SW1
☎ 071 493 3175

With a chance to see 18 big rooms in the palace including the Throne Room, State Dining Room and Picture Gallery, tickets are snapped up fast and the daily allocation is mostly gone by noon. Unless you get on the Honours List, this is your best chance to see inside the palace.

🕐 Daily, early Aug–early Oct, 9.30–5.30
🅴 Ad £8, Chd £4, SC £5.50
✳ Tkt office opens 9am
Victoria/Charing X
⊖ Green Pk/St James's Pk/Victoria
🛆 (prior notice)

Cabaret Mechanical Theatre

33/34 The Market,
Covent Garden WC2E 8RE
☎ 071 379 7961

Bang in the middle of the bustling stalls and street entertainers, this smallish shop offers more than 50 hand-made mechanical figures and scenes, all of which you can move by pushing buttons or feeding in a coin.

🕐 All year, daily 10–6.30
🅴 Ad £1.95, Chd(6+)/SC £1.20, f/t
Charing X
⊖ Covent Garden
🛆 🛍

Cabinet War Rooms

Clive Steps, King Charles St,
London SW1A 2AQ
☎ 071 930 6961

This 3-acre underground bomb-proof complex within spitting distance of the Houses of Parliament was where the Government ran Britain during World War II. There are 21 rooms (of 70) to see, including Churchill's bedroom with his siren suit and gas mask (and cigar).

🕐 All year, daily 10–6 (last adm 5.15)
💷 Ad £3.90, Chd £1.90, SC £3
🚇 Victoria/Charing X
🚇 Westminster
♿

Changing of the Guard

Buckingham Palace/Horse Guards,
Whitehall/St James's Palace
☎ 0839 123411

One of London's really great free shows. The Queen's Guard Change at Buckingham Palace takes about 30 min, in Horse Guards, Whitehall about 25 min. The Guard at St James's Palace changes between 11.15 and noon on the same days as the Change at Buckingham Palace.

🕐 Phone for details
💷 Free
🚇 Victoria/Charing X
🚇 Green Pk/Westminster
♿

Chislehurst Caves

Old Hill, Chislehurst, Kent BR7 5NB
☎ 081 467 3264

People have been sheltering here for around 8,000 years. Miles of caves carved in chalk include early caves, Druid altars, Royalist Civil War hideouts and World War II air raid shelters. Best time to go is the 2.30 Sunday or Bank Holiday tour which goes to parts of the system not usually open to the public.

🕐 Daily: Easter–Sep 10–5,
   Sep–Mar 11–4.30
💷 Ad £3, Chd/SC £1.50;
   long tour: £5/£2.50
🚇 Chislehurst 10 min
♿ (res) ☕ 🅿

Commonwealth Institute

Kensington High St, London W8 6NQ
☎ 071 603 4535

Commonwealth countries tell you about themselves and show off their crafts and skills. You can find a vibrant dancing dragon from Hong Kong, sitar lessons from India, or a Canadian snomobile to ride (well, sit on).

🕐 All year, Mon–Sat 10–5, Sun 2–5
💷 Adm free
🚇 High St Kensington/Earls Ct/Olympia
♿ 🍴 🛍

Cutty Sark

King William Walk, Greenwich SE10 9HT
☎ 081 858 3445

Once the fastest clipper of her time,
the *Cutty Sark*, with a 44m mainmast,
an acre of sail and 10 miles of
rigging, could travel 363 miles a day
with a cargo of tea from China. The
cargo now is the world's largest
collection of ship's figureheads.

🕐 Apr–Sep, Mon–Sat 10–6, Sun 12–6;
  Oct–Mar, Mon–Sat 10–5, Sun 12–5
£ Ad £3.25, Chd/SC £2.25, f/t
🚹 Also river bus
🚏 Greenwich/DLR Island Gardens
  (+Thames foot tunnel)

Design Museum

Butlers Wharf, Shad Thames,
Tower Bridge SE1 2YD
☎ 071 403 6933/407 6261 info

It might seem odd to fill a museum
with cars, computers, kettles,
climbing frames and things you can
still buy in High Street shops, but a
lot of the stuff is touchable, it is all
bright, and presented as fun.

🕐 All year, daily (phone re times)
£ Ad £4.50, Chd/SC £3.50
🚹 Also river bus
🚏 London Bridge; DLR Tower Gateway
⊖ Tower Hill/London Bridge
♿ 🚻 🍴

Fan Museum

12 Crooms Hill, Greenwich SE10 8ER
☎ 081 305 1441

The only museum in the world
devoted only to fans. They have
thousands here: elaborate, simple,
beautiful, cooling and relaxing.
Georgian house with Japanese
garden.

🕐 All year, Tue–Sat 11–4.30,
  Sun 12–4.30
£ Ad £2.50, Chd/SC £1.50, f/t
🚏 Greenwich 5 min

Geffrye Museum

Kingsland Rd, London E2 8EA
☎ 071 739 9893

Once a set of East End almshouses,
this is now a bright and imaginative
museum which has a room setting
for almost every social era from
Elizabethan times onwards.

🕐 All year, Tue–Sat 10–5, Sun/BH 2–5
  (not Good Fri)
£ Adm free
✳ Gardens
🚏 Liverpool St 20 min
⊖ Old St/Liverpool St
♿ 🚻 🛍

Guinness World of Records

Trocadero Centre, Coventry St,
London W1V 7FD
☎ 071 439 7331

Think thin...stand beside the life-size model of the world's heaviest man. Think big...beside the world's smallest things, as recorded in the *Guinness Book of Records*. The world of trivia joins forces with the latest in electronic and audio-visual techniques to make compulsive viewing.

🕐 All year, daily 10–10
£ Ad £5.75, Chd £3.75, SC £4.50, f/t
♯♯♯ Charing X
⊖ Piccadilly/Leicester Sq
♿ ☕ 🍽 🛍

Hampton Court Palace

East Molesey, Surrey KT8 9AU
☎ 081 781 9500/977 8441 info

Henry VIII, Anne Boleyn, Cardinal Wolsey all walked the same corridors as today's visitors (although Henry might not have visited the fascinating kitchens). The oldest Tudor palace in Britain has a magnificence to remember. Don't miss the maze and the vine in the Thameside gardens.

🕐 Mid Mar–mid Oct, Mon 10.15–6,
   Tue–Sun 9.30–6; Mid Oct–mid Mar,
   Mon 10.15–4.30, Tue–Sun 9.30–4.30
£ Ad £7, Chd £4.70, SC £5.30, f/t
/🛈 Also river bus
♯♯♯ Hampton Court
♿ ☕ 🍽 🛍 🅿

HMS Belfast

Morgans Lane, Tooley St, London SE1 2JH
☎ 071 407 6434

The largest preserved warship in Europe stands to, her systems set at battle stations. The *Belfast*, a World War II cruiser, has 7 decks, and marked routes take you through them all, from boiler room to bridge via the big guns.

🕐 Daily: summer 10–6 (last adm 5.15);
   winter 10–5 (last adm 4pm)
£ Ad £4, Chd £2, SC £3
/🛈 Also river bus
♯♯♯ London Bridge/DLR Tower Gateway
⊖ Tower Hill/Monument/London Bridge
☕ 🛍

Horniman Museum & Gardens

100 London Rd, Forest Hill SE23 3PQ
☎ 081 699 2339/1872

Mr Horniman was a Victorian tea merchant who roamed the world for the unusual, the rare, the lovely. The result is this museum, which includes 1,500 musical instruments ranging from whistling Peruvian pots to jungle drums, via violins and more familiar sounds. And you can hear them.

🕐 All year, Mon–Sat 10.30–5.30,
   Sun 2–5.30
£ Adm free
✳ Chd Workshop: Sat 10.30–12.30
   (Mon–Sat/sch hols)
♯♯♯ Forest Hill 15 min
♿ ☕

Houses of Parliament

Westminster, London SW1
☎ 071 219 4273

Mother of parliaments, home of democracy, or the bad-mannered talking shop? You can decide by visiting the echoing Victorian building. You need a ticket (from your MP) to get in at 2.30, or for question times, or for a tour. Other times, turn up and join the queue.

🕐 Mon–Thu 2.30–10.30, Fri 9.30–3.
   Question Time: Mon–Thu 2.30–3.30
   (PM questions Tue/Thu)
🅴 Visitors' Gallery: adm free
⊖ Westminster
♿

Imperial War Museum

Lambeth Rd, London SE1 6HZ
☎ 071 416 5000

Be terrified in the trenches of World War I, shudder in a shelter or fly on a

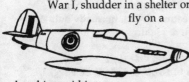

bombing raid in World War II. The museum has the best sight, sound and smell re-creations of history anywhere in London, plus a real U-boat, Spitfires and well-displayed galleries.

🕐 All year, daily 10–6
🅴 Ad £3.90, Chd £1.95, SC £2.90, f/t
🚉 Waterloo
⊖ Lambeth N/Elephant & Castle
♿ ☕ 🛍

Kensington Palace

Kensington Gardens, London W8 4PX
☎ 071 937 9561

William and Mary had Sir Christopher Wren in to do alterations, Queen Victoria was born here, and you can see the cot used by all 9 of her children. Another highlight, apart from the State Apartments, is the great collection of court dress: 200 and more years of what Europe's richest and best-dressed women wore.

🕐 All year, Mon–Sat 9–5, Sun 11–5
   (last adm 4–15)
🅴 Ad £4.50, Chd £3, SC £3.40, f/t
⊖ Queensway/High St Kensington
☕ 🛍

Kenwood House

Hampstead Lane, Kenwood,
London NW3 7JR
☎ 081 348 1286

A beautiful house and grounds near Hampstead Heath. Fine paintings, but more unusual are the collection of shoe buckles and jewellery. On summer evenings they have classical music concerts beside the lake.

🕐 Daily: Apr–Oct 10–6, Nov–Mar 10–4
🅴 Adm free
⊖ Golders Green/Archway
♿ ☕ EH

London Dungeon

28–34 Tooley St, London SE1 2SZ
☎ 071 403 0606

Convincing special effects bring
London's violent past to gruesome
life, getting you close to Jack the
Ripper, the medieval axeman and
the more modern hangman. Not for
the nervous, and not recommended
for young children.

🕐 Daily: Apr–Sep 10–6.30,
   Oct–Mar 10–5.30 (last adm 1hr before)
💷 Ad £6.50, Chd £4, SC £5.50
🚇 London Bridge
✚ London Bridge
☕ 🍴 🏠

London Planetarium

Marylebone Rd, London NW1R 5LR
☎ 071 486 1121

Shows which move the earth and
give a guided tour of the universe
are a fascinating and impressive
introduction to astronomy. They
last half an hour and are held every
40 minutes, leaving time to pop
next door to Madame Tussauds
[qv]. An activity area gives you a
closer look at the constellations.

🕐 All year, Mon–Fri
   12.20–5, Sat/Sun/sch
   hols 10.20–5
💷 Ad £4.20,
   Chd (5–15) £2.60,
   SC £3.25, f/t
✚ Baker Street
☕ 🏠

London Transport Museum

The Piazza, Covent Garden WC2E 7BB
☎ 071 379 6344

After a £4m refurbishment the
museum has 3 new galleries. There
are Underground steam trains,
buses which went to the front in
World War I, hansom cabs from
Sherlock Holmes times. And more.

🕐 All year, daily 10–6 (last adm 5.15)
💷 Ad £3.95, Chd (5–15)/SC £2.50, f/t
✚ Covent Garden
♿ ☕ 🏠

London Zoo

Regent's Park, London NW1 4RY
☎ 071 722 3333

More than 8,000 animals and a
comprehensive, accessible
Children's Zoo. Big effort made to
inform visitors about animals and to
encourage getting close. The
nocturnal showcase lets you see
creatures which normally only come
out at night.

🕐 All year, daily 10–5
💷 Ad £6.50, Chd £4.50, SC £5.50, f/t
✚ Camden Town
♿ ☕ 🍴 🏠 🅿

Lord's Cricket Tour

MCC, Lords Ground, London NW8
☎ 071 266 3825

 You can see the Ashes, and relics of cricketing greats from before W.G.Grace right up to today's heroes. Male visitors can even see the Long Room, through which the sport's most famous names have passed on the way to fame; but not during match days.

🕐 All year, phone for details
£ Ad £4.95, Chd/SC £3.50
🚇 Paddington 25 min
🚇 St John's Wood
♿ (prior notice) 🛍

Madame Tussaud's

Marylebone Rd, London NW1R 5LR
☎ 071 935 6861

Continuous updating ensures that the waxworks collection is packed with the famous and fashionable. The Chamber of Horrors contains the notorious, while Spirit of London has a taxi 'time machine' which uses high-tech and wax figures to give a moving history of London.

🕐 All year, Mon–Fri 10–5.30, Sat/Sun 9.30–5.30
£ Ad £7.95, Chd(5+) £4.95, SC £5.95, f/t
🚇 Baker Street
♿ (prior notice) 🍴 🛍

Monument

Monument St, London EC2 8AH
☎ 071 626 2717

You can climb to the top of this pillar, put up to commemorate the Great Fire of London in 1666. The column is 62m high, exactly the distance from its base to the point in Pudding Lane where the fire started. The view has changed.

🕐 Apr–Sep, Mon–Fri 9–6, Sat/Sun 2–6 (closed May Day); phone re winter
£ Ad £1, Chd 25p
🚇 Monument

Museum of London

150 London Wall, London EC2Y 5HN
☎ 071 600 3699

The story of London from prehistoric times to the present. Highlights are the Fire of London display, the Lord Mayor's coach, the Cheapside hoard of Elizabethan jewels and the Victorian shops.

🕐 All year, Tue–Sat 10–6, Sun 12–6
£ Ad £3, Chd £1.50; ♿ free
🚇 Moorgate
🚇 Barbican/St Pauls/Moorgate
♿ 🍴 🛍

Museum of Mankind
6 Burlington Gardens, London W1
☎ 071 437 2224

Full battle gear for a Zulu warrior,
fishing tackle for Eskimos, more
Red Indians than you could shake a
tomahawk at, enough Maori tattoos
to frighten an All Black...all here in
a great collection of customs and
cultures from all over the world.

🕐 All year, Mon–Sat 10–5, Sun 2.30–6
£ Adm free
⊖ Piccadilly
♿ ☕ 🛍

 Museum of the Moving Image
South Bank, London SE1 8XT
☎ 071 928 3535

The moving story of film, from the
first flickering home movies to the
latest Oscar winners and TV soaps.
More than 50 displays of stardom
and technical wizardry. Lots of
hands-on activities and actors in
costume.

🕐 All year, daily 10–6 (last adm 5pm)
£ Ad £5.50, Chd/SC £4, f/t
🚌 Waterloo
⊖ Waterloo
♿ ☕ 🍽 🛍

Musical Museum
368 High St, Brentford TW8 0BD
☎ 081 560 8108

This old church houses instruments
which play by themselves. You can
listen to a fully automatic Wurlitzer
theatre organ, polyphons in plenty
and even an automatic violin.

🕐 Jul/Aug, Wed–Fri 2–4, Sat/Sun 2–5;
Apr–Jun/Sep/Oct, Sat/Sun 2–5
£ Ad £3.20, Chd/SC £2.50, f/t
⊖ Gunnersbury
♿ 🛍

National Army Museum
Royal Hospital Rd, London SW3 4HT
☎ 071 730 0717

Six centuries of British feats of arms,
many exhibits heightened by sound
effects and atmospheric re-creation.
You can also see the original
message which led to the disastrous
Charge of the Light Brigade, and
other famous memorabilia.

🕐 All year, daily 10–5.30
£ Adm free
⊖ Sloane Square
♿ ☕ 🛍

National Gallery

Trafalgar Square, London WC2N 5DN
☎ 071 839 3321

The pictures might not move, but
they are among the best paintings
by the world's best artists and not
to be missed. Well organised trails
help adults find the famous pictures
and children to discover intriguing
and beautiful details.

🕓 All year, Mon–Sat 10–6, Sun 2–6
💷 Adm free (not major exhibs)
⌗ Charing X
⊖ Leicester Square
♿ ☕ 🛍

National Portrait Gallery

St Martin's Place, London WC2H 0HE
☎ 071 306 0055

Now has photographs of the great
and the good as well as paintings. It
means you can see how Princess Di
looked when she became engaged,
how Charles I looked before he was
beheaded and whether Anne Boleyn
might really have had six fingers.

🕓 All year, Mon–Sat 10–6, Sun 12–6
(not May Day/Good Fri)
💷 Adm free
⌗ Charing X
⊖ Leicester Sq
♿ 🛍

National Maritime Museum

Romney Rd, Greenwich SE10 9NF
☎ 081 858 4422

The British as sailors
from their days of
dugout canoes to the
times when the
great liners strutted
the world's oceans.
Lots of exhibits,
but the display
everyone
remembers is
Nelson's uniform,
still bloodstained
from Trafalgar.

🕓 Apr–Sep, Mon–Sat
10–6, Sun 12–6; Oct–Mar, Mon–Sat
10–5, Sun 2–5
💷 Ad £3.95–£7.95,
Chd(7+)/SC £2.95–£5.45, f/t
⚠ Also river bus
⌗ Greenwich/DLR Island Gardens
(+Thames foot tunnel)
♿ ☕ 🛍

Natural History Museum

Cromwell Rd, London SW7 5BD
☎ 071 938 9123

See the great dinosaur collection
which has living, moving, hunting
models, and the life-size model of
the world's biggest creature, the
blue whale. There is a special
display on the world's most
dangerous creature - man - and
Plant Power shows how we are
dependent on plants for food, light
and shelter.

In the **Geological Museum**,
which is in the same building, you
can watch a volcanic eruption or an
earthquake. There is also a fabulous
display of diamonds, emeralds,
rubies and other precious minerals
and crystals.

🕓 All year, Mon–Sat 10–6, Sun 11–6
💷 Ad £5, Chd/SC £2.50, f/t
⊖ South Kensington
♿ ☕ 🍴 🛍

Pollock's Toy Museum

1 Scala St, London W1P 1LT
☎ 071 636 3452

Old-fashioned
collection of
toys, dolls,
dolls' houses and
teddy bears, and
miniature
Victorian
theatres in
which, with
cut-out
cardboard
figures,
children
used to stage their own plays.

🕐 All year, Mon–Sat 10–5.30
💷 Ad £2, Chd 75p (Sat: free with adult)
⊖ Goodge Street
📖

Rock Circus

London Pavilion, 1 Piccadilly,
London W1V 9LA
☎ 071 734 7203

The history of rock music (almost)
live! High-tech audio and video
offers you moving, speaking,
singing greats of rock including the
Beatles and Elvis Presley
performing their top numbers.

🕐 All year, daily 11–9
    (later in summer)
💷 Ad £6.95, Chd/SC
    £4.95, f/t
⊖ Piccadilly
♿ ☕ 📖

Royal Mews

Buckingham Palace Rd, London SW1W 0QH
☎ 071 799 2331

This is a working area and what
you can see varies. Among the
magnificent royal conveyances here
are George III's Gold State Coach
and the famous Glass Coach. Also
the horses that pull them, and the
fleet of royal Rolls-Royces.

The nearby **Queen's Gallery** has
much of the priceless royal art
collection (Mar-Dec; phone for
details 071 799 2331).

🕐 Jan–Mar/Oct–Dec, Wed only 12–4;
    Apr–Sep, Tue–Thu 12–4
💷 Ad £3, Chd £1.50, SC £2, f/t
✳ Cmbd tkt with Queen's Gallery:
    £5/£2.20/£3.50, f/t
🚉 Victoria
⊖ Victoria
♿ (not Queen's Gallery)

Rugby Football Union Museum

National Stadium, Rugby Rd,
Twickenham TW1 1DZ
☎ 081 892 8161

Jerseys worn by the famous, caps of
conquerors, even tide marks in the
big double baths, are objects of
deep respect to true fans. Video of
pre-match preparations. Guided
tours have to be booked in advance.

🕐 All year, Mon–Fri 9.30–1
    & 2.30–5
💷 Tour: Ad £1, Chd 50p
🚉 Twickenham 10 min
⊖ Hounslow
    East/Richmond
♿ 📖 🅿

St Edward's Tower

Westminster Cathedral, Victoria St,
London SW1P 1QW
☎ 071 834 7452

One of the best views of London's riverside. Ride 83m up in the lift to the top of the bell tower of the great liquorice allsort-striped Roman Catholic cathedral, and gaze in wonder.

🕐 Apr–Oct, daily 9.30–5
💷 Ad £2, Chd/SC £1, f/t
🚇 Victoria
🚇 Victoria

St Paul's Cathedral

St Paul's Churchyard, London EC4
☎ 071 248 2705/236 0752 info

Christopher Wren's most famous church. In the Whispering Gallery, the sound hurtles across 34m to be heard on the other side. Golden Gallery gives a wonderful view of the City. Look for the peapod 'signature' on the decorative wood carvings of Grinling Gibbons.

St Paul's took 38 years to build. As well as being one of the greatest architects of all time, Christopher Wren was a mathematician and astronomer, and twice, briefly, a Member of Parliament. Busy fellow.

🕐 Mon–Sat 8.30–4.30
(Crypt 9–4.15/Galleries 9.45–4.45)
💷 Ad £2.50, Chd £1.50 (donation)
✳ Guided tours
🚇 St Paul's
♿

Science Museum

Exhibition Rd, South Kensington,
London SW7 2DD
☎ 071 938 8000

Science from the first steam engine to the latest space probe, lightning flashes, pioneer cars and a full-size Apollo moon-lander are all here to see. The children's gallery lets you test reflexes, star in a special effects video, and shake hands with yourself.

🕐 All year, Mon–Sat 10–6, Sun 11–6
💷 Ad £4.50, Chd/SC £2.40, f/t
🚇 South Kensington
♿ ☕ 🍴 🛍

Shakespeare Globe Museum

1 Bear Gardens, Bankside,
London SE1 9EB
☎ 071 620 0202

Find out what it was like to go to the theatre when Will Shakespeare was still exercising his quill. Models, replicas and memorabilia. Part of the project to rebuild the Globe Theatre.

🕐 All year, Mon–Sat 10–5, Sun 2–5.30
💷 Ad £3, Chd/SC £2
🚇 London Bridge/Cannon St
🚇 London Bridge/Cannon St/Mansion Hse
♿ 🛍

Sir John Soane's Museum

13 Lincolns Inn Fields, London WC2A 3BP
☎ 071 405 2107

Soane (1753-1837) was one of the most famous architects of his time, and he designed this extraordinary little house for himself. It has a rustic grotto, the sarcophagus of one of ancient Egypt's pharaohs, Seti I, and an art gallery with hinged walls which swing back and forward to give 4 sets of pictures in the same space. Fascinating and fun.

🕘 All year, Tue–Sat 10–5
£ Adm free
✳ Guided tour Sat 2.30
⊖ Holborn

Spencer House

27 St James's Pl, London SW1A 1NR
☎ 071 499 8620

Recently restored, this private palace was once owned by Earl Spencer, an ancestor of Princess Di. You can see 9 State Rooms once graced frequently by royalty, and now looking as they did in Georgian times.

🕘 Feb–July/Sep–Dec: Sun 11–5.30,
last adm 4.45
£ Ad £6, Chd £5
✳ Advisable to book
⊖ Green Park
♿

Tate Gallery

Millbank, London SW1P 4RG
☎ 071 887 8000

The Tate is full of paintings you already know or want to see. Children will like Andy Warhol's Coke bottles and soup cans, and the mystic pixie people in *The Fairy Feller's Master Stroke*. Beatrix Potter's original illustrations for *The Tailor of Gloucester* are here, too.

🕘 All year, Mon–Sat 10–5.50, Sun 2–5.50
£ Adm free (not major exhibs)
⊖ Pimlico
♿ (prior notice) ☕ 🍽 🛍

Thames Barrier Visitor Centre

Unity Way, Woolwich SE18 5NJ
☎ 081 854 1373

See the largest movable flood barrier in the world, and learn, in a slick audio-visual presentation, how it saves London from drowning.

🕘 All year, Mon–Fri 10–5,
Sat/Sun 10.30–5.30
£ Ad £2.50, Chd/SC £1.55, f/t
⚠ Also river bus
🚆 Charlton 20 min
♿ ☕ 🛍 🅿

Theatre Museum

1E Tavistock St, London WC2E 7PA
☎ 071 836 7891/7624 info

A kind of touring company from the Victoria & Albert, with quality theatrical exhibits. Items range through theatre, ballet and circus with just a touch of music hall. Stage struck visitors may want an encore.

🕐 All year, Tue–Sun 11–7
💷 Ad £3, Chd £1.50
⊖ Covent Garden
&. ▪

Theatre Royal Drury Lane

Catherine St, London WC2
☎ 071 494 5091

Claims to be the world's oldest operational theatre, and the 75-minute tour covers everything from the staging of the current show to more than 300 years of royal scandals, a murder or two, and the friendly ghost.

🕐 All year. Phone for details
💷 Ad/Chd £3.50
⊖ Covent Garden

Tower Bridge

London SE1 2UP
☎ 071 403 3761

High level, double-glazed walkways between the two towers give panoramic views of London and of the 1,000-ton drawbridges as they open to let ships through. High-tech exhibition tells the story of the bridge-building. Don't miss the wonderful Victorian engines.

🕐 Daily: Apr–Oct 10–6.30; Nov–Mar
   10–5.15 (last adm 75 min before)
💷 Ad £5, Chd (5–15)/SC £3.50, f/t
🛆 Also river bus
▦ Charing X/DLR Tower Gateway
⊖ Tower Hill
&. ▪

Tower Hill Pageant

Tower Hill Tce, London EC3N 4EE
☎ 071 702 0982

Your automated ride treks you through 900 years of London history ('See the Romans, hear the Vikings, avoid the Plague'), topped off with a display of recent Thameside archaeological finds.

🕐 All year, daily 9.30–5.30
   (4.30 Nov–Mar)
💷 Ad £5.45, Chd/SC £3.45, f/t
▦ DLR Tower Gateway
⊖ Tower Hill
&. ▪ 🍴 ▪

Tower of London
Tower Hill, London EC3N 4AB
☎ 071 709 0765

Plan to spend a long time. The
Beefeaters give free 1-hour
guided tours every 30 minutes,
then you can look
more closely at
the mind-
boggling
 armour
collection,
the torture
chamber and
execution
ground, and
the ravens.
Then there
are the
Crown
Jewels.
The nightly
ritual closing
of the
Tower has
gone on
for 700 years. Admission to the
Ceremony of the Keys (9.35-
10.05pm) is free but by ticket
application only, and you must
write at least 2 months before your
chosen date, offer alternative dates,
and enclose a SAE. Write to: The
Resident Governor, Queen's House,
at the above address.

🕐 Mar–Oct, Mon–Sat 9–6, Sun 10–6;
   Nov–Feb, Mon–Sat 9–5, Sun 10–5;
   last adm 1hr before
£ Ad £7.95, Chd (5–15) £5.25,
   SC £5.95, f/t
⚠ Also river bus
▦ DLR Tower Gateway
⊖ Tower Hill
⎕ 🍽 🛍

Victoria & Albert Museum
Cromwell Rd, London SW7 2RL
☎ 071 938 8500

There are 7 miles of galleries in this,
the world's best museum of
decorative arts. Draperies with gold
thread, samurai swords, musical
instruments, ivory chess men,
medieval beds...Real treasury stuff.

🕐 All year, Tue–Sun 10–5.50,
   Mon 12–5.50
£ Ad £4.50, Chd(12+)/SC £1.50
   (donation)
⊖ South Kensington
⎕ 🍵 🍽 🛍

Wembley Stadium Tours
Empire Way, Wembley HA9 0DW
☎ 081 902 8833

The 80-minute tour includes a
video of historic highlights, then it is
off to the dressing rooms and
players' tunnel. You can imagine
you have won the Cup! Tour every
45 minutes.

🕐 All year, daily 10–3 (not events days)
£ Ad £5.95, Chd/SC
   £4.25, f/t
⊖ Wembley Park
⎕ (prior notice)
⎕ 🛍 Ⓟ

Westminster Abbey

Dean's Yard, Parliament Square SW1P 3PA
☎ 071 222 5152

English kings and queens have been crowned (and christened and buried) here since William the Conqueror. Statues, memorials and graves of the good and famous. Poets' Corner includes Chaucer's tomb. Very busy early in the day.

🕐 Daily 9.20–4
 (Chapels closed 2–3.45 Sat)
💷 Nave: free. Chapels: Ad £4, Chd £1,
 SC £2. Museum: £2/£1/£1.50
✳ Brass rubbing Mon-Sat (071 222 2085)
⊖ Westminster
♿ EH

Wimbledon Lawn Tennis Museum

All England Club, Church Rd,
Wimbledon SW19 5AE
☎ 081 946 6131

History, magic memories on video, and a racket-making demonstration. Displays feature long skirts, short skirts and John McEnroe's trainers. Open only to spectators during Championships.

🕐 All year, Tue–Sat 10.30–5, Sun 2–5
💷 Ad £2, Chd/SC £1
⊖ Southfields
♿

Winston Churchill's Britain at War Museum

64–66 Tooley St, London SE1 2TF
☎ 071 403 3171

Themed museum about Britain at war, with emphasis on the Home Front and 'how we lived then'. Churchill speeches, Blitz sound effects, the buzz of rockets. Sights, sounds, smells - and all very patriotic.

🕐 Daily: Oct–Mar
 10–4.30,
 Apr–Sep 10–5.30
💷 Ad £5, Chd £2.75,
 SC £3.75, f/t
🚇 London Bridge
⊖ London Bridge
♿ ☕ 🛍

Bedfordshire
Buckinghamshire (N)
Derbyshire
Hertfordshire
Leicestershire
Lincolnshire
Northamptonshire
Nottinghamshire and
S Yorkshire borders

Aeropark & Visitor Centre

East Midlands Airport,
Castle Donington DE74 2SA
☎ 0332 810621

Set in a 12-acre park near the airport
so that, as well as watching modern
jets landing, you can examine
exhibits like the Lightning
jet fighter and Vulcan bomber.
Display of history and technology
of flying.

🕐 Daily, dawn–dusk. Centre: Easter–Oct
  Mon–Fri 10–5, Sat 11–4, Sun 11–6;
  Nov–Mar Sat/Sun 11–4
💷 £2 per car
🛣 M1 jnct 24, A453
♿ ⛲ 🎁 🅿

American Adventure Theme Park

Pit Lane, Ilkeston, Derbys DE7 5SX
☎ 0773 531521/769931 info

Dare you try Nightmare Niagara,
'the world's highest triple-drop log
flume'? If so, there is also
MotionMaster and The Missile, top
3 among more than 100 rides.
Pioneer Playland is for little 'uns;
plus live shows, Western shoot-
outs, and a golf game where a hole-
in-one wins £1,000.

🕐 Easter–Oct, daily from 10am
  (w/ends only mid Sep/Oct)
💷 Ad/Chd £10.99
🛣 M1 jnct 26
♿ ☕ 🍴 🎁 🅿

Baytree Owl Centre

Baytree Nursery, Weston,
Spalding PE12 9RA
☎ 0406 371907

Owls
from all
over the
world
inhabit a
specially
landscaped
area. You
can see them flying free, and there
is a conservation pond with
peafowl, ducks and swans.

🕐 Daily: summer 9.30–5.30;
    winter 9.30–4
💷 Ad £1.80, Chd £1.30
🅰 A151
  ♿ ☕ 🍴 🛍 🅿

Bellfoundry Museum

Freehold St, Nottingham Rd,
Loughborough LE11 1AR
☎ 0509 233414

Not a museum but a working
foundry, with displays of historic
bell-making in the largest complex
of its kind in the world.

🕐 All year, Tue–Sat
    9.30–12.30/1.30–4.30
💷 Ad 75p, Chd 50p
🅰 N of town centre
🚉 Loughborough 10 min
♿ 🅿

Belvoir Castle

Belvoir, Grantham, Lincs NG32 1PD
☎ 0476 870262

Pronounced 'Beaver'. The first castle
(this is the 4th) was built by one of
William the Conqueror's barons.
The castle is filled with treasures
and history, but current highlights
are the well-staged jousting
tournaments, held here on summer
Sundays and bank holidays.

🕐 Easter–Sep, Tue–Thu/Sat 11–5,
    Sun/BH 11–6; Oct, Sun 11–5
💷 Ad £4, Chd £2.50, SC £2.75
✳ Extra on jousting days
🅰 A607, SW of Grantham
⛺ 🍴 🛍 🅿

Blue John Cavern & Mine

Castleton, Sheffield S30 2WP
☎ 0433 620638/620642

Source of the rare, semi-precious
Blue John stone, mined here for
centuries. Visitors are guided
through workings including the
Grand Crystalised Cavern and
Waterfall Cavern to see
dramatically tinted stalactites.

🕐 Summer, daily 9.30–dusk.
    Phone re winter
💷 Ad £4, Chd £2,
    SC £2.50, f/t
🅰 A625, W of Castleton
☕ 🛍 🅿

73

Bosworth Battlefield & Country Park

Sutton Cheney, Market Bosworth,
Nuneaton CV13 0AD
☎ 0455 290429

Relive the battle that ended
the Wars of the Roses and let
Shakespeare write 'My
kingdom for a horse'.
Marked battle trails show
where it all happened, the
visitor centre displays arms
and armour and film clips from
Richard III. Special events such as
jousting during summer.

🕐 Easter–Oct. Park: dawn–dusk.
Centre: Mon–Fri 1–5, Sat/Sun/BH 11–4
(Jul–Aug daily 11–5)
💷 Park: free. Centre: Ad £2,
Chd/SC £1.30
🅰 A5, A444, A447
♿ 🚻 ☕ 🏪 🅿

Bradgate Country Park

Newtown Linford, Leics
☎ 0533 362713

Romantic ruined house in the centre
of wooded parkland was the home
of Lady Jane Grey, queen of
England for just 9 days. Now, deer
and picnickers occupy the hillsides,
and the Centre displays Lady Jane's
sad tale and local flora and fauna.

🕐 Apr–Oct, Tue–Fri 2–5, Sat/Sun/BH 1–6;
Nov–Mar, Sat/Sun 2–5.
Park: daily dawn–dusk
💷 Centre: Ad £1.20, Chd/SC 60p, f/t
🅰 B5327, NW of Leicester
♿ 🚻 🅿

Bransby Home of Rest for Horses

Bransby, Saxilby, Lincoln LN1 2PH
☎ 0427 788464

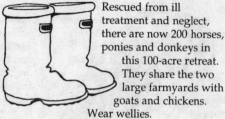

Rescued from ill
treatment and neglect,
there are now 200 horses,
ponies and donkeys in
this 100-acre retreat.
They share the two
large farmyards with
goats and chickens.
Wear wellies.

🕐 All year, Mon–Fri 8–4, Sat 9–3, Sun 1–4
💷 Adm free
🅰 A57
🚻 🏪 🅿

Brittain Pit Farm

Swanwick Jnct, Butterley Park, Ripley,
Derbys DE5 3QW
☎ 0773 512767

Ambitious idea which combines
building a farm at an abandoned pit
head, running an animal rescue and
making the pair a 'community
touch farm'. Rescued animals range
from gerbils to shire horses.

🕐 All year, daily 9–dusk
💷 Donations
🅰 A38
♿ 🚻 🏪 🅿

Burghley House
Stamford, Lincs PE9 3JY
☎ 0780 52451

The Cecil family have lived in this
great house for 400 years, collecting
some fine treasures including beds
slept in by royalty, letters from
kings and queens, as well as an
amazing painted room called,
modestly, The Heaven Room. Even
the kitchen makes people gasp. The
herd of fallow deer in the Deer Park
dates back to 1562.

🕒 Apr–beg Oct, daily 11–5
   (closed 1st Sat/Sep)
💷 Ad (+1 Chd) £5.10, Chd £2.50,
   SC £4.80, f/t
🅰 B1433, SE of Stamford
☕ 🍴 🎁 🅿

Butterfly & Falconry Park
Long Sutton, Spalding, Lincs PE12 9LE
☎ 0406 363833

Landscaped with tropical
plants, ponds and
waterfalls, the
butterfly area has
around 500
butterflies flitting
about. Outside,
falcons, eagles and
owls swoop down in
display twice a day at 12 and 3.
Elsewhere are acres of wildflowers,
farm animals, a mini-assault course
and an insectarium.

🕒 Daily, mid Mar–Oct 10–6
💷 Ad £3.40, Chd £2.20, SC £3
🅰 A17, Spalding/King's Lynn
♿ 🧒 ☕ 🎁 🅿

Calke Abbey Park
Ticknall, Melbourne, Derbys DE73 1LE
☎ 0332 863822

Built in 1701, the house is virtually
unchanged since the death of the
last owner in 1924, leaving a kind of
time capsule. Fascinating natural
history collections, carriages, even a
beer cellar. Set in 750 acres with
ambling Portland sheep and lovely
gardens.

🕒 Easter–Oct Sat–Wed: Hse 1–5.30;
   Gdn 11–5.30. Park: all year, dawn–dusk
💷 Ad £4.50, Chd £2.20, f/t. Gdn only: £2
✳ Braille guide
🅰 A514, S of Derby
♿ 🍴 🎁 🅿 NT

Carriage Museum
Red House Stables, Old Road,
Darley Dale, Matlock DE4 2ER
☎ 0629 733583

More than just a
collection of
broughams,
landaus and
diligences, for
you can
actually take
rides aboard
carriages,
and have
driving lessons in 1hp vehicles.
Afterwards you can, on most days,
watch the blacksmith at work.

🕒 All year, daily 10–5
💷 Ad £2, Chd £1, SC £1.50, f/t
🅰 A6, N of Matlock
🚆 Darley Dale 10 min
♿ ☕ 🅿

Carsington Water

Ashbourne, Derbys DE6 1ST
☎ 0629 85696

Britain's newest reservoir, providing
water for 3 million people, also
provides good recreation spots.
Wind-surfing, riding, canoeing and
cycle hire are all available at the
visitor centre, with displays about
the reservoir and the countryside
around.

🕐 Apr–Sep, Mon–Fri 10–6, Sat/Sun/BH
10–10. Oct–Mar/phone
💷 Adm free, pkg £1
🅰 B5035, SW of Wirksworth
♿ ☕ 🅿

Chestnut Centre Conservation Park

Castleton Rd, Chapel–en–le–Frith,
Derbys SK12 6PE
☎ 0298 814099

An otter haven and owl sanctuary
where you can see and learn about
different species of both. The Centre
has a notable record of breeding and
of rearing injured animals. Nature
trails. Special displays for children.

🕐 Mar–Dec, daily 10–5.30;
Jan/Feb Sat/Sun (phone/times)
💷 Ad £3.50, Chd £2
🅰 A625
☕ 🎁 🅿

Chatsworth House & Garden

Bakewell, Derbys DE45 1PP
☎ 0246 582204

The house has been furnished and
decorated through 450 years with
little expense spared, and it takes at
least an hour to walk through the
stunning display. Outside, the 100-
acre garden was landscaped by
Capability Brown, and the cascade
in the grounds is one of Europe's
gardening wonders, while the maze
(open some summer Sundays) is a
baffling delight.

🕐 Late Mar–Oct, daily. Hse: 11–4.30;
Gdn 11–5
💷 Hse/Gdn: Ad £5.50, Chd £2.75,
SC £4.75, f/t.
Gdn: £3/£1.50/£2.50, f/t.
Farm/Adv Playgnd: £2
🅰 B6012, N of Matlock
♿ (not house) ☕ 🍴 🎁 🅿

Clumber Park

Worksop, Notts S80 3AZ
☎ 0909 476 592

This 3,800-acre estate once held a
huge mansion; now you have access
to parkland,
farmland, woodland,
an 80-acre lake and
a chance to
wander down the
longest avenue
of lime trees in
Europe. For a
small fee you can
take boat trips, visit
the vineries, hire a bike,
fish or go orienteering.

🕐 Park: all year, dawn–dusk;
activities 10.30–5
💷 Adm free, pkg £2.50
🅰 A1/A57, SE of Worksop
♿ 🚲 ☕ 🍴 🅿 NT

Costume Museum

Wygston's House, 12 Applegate, Leicester
☎ 0533 473056

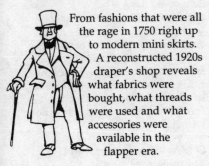

From fashions that were all the rage in 1750 right up to modern mini skirts. A reconstructed 1920s draper's shop reveals what fabrics were bought, what threads were used and what accessories were available in the flapper era.

🕐 All year, Mon–Sat 10–5.30, Sun 2–5.30
£ Adm free
⚠ Nr city centre
🚻 Leicester 15 min
♿ (res) ℗

Deene Park

Deene, Corby, Northants NN17 3EW
☎ 0780 450223/450278

Lovely Tudor house and garden, and the Brudenells have lived here since 1514. But the main reason to visit is the collection of military uniforms and mementos inside, including those of Lord Cardigan, the Brudenell responsible for the Charge of the Light Brigade.

🕐 Jun–Aug, Sun/BH 2–5 (+Easter/May BH);
   Park 1–5
£ Ad £3.50, Chd £1
⚠ A43, NE of Corby
♿ ☕ 🛍 ℗

Doddington Hall

Lincoln LN6 4RU
☎ 0522 694308

Doddington looks today almost exactly as it did when it was finished in 1600, so it is good for history projects. Look out for the Duke of Cumberland's 4-poster: he was 5 feet tall and weighed 23 stone, so the springs must be good.

🕐 May–Jul/Sep, Wed/Sun/BHM 2–6;
   Aug, Sun–Fri
£ Hse/Gdn: Ad £3.50, Chd £1.75, f/t.
   Gdn: £1.75/85p
⚠ A46, A57
♿ (res) ⚜ 🍴 🛍 ℗

⚑ Donington Collection/Grand Prix Racing Cars

Donington Park, Castle Donington,
Derbys DE7 2RP
☎ 0332 810048

Not only do they have Ayrton Senna's Marlboro Grand Prix machine, they have other top speed motors and motorbikes once driven by champion Mike Hailwood and others. A total of 130 *brrms* which once swept the tracks clean.

🕐 All year, daily 10–4
£ Ad £4, Chd £1.50
⚠ M1 jnct 24, A453
☕ 🛍 ℗

East Carlton Countryside Park

Market Harborough, Leics
☎ 0536 770977

This 100-acre park cleverly combines caring for the environment with a nostalgic look at the art of making quality steel. Surprisingly, a smithy and a nature trail get along very happily with craft workshops. Rare hardwood trees and a heritage centre.

🕐 Daily: Easter–Oct 10–6;
  Nov–Easter 11–4
£ Adm free
🅰 A427, W of Corby
♿ ☕ 🅿

Eco House

Western Park, Hinckley Rd,
Leicester LE3 6HX
☎ 0533 856675

Instead of talking about saving the planet's resources, this house tries to do something about it - and shows you how you can, too. Triple glazing, solar panels, heat-exchanger and organic gardening are all here and ·working. Leaves you thinking, while the youngsters use the Energy Playground.

🕐 All year, Wed–Fri 2–5,
  Sat/Sun 10–5
£ Adm free (donation)
🅰 A47 to Hinckley
♿ ☕ 🛍 🅿

Eyam Hall

Eyam, Sheffield S30 1QW
☎ 0433 631976

In the 300-odd years the Wright family have lived here, they have kept buying toys for the children... and clothes...and pictures of the family. Visitors are amazed at how much survives. It makes the visit to this Jacobean house a little bit special - and you won't believe the kitchen.

🕐 Easter–Oct, Wed/Thu/Sun/BH 11–5.30
  (last adm 4.30)
£ Ad £3.25, Chd £2.25, SC £2.75, f/t
🅰 B6521
☕ 🛍 🅿

Farmworld

Stoughton Farm Park, Gartree Rd, Oadby,
Leicester LE2 2FB
☎ 0533 710355

Will you have time for a spot of 'hands-on' milking of a Holstein cow as well as a cart ride with a shire horse? There is much to do, what with a children's farmyard, wood and lake walks and a toy tractor park. Leave time to meet the rare animals.

🕐 Daily: Easter–Oct
  10–5.30; Oct–Mar
  10–5
£ Ad £4, Chd £2.25,
  SC £3, f/t
✳ Organic farm produce
🅰 A6, S of city centre
♿ 🎠 ☕ 🛍 🅿

Flag Fen
Fourth Drove, Fengate,
Peterborough PE1 5UR
☎ 0733 313414

This huge Bronze Age
settlement has been described
as one of the most exciting
archaeological finds this
century. You can see how the
experts are getting on
uncovering the 3,000-year-old
platform with its 4 million
timbers, and see some of the
swords, spears and other
dramatic finds. The landscape
park alongside has
reconstructed prehistoric buildings.

🕐 All year, daily 11–4
£ Ad £2.80, Chd £1.95, SC £2.55
✱ Visitor centre
⚠ A47, E of Peterborough
♿ ☕ 🛍 Ⓟ

Foxton Locks Country Park
Gumley Rd, Foxton,
Market Harborough, Leics
☎ 0533 656914

The park takes a woodland route to
follow the towpath of the Grand
Union Canal, so you can see boats
lifted up and down as they move
along, have a picnic or think of it as
studies in hydraulics.

🕐 All year, daily dawn–dusk
£ Adm free, pkg 50p
⚠ A6 Foxton/Gumley
♿ 🍴 ☕ Ⓟ

Great Central Railway
Great Central Rd, Loughborough LE11 1RW
☎ 0509 230726

Live and breathe steam as one of
the 18 full-size locos travels the 8½-
mile route from Loughborough
to Leicester,
long enough to
get up speed
and give you a feeling for the
romance of it all. Special events
include night steam trains.

🕐 May–Sep daily; Oct–Apr Sat/Sun.
Phone re timetable
£ Rtn: Ad £9, Chd £6.
Cheap Day: £6/£4. f/t
✱ Thomas the Tank specials etc
⚠ SE of town centre
🚉 Loughborough 15 min
♿ ☕ Ⓟ

Grimsthorpe Castle
Grimsthorpe, Bourne, Lincs PE10 0NB
☎ 0778 32205

Three things to look for: feeding
tame red deer beside the castle,
secondhand thrones and furnishings
from the old House of Lords - as
Lord Great Chamberlains, the de
Eresby family collected these as a
perk - and the vegetable garden,
designed to be ornamental as well
as edible. Nature trails and lake
fishing.

🕐 Park/Gdn: Easter/May–mid Sep,
Thu/Sun/BH 12–6.
Castle: Easter/Jun–mid Sep, Sun/BH 2–6
£ Castle: Ad £2.50, Chd/SC £1.25.
Park/Gdn: £1/50p
⚠ A151, NW of Bourne
♿ 🍴 ☕ Ⓟ

Gulliver's Kingdom

Temple Walk, Matlock Bath, Matlock,
Derbys DE4 3PG
☎ 0629 580540

Rides, an entire Wild West town, a
ghostly hotel and scaled-down
peaks and alps in Little Switzerland.
Good chairlift and imaginative
adventure playground.

🕐 Easter/Jun–Sep, daily 10.30–5;
 other times/phone
£ Ad/Chd £4.50, SC £3.95
🚗 A6
♯♯♯ Matlock 15 min
♿ ☕ 🍴 🅿

Heights of Abraham Country Park

Matlock Bath, Derbys DE4 3PD
☎ 0629 582365

Getting there is fun, for access is by
cable car which lifts you high up
the mountain where you can have
guided tours of 2 show caves and a
mine, puzzle your way through a
maze, roam nature trails or bounce
on trampolines in the play area.

🕐 Mid Feb–Mar, Sat/Sun 10–5;
 Easter–Oct, daily 10–5 (later Jul/Aug)
£ Ad £5.30, Chd £3.25, SC £4.30
🚗 A6
♿ 🧒 ☕ 🍴 💼 🅿

Haddon Hall

Bakewell, Derbys DE45 1LA
☎ 0629 812855

Fortified medieval manor house,
reckoned to be most complete
survivor of its era. The banqueting
hall is particularly grand, and the
house has many romantic legends
connected with it.

🕐 Apr–Sep, Tue–Sun 11–6
 (not Sun Jul/Aug)
£ Ad £4, Chd £2.50, SC £3, f/t
🚗 A6, SE of Bakewell
☕ 🅿

High Peak Trail

Peak National Park Office,
Bakewell DE4 1AE
☎ 0629 814321

The trail goes from High Peak
Junction near Cromford to Dowlow
near Buxton, a total of 17½ miles
along the route of the old Cromford
and High Peak railway. Wildflower
lovers can spot rarities like
cranesbill and wild thyme, but may
be distracted by the song of the
skylark.

🕐 All year, all day
£ Adm free
✳ Bike hire at Middleton
 Top/Parsley Hay
🚗 A6, A5012, A515
🧒 🅿

Horse World

Sand Lane, Osgodby, Market Rasen,
Lincs LN8 3TE
☎ 0673 843407

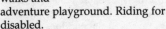

Horses galore
at work, rest
and play.
Range of
allied
activities from
simple riding
to cart rides,
hacking,
competitions,
plus forest
walks and
adventure playground. Riding for
disabled.

🕐 All year, daily 10–8
£ Ad £1.50, Chd 75p
🅰 A46, A1103
♿ ☕ 🛍 🅿

Incredibly Fantastic
Old Toy Show

26 Westgate, Lincoln LN1 3BD
☎ 0522 520534

Fascinating quick stop to see a one-
man collection of more than 1,000
toys, from dolls' houses and rocking
horses to train sets and teddies.
End-of-pier machines let you push
buttons, distorting mirrors make
you laugh.

🕐 Apr–Sep Tue–Sat 11–5, Sun/BH 12–4;
   Oct–Xmas Sat/Sun/sch hols
£ Ad £1.50, Chd 75p, SC £1
🅰 Nr castle
🚉 Lincoln 10 min
♿ 🅿

Knebworth House & Gardens

Knebworth, Stevenage, Herts SG3 6PY
☎ 0438 812661

Of film, TV and pop concert
fame. The house is richly
decorated, the gardens are
green and lovely, the park is
huge and filled with deer,
the adventure playground
big enough to charge a
separate entrance fee. What
more do you want in a
stately home?

🕐 Easter/end May–beg Sep.
   Park: daily 11–5.30. Hse/Gdn: 12–5
   (not Mon exc BH)
£ Hse/Gdn/Park: Ad £4.50, Chd/SC £4.
   Park/playgnd: £3
🅰 A1(M) jnct 7
🎡 ☕ 🛍 🅿

Leicester City Football Club

City Stadium, Filbert St, Leicester LE2 7FL
☎ 0533 854000

Behind-the-scenes tour of a major
soccer club includes not
just the trophy
room but training
facilities,
dressing rooms,
even the ref's
sanctuary.

🕐 Phone to book
£ Free
🅰 M1 jnct 21
🚉 Leicester 3 miles
♿ ☕ 🛍 🅿

Leighton Buzzard Railway

Page's Park Station, Billington Rd,
Leighton Buzzard LU7 8TN
☎ 0525 373888

Beautifully preserved narrow gauge
engines and rolling stock. Steam
locos - they include 9 from overseas
- puff proudly round a varied 3-mile
route.

🕐 Mid Mar–Oct; phone re timetable
💷 Ad £4, Chd £1, SC £3
🅰 A4146
♯ Leighton Buzzard 2 miles
♿ ☕ 🎁 🅿

Mablethorpe's Animal Gardens

North End, Mablethorpe, Lincs LN12 1QG
☎ 0507 473346

Local wildlife past and present,
including arctic foxes and
snowy owls as well as deer

and herons.
Overseas
visitors
include
alligators, porcupines and emus.
There is also a sanctuary for injured
animals - mainly seals and sea birds
- and a special display of tawny,
barn and little owls.

🕐 Sun before Easter–last Sun/Oct, daily 10–6
💷 Ad £2.50, Chd £1.50, SC £2
🅰 N of town
♿ ☕ 🎁 🅿

Mallory Park Racing Circuit

Kirkby Mallory,
Leics LE9 7QE
☎ 0455 842931

Friendly circuit where you can see
all the motorbike or racing car
action from grassy banks. Hairpin
and ultra-fast bends make it all the
more exciting, and you can get very
close to cars in the paddock.

🕐 Mar–Oct, Sun/BHM
   phone for details
💷 Ad £5.50–£8, Chd free
🅰 Off A47
♿ ☕ 🎁 🅿

Micrarium, The

The Crescent, Buxton,
Derbys SK17 6BQ
☎ 0298 78662

Microscopic images on large flat
screens. Plants, insects, bacteria and
crystals change and grow in
brilliant colours as you watch. An
award winner.

🕐 End Mar–Oct, daily 10–5.
   Some winter w/ends
💷 Ad £2.50, Chd £1.50, SC £2
🅰 Town centre
♯ Buxton 5 min
♿ 🎁

Mill on the Soar Falconry Centre

Coventry Rd, Sutton In the Elms,
Leics LE9 6QD
☎ 0455 285924

In between regular flying/hunting
demonstrations, the idea is to get
visitors as close as possible to the
resident owls, hawks, falcons and
wide-winged buzzards.

🕒 All year, daily 11–dusk
£ Ad £1.60, Chd/SC 80p
🅰 B4114, SW of Leicester
♿ ☕ 🅿

Museum of Entertainment

Millgate, Whaplode St Catherine,
Spalding, Lincs
☎ 0406 540379

Mechanical music at fairgrounds,
circuses, cinemas and theatres...that
is what enthusiasts remember and
lovingly preserve here. Exhibition
includes rare posters, live music and
guided tours.

🕒 Easter–Oct, Sat/Sun/BH 10–6;
    Jul–Sep, Mon–Fri 1–5
£ Ad £2, Chd £1.50, SC £1.80, f/t
🅰 A151, B1165
♿ ☕ 🅿

Museum of Lincolnshire Life

Burton Rd, Lincoln LN1 3LY
☎ 0522 528448

Lincolnshire folk are called
Yellowbellies; poet Alfred Lord
Tennyson started life with an accent
you could cut with a knife; the
world's first tank was made in
Lincoln and called Little Willie; cast
iron urinals made here sold all over
the world. Look and learn.

🕒 Daily: May–Sep 10–5.30;
    Oct–Apr Mon–Sat 10–5.30, Sun 2–5.30
£ Ad £1, Chd 50p, f/t
🅰 City centre
🚉 Lincoln 20 min
♿ ☕ 🛍 🅿

National Cycle Museum

The Lawn, Union Rd, Lincoln LN1 3BU
☎ 0522 545091

Climb aboard a penny-farthing,
examine a very ancient hobby-horse
bike and look at a magnesium racer;
and if you have never seen
unicycles, dicycles, tricycles, triplets
or quadricycles, now's your chance.

🕒 All year, daily 10–5
£ Ad £1, Chd 50p
🅰 Nr castle
🚉 Lincoln 20 min
♿ 🛍 🅿

National Stone Centre

Porter Lane, Wirksworth, Derbys DE4 4LS
☎ 0629 824833/825403

A quarry, mine and nature trail lays the ground for the presentation of everything from fossils to stone axes and knives, right on to decoration, sculpture and the 300 million tons of stone used in building in Britain every year. Thought provoking.

🕐 Daily: Easter–Oct 10–5; Nov–Mar 10–4
💷 Exhibition: Ad £1.80, Chd 90p,
    SC £1.20
🛣 B5035, N of Wirksworth
🚆 Cromford 2 miles
♿ ☕ Ⓟ

National Tramway Museum

Crich, Matlock, Derbys DE4 5DP
☎ 0773 852565

Some glided, some rattled, some were drawn by horses and some were powered by steam or electricity, yet for 50 years trams were kings of the road. Here you can see more than 50 of them, most in working order, and take mile-long rides through the complex, cruising past period street scenes.

🕐 Mar–Dec. Days/times vary, phone
💷 Ad £4.50, Chd £2.60, SC £3.80, f/t
✳ Special events
🛣 A6, SE of Matlock
♿ 🧺 ☕ 🎁 Ⓟ

Naturescape Wildflower Farm

Coach Gap Lane, Langar, Notts NG13 9HP
☎ 0949 51045/60592

Thirty acres of summer wildflowers, with birds, butterflies and all the visitors enjoying the sights and the scents. Separate wildlife garden shows what creatures are attracted, and gives ideas on how to encourage it all at home.

🕐 Apr–Sep, daily 11–5.30
💷 Ad £1.50, Chd/SC £1
    (mid Jun–mid Aug only)
🛣 Off A52 at Bingham, signs Langar
♿ ☕ Ⓟ

Nene Valley Railway

Wansford Station, Stibbington,
Peterborough PE8 6LR
☎ 0780 782854/782921 info

The 15-mile round trip between Wansford and Peterborough runs through the Nene Valley, and you can stop off at sites with parkland, nature trails, boat rides, even a miniature railway. A collection of 28 steam and diesel locos, including the original Thomas the Tank Engine, plus things like a Wagon Lits dining car and a water tower for the engines.

🕐 Mar–Oct. Days vary, phone
💷 Ad £6, Chd £3, SC £4.50, f/t
🛣 A1/A47 (Wansford); A605 (P'boro)
🚆 Peterborough 15 min
♿ 🧺 ☕ 🎁 Ⓟ

Newark Air Museum

The Airfield, Winthorpe, Newark NG24 2NY
☎ 0636 707170

More than 40 planes
to see.
Ansons,
Swifts and
Sycamores,
as well as
the more
familiar
Provost
trainer and
Vulcan, Meteor and
Vampire jets. Good
selection of memorabilia, well
displayed.

🕓 Daily: Apr–Oct Mon–Fri 10–5,
  Sat/Sun 10–6; Nov–Mar 10–4
💷 Ad £3, Chd/SC £2
🅰 A46, N of Newark
♿ ☕ 📷 Ⓟ

Northampton Central Museum

Guildhall Rd, Northampton, NN1 1DP
☎ 0604 39415

The museum has the largest
collection of shoes in the world.
Styles from pre-Roman sandals to
the latest in platform soles explain,
perhaps, why Britain has more shoe
shops per head of population than
anywhere else in Europe. Eat your
heart out Imelda Marcos.

🕓 All year, Mon–Sat 10–5, Sun 2–5
💷 Adm free
🅰 Town centre
🚌 Northampton 10 min
♿ 📷

Northcote Heavy Horse Centre

Great Steeping, Spilsby, Lincs PE23 5PS
☎ 0754 830286

Heavy horses are alive, well and
still working here. Not only can you
meet them and take wagon and cart
rides, you can listen to talks about
their life and history. Rare breeds
on show, too.

🕓 Days/times vary, phone
💷 Ad £3.75, Chd £2.55, SC £3.25
🅰 B1195, E of Spilsby
♿ ☕ Ⓟ

Our Little Farm

Lodge Farm, Plungar, Notts NG13 0JH
☎ 0949 60349

Set beside the Grantham Canal,
where you can walk a nature trail
after meeting Samson the shire
horse. A selection of interesting rare
breeds share the farm with goats
and ducks and more.

🕓 Mid Mar–Oct, Tue–Sun/BH 10.30–5.30
💷 Ad £2.20, Chd £1.20, SC £1.60
🅰 S off A52 at Bingham
♿ 🐾 ☕ 📷 Ⓟ

Patching's Farm Art Centre

Oxton Rd, Calverton, Notts NG14 6NU
☎ 0602 653479

Working pottery and artists' studios, with 50 acres planted specially for artists who buy tickets to paint here for the day. One part of the gardens is a reconstruction of the bridge and water-lily patch painted so often by Claude Monet.

🕐 All year, daily 9–10.30pm.
 Grounds: 9.30–6
💷 Grounds: Ad £1, Chd 50p. Centre: free
✳ Art courses, gallery
🛣 B6386, N of Nottingham
♿ 🍴 🛍 🅿

Peak Cavern

Castleton, nr Sheffield
☎ 0433 620285

The huge open mouth of this cave once housed a whole community of local ropemakers, and the Grand Entrance Hall is supposed to be the largest entry to any cave in Europe. Inside, the Orchestral Chamber produces wonderful sounds for people who only sing in their bath.

🕐 Apr–Oct, 10.30–4.30
💷 Ad £2.60, Chd £1.60
🛣 Below Peveril Castle
🅿

Poole's Cavern & Buxton Country Park

Green Lane, Buxton, Derbys SK17 9DH
☎ 0298 26978

Huge cave with thousands of stalactites stained into bright colours by iron deposits. Lived in by Stone Age tribes, Iron Age Celts, even Romans, it is named after a 15th-century outlaw who used it as a hideaway. Nature trails in 100-acre park which contains rare orchids and bird life.

🕐 Park: all year, dawn–dusk.
 Cavern: Easter–Oct, daily 10–5 (not Wed, Apr/May/Oct)
💷 Ad £3.20, Chd £1.60, SC £2.50
🛣 A53, A515
🚇 Buxton 20 min
♿ 🚶 🚼 🛍 🅿

Royal Crown Derby

194 Osmaston Rd, Derby DE3 8JZ
☎ 0332 712800

Royal Crown Derby, perhaps England's best known porcelain manufacturer, show you the making of it from clay to glazed and gilded dinner services and vases. Hand decoration skills are what visitors admire most.

🕐 All year. Museum: Mon–Fri 9.30–12.30/2–4.30.
 Tours: Mon–Fri/phone
💷 Tour: Ad £2.50, Chd £2.25 (no under 10s), f/t
🛣 A514
🚇 Derby 10 min
🛍 🅿

Rutland Water

Info Centre, Sykes Lane, Empingham,
Oakham, Leics LE15 8PX
☎ 0780 460321/0832 276427

The biggest man-made lake in
Western Europe
offers a range of
facilities. You can
hire bikes and stop off
perhaps at the Butterfly &
Aquatic Centre to see
what is happening
under the lake, or at Egleton
Nature Reserve to watch the
waterfowl. The *Rutland Belle* runs
pleasure cruises from near the
Whitwell car park.

🕐 All year, daily dawn–dusk
💷 Nature Res: Ad £3, Chd £1.50.
   Aqua Centre: £2.75/£1.
   Cruise: £2.80/£1.90. f/t
🅰 A606, E of Oakham
♿ 🧺 🍴 🛍 🅿

Sherwood Forest Visitor Centre & Country Park

Edwinstowe, Mansfield, Notts NG21 9HN
☎ 0623 823202/824490

The 450 acres of ancient forest
where Robin, Marian and the Merry
Men operated. There is a Robin
Hood exhibition and films, but the
park itself is good to walk and
picnic in. You can see why Robin
liked the place.

🕐 Daily. Park: dawn–dusk.
   Centre: Apr–Oct 10.30–5;
   Nov–Mar 10.30–4.30
💷 Adm free
🅰 B6034, W of Ollerton
♿ 🧺 🍴 🛍 🅿

Shuttleworth Collection

Old Warden Aerodrome,
Biggleswade, Beds SG18 9ER
☎ 0767 627288

Biggles lives! This collection of
vintage aeroplanes sits beside a
1920s grass aerodrome, and men in
goggles and leather jackets can make
them fly. The magnificent flying
machines range from a 1909 Bleriot
to a 1940s Spitfire, all kept in
working condition. Summer displays.

🕐 Daily: Apr–Oct 10–5; Nov–Mar 10–4;
   last adm 4/3
💷 Ad £4, Chd/SC £2.50
🅰 A1, 2 miles W of Biggleswade
🚌 Biggleswade 3 miles
♿ 🍴 🍽 🛍 🅿

🏝 Snibston Discovery Park

Ashby Rd, Coalville, Leics LE67 3LN
☎ 0530 510851/813608 info

You can travel in time, stroll
through a tornado and cycle with a
skeleton, thanks to the wonders of
science in this hands-on show. Or
you can go down a mine, or walk a
nature trail. This former colliery has
it all.

🕐 Daily: Apr–Oct 10–6; Nov–Mar 10–5
💷 Ad £4, Chd/SC £2.75, f/t
🅰 M1 jnct 22, A50
♿ 🍴 🛍 🅿

Speedwell Cavern

Winnats Pass, Castleton,
Sheffield S30 2WA
☎ 0433 620512

Your visit starts with a mile-long
underground boat journey to reach
the complex system of caves and
streams, including a subterranean
lake which once absorbed 40,000
tons of waste rock without the
water level rising an inch. They call
it the Bottomless Pit.

🕒 All year, daily 9.30–4.30
£ Ad £4/£4.50, Chd £2.50/£2.75,
   SC £3.25/£3.50
🅰 A625, W of Castleton
🍽 🛍 🅿

Stamford Steam Brewery Museum

All Saints St, Stamford, Lincs PE9 2PA
☎ 0780 52186

See what inspired the Victorian
worker, and find out how he was
treated. The brewery still has all the
traditional gear to move the amber
nectar from barley to bottle.

🕒 Mar–Oct, Wed–Fri 10–4, Sat/Sun 10–6
£ Ad £1.50, Chd/SC £1
🅰 Town centre
🚉 Stamford 5 min
🍽 🛍 🅿

Stockwood Craft Museum & Mossman Collection

Stockwood Country Park, Farley Hill,
Luton LU1 4BH
☎ 0582 38714

The craft museum shows
woodworking, brick-making and
various rural skills. The gardens
cover 900 years of garden history.
But the big draw for many will be
the Mossman Collection of horse-
drawn vehicles, which has
everything from milk carts to
vehicles made for films like *Chitty
Chitty Bang Bang*.

🕒 Apr–Oct, Tue–Sat 10–5, Sun 10–6;
   Nov–Mar, Sat/Sun 10–4
£ Adm free
🅰 M1 jnct 10
🚉 Luton 30 min
♿ 🍴 🍽 🛍 🅿

Stonehurst Family Farm

Loughborough Rd, Mountsorrel,
Loughborough LE12 7AR
☎ 0509 413216

Small animals can be cuddled and
stroked, but you just say hello to
Priscilla Pig and Dink the donkey
before you take a walk round the
farm. Then you can look in the
motor museum, which lets you get
close to vintage cars and
motor-bikes. The farm
shop sells freshly baked
bread.

🕒 Easter–Xmas, Thu–Tue 10–5
£ Ad £1.95, Chd 95p.
   Museum: Ad/Chd £1
🅰 A6, S of Loughborough
🍽 🛍 🅿

Stowe Landscape Gardens

Buckingham MK18 5EH
☎ 0280 822850

It takes 2 hours to cover the route in this unbelievable landscape. The grounds began being laid out in the 1730s, and what you see now - lawns, trees, follies, bridges, classical temples in groves, monuments and arches - is so astonishing that someone once called it 'Britain's largest work of art'.

🕐 Times vary/phone
💷 Ad £3.60, Chd £1.80, f/t
🅰 A422, 3 miles NW of Buckingham
♿ ☕ 🛍 🅿 NT

🔻 Sudbury Hall & NT Museum of Childhood

Sudbury, Ashbourne, Derbys DE6 5HT
☎ 0283 585305

The staircase, plasterwork and carvings send adults away delighted, but the bit to savour is the childhood museum, where you can see how children have lived in Britain throughout the ages. Different room settings, one of which offers children small and brave enough the chance to be a chimney sweep. Hall closing end September 1994 for restoration.

🕐 Apr–Oct, Wed–Sun/BHM 1–5.30/dusk
💷 Jnt tkt: Ad £4.40, Chd £2.20.
　 Mus only: £2.20/£1.10. f/t
🅰 A50, E of Uttoxeter
♿ (res) ☕ 🛍 🅿 NT

Sundown Kiddies Adventureland & Pets Garden

Treswell Rd, Rampton, Retford,
Notts DN22 0HX
☎ 0777 248274

Fun for the under 10s. They can play safely in the Smugglers' Cove, see animated fairy tales and be close enough to touch small tame animals in the garden.

🕐 Daily: Jun–Sep 10–6; Oct–May 10–5
💷 Ad/Chd £3.25
🅰 Off A57, E of A1
♿ ☕ 🛍 🅿

Tales of Robin Hood

30–38 Maid Marian Way,
Nottingham NG1 6GF
☎ 0602 483284/414414

Adventure car ride takes you into medieval England, where you escape the evil sheriff to shelter with Robin and his band. Noise, animation, scents (some not so sweet) bring the journey to life. Afterwards, try your hand at archery or watch the audio-visual on the Hood legend.

🕐 Daily: summer 10–6; winter 10–5;
　 last adm 1½hr before
💷 Ad £3.95, Chd/SC £2.95, f/t
🅰 Nr castle
🚉 Nottingham 10 min
♿ ☕

Temple Mine & Peak District Mining Museum

Temple Rd, Matlock Bath, Derbys DE4 3PS
☎ 0629 583834

Encounter 2,000 years of lead mining with ancient tools, smelting hearth and tunnels. Temple Mine, where you can go underground, is a working lead and fluorspar mine where gold was discovered in 1933. You can have a go at panning for it yourself.

🕐 Daily: summer 11–5; winter 12–4
£ Ad £1.50, Chd/SC £1.
   Mine & Museum: £2.50/£1.60
🅰 A6
♿ ☕ 🎁 ℗

Tours of the Unexpected

Tourism Unit, Northamptonshire Enterprise Agency Ltd, Royal Pavilion, 2 Summerhouse Rd, Moulton Park, Northampton NN3 6BJ
☎ 0604 671400

An intriguing variety of tours which take you behind the scenes of industry, business and community services in the county. There are almost 50 to choose from, but they only operate on certain days, are in great demand, and can only be booked through the above address. A few samples:

Ark Farm Dairy Products
Tiffield, nr Towcester

Large-scale sheep dairy farm. See it all, from ewes in fields to ice cream and yoghurt in pots.

Tour: 2–2½ hours
£ Ad/Chd £1

British Waterways
Braunston, nr Daventry

What it takes to keep Britain's canals up to scratch. Displays, demonstrations and boat trip.

£ free

DB Shoes
Northampton

You start with a piece of leather and end up with a gleaming, polished pair of shoes. Follow the footsteps of the manufacturing process from start to finish.

Tour: 1½–2 hours
£ Ad/Chd £1.50. Minimum age 10

Derngate
Northampton

The show must go on, but how? See the scene changes at this multi-media theatre, concert and conference venue.

Tour: 1 hour
£ Ad £1, Chd 75p. Minimum age 8

Forest Enterprise (Forestry Commission)
Fineshade, nr Corby

A visit to Rockingham Forest makes it clear that there is a lot more to managing woodland than shouting 'timber'.

Tour: 2 hours
£ Ad £2, Chd £1.50

Holdenby Falconry Centre
Holdenby House, Northampton

They have 19 species of birds in the grounds. Visitors can handle some and learn how to feed and train our feathered friends.

Tour: 1½ hours
£ Ad £2.50, Chd £1.50. Minimum age 7

Northampton Football Club
Northampton

The Saints are one of England's top rugby clubs. You see all the club facilities including the dressing rooms, gym and medical set-up, and might learn a thing or two about the scrum.

Tour: 1½ hours
£ free. Minimum age 10

Northampton Mercury Company
Northampton

Publishers of the *Chronicle & Echo*. See how the local evening newspaper is put together, and watch it rolling off the presses.

Tour: 1½–2 hours
£ Ad £2.50, Chd/SC £1

Northamptonshire County Cricket Club
Northampton

Recent stars have included Allan Lamb and Curtley Ambrose. Learn about the history of the club and how it manages in the modern game.

Tour: 1 hour
£ free. Minimum age 7

Royal Theatre
Northampton

Opened in 1884, the Royal is a handsome example of a Victorian pit theatre, and home to the Northampton Rep. On stage, backstage, but not upstaged.

Tour: 1 hour
£ Ad/Chd £2. Minimum age 5

Treak Cliff Cavern
Castleton, Sheffield S30 2WP
☎ 0433 620571

They still mine about half a ton of Blue John from here every year. It has the most spectacular stalagmites and stalactites, imaginatively stage-lit. A site of special scientific interest.

🕐 Daily: summer 9.30–5.30;
    winter 9.30–4
£ Ad £3.80, Chd £1.90, SC £3, f/t
🅰 A625, W of Castleton
🍴 🎁 Ⓟ

Tumble Town

107 High St, Arnold, Nottingham NG5 7DS
☎ 0602 671161

Children only. The play areas, which feature slides, bouncy castles, climbing frames, helter-skelters and more, are all supervised.

🕐 All year, Mon–Fri 10–6.30, Sun 10–4, Sat/sch hols 9.30–5.30
£ Chd £2.75
🅰 A60
♿ ☕ Ⓟ

Twycross Zoo

Twycross, Atherstone, Warwicks CV9 3PX
☎ 0827 880250

Underwater views of penguins and sea lions taking showers in a waterfall are highlights, but the pride of the zoo is the collection of primates. Spread over 50 busy acres are also lions, elephants, giraffes and more.

🕐 Daily: Apr–Oct 10–6, Nov–Mar 10–4
£ Ad £4, Chd (3–14) £2.50, SC £3
✳ Adv playgnd, rides
🅰 A444, N of Nuneaton
♿ 🍴 ☕ 🎁 Ⓟ

Whipsnade Wild Animal Park

Dunstable, Beds LU6 2LF
☎ 0582 872171

You can use the Great Whipsnade Railway or the road train to roam the 600 acres, where there are more than 2,500 endangered animals. Sea lion demonstrations, elephant encounters and birds-in-flight show, as well as a children's farm and 'run wild' play centre.

🕐 Daily: summer 10–6 (7pm Sun/BH); winter 10–4
£ Ad £6.95, Chd £5.45, SC £5.95
✳ Special events
🅰 M1 jnct 9/12
♿ ☕ 🎁 Ⓟ

White Post Modern Farm Centre

White Post Farm, Farnsfield,
Newark NG22 8HL
☎ 0623 882977

Almost 3,000 animals from day-old chicks to llamas, owls and quails. See the 8,000-egg incubator, follow the indoor 'night time' country walk. It is also a working farm, and you can tour it.

🕐 All year, Mon–Fri 10–5, Sat/Sun 10–6
£ Ad £2.75, Chd/SC £1.75
🅰 A614, N of Nottingham
♿ 🍴 ☕ Ⓟ

Woburn Safari Park
Woburn, Beds MK17 9QN
☎ 0525 290407

The stately home might be next door, but the stately animals are here, in Britain's largest drive-through game reserve. It is like being on a real safari. Then try the boating lake, amusement park and sea lion shows.

🕒 Daily,
  Mar–Oct 10–5
💷 Ad £7.50, Chd £5
🅰 M1 jnct 12/13
♿ ⛺ 🍴 🎁 🅿

World of Robin Hood
Haughton Farm, Haughton, Retford, Notts DN22 8DZ
☎ 0623 860210

Actors in doublets and armour go with you from a Crusader battle back to a medieval village and to Sherwood and the outlaws. Shoot an arrow, see the dungeons, visit a banqueting hall. History comes to life outdoors.

🕒 Apr–Oct, daily 10.30–4.30
💷 Ad £3.95, Chd/SC £2.95, f/t
🅰 B6387
♿ ☕ 🍴 🎁 🅿

Yew Tree Avenue
Clipsham Park Wood, Clipsham, Leics
☎ 0780 83394 info

An amazing line of trees, 150 in all and stretching half a mile, clipped, trimmed, shaved and coaxed into the shapes of animals, people, local characters and astronomical events. A one-off walk.

🕒 All year, dawn–dusk
💷 Adm free
🅰 B1176, N of Stamford
♿ 🅿

Midlands - West

Gloucestershire
Hereford & Worcester
Oxfordshire (N)
Shropshire
Staffordshire
Warwickshire
W Midlands

Acton Scott Historic Working Farm

Wenlock Lodge, Acton Scott, Shrops
☎ 0694 781306/7

No thudding tractor engines, chainsaws or combine harvesters. Here the clock winds back to Victorian techniques and quieter days: shire horses for ploughing, billhooks for hedging and scythes for harvest. Fascinating, instructive, organic...and you'll find the scones taste better, too.

🕐 Apr–Oct, Tue–Sat 10–5, Sun/BH 10–6
💷 Ad £2.75, Chd(5+) £1.50, SC £2, f/t
🅰 A49, S of Church Stretton
♿ 🧺 ☕ 🏪 🅿

Aerospace Museum

Cosford, Shifnal, Shrops TF11 8UP
☎ 0902 374112/374872

Not one, but 4 museums: warplanes, transport planes, research planes and missiles. The missile collection has a rocket made from concrete, and there are some exotic aircraft in the R&D section, some of which never made it off the ground. Transport planes take you back to Imperial Airways, when flying might have been slower but was a lot more fun.

🕐 All year, daily 10–5, last adm 4
💷 Ad £4, Chd £2.30, SC £3, f/t
🅰 M54 jnct 3, A41
♿ 🧺 ☕ 🏪 🅿

Alton Towers
Alton, Staffs
☎ 0538 702200

With 500 acres of parkland and
gardens and dozens of giant rides,
white-knuckle or just plain exciting,
there seems to be just too much to
do in one day. You may have to
face a second day after trying out
the Beast roller coaster, the
Runaway Mine Train, the
Thunderlopper, or the gentle Land
of Make Believe.

🕒 Mid Mar–beg Nov, daily 9am.
   Rides: 10–5/6/7 (vary per season)
💷 Pk/Off Pk: Ad £14/£15,
   Chd £10.50/£11, SC £5.50
🅰 B5032, 12 miles E of Stoke
♿ ⚲ 🚼 🍴 🎁 🅿

Amerton Working Farm
Stowe-by-Chartley, Stafford ST18 0LA
☎ 0889 270294

Working farm with close-ups of
feeding the animals, then seeing the
pedigree Jersey herd being milked
and watching ice cream being made
from the very same milk. You get to
eat it later.

🕒 Daily:
   Apr–Sep 9–6;
   Oct–Mar 9–5
💷 Adm free
🅰 A518, E of
   Weston
♿ ⚲ 🚼 🍴
🎁 🅿

Antique Doll Collection
Golden Cross, Wixford Rd,
Ardens Grafton, Warwicks B50 4LG
☎ 0789 772420

A fine collection
of 300 antique
dolls and
Victoriana
housed in a
grey stone
country
inn. It
makes a
pleasant

stop in lovely country, and
keeps both adults and children
happy.

🕒 All year, daily
   11–2.30/6–10
💷 Adm free
✱ Dolls & teddy
   bears for sale
🅰 Off A439, E of Bidford-on-Avon
♿ 🍴 🅿

Ashorne Hall Nickelodeon
Ashorne Hill, Warwick CV33 9QN
☎ 0926 651444

A real theatre organ rises up
through the floor, playing tunes
everyone knows. Elsewhere there
are more musical machines, from
player pianos to music boxes
and, of course, nickelodeons.
Sounds great.

🕒 All year (not Jan/1st 2 wks Jun);
   phone for details
💷 Varies/activities
✱ Parkland & gardens
🅰 M40 jnct 13/14
♿ 🚼 🅿

Avoncroft Museum of Buildings

Stoke Heath, Bromsgrove, Worcs B60 4JR
☎ 0527 831886/831363

A collection of whole buildings:
windmills, barns, medieval houses,
prefabs - even a 3-seater outside loo
- with traditional activities like
blacksmithing, brick-making and
wagon rides. A very different kind
of museum.

🕐 All year. Jun–Aug, daily 11–5.30;
other times/phone
💷 Ad £3.10, Chd £1.55, SC £2.20, f/t
🅰 A38
⛟ Bromsgrove 1½ miles
♿(res) ☕ 🏬 🅿

Bewdley Museum

The Shambles, Load St, Bewdley,
Worcs DY12 2AE
☎ 0299 403573

Must be the only museum
anywhere which makes clay pipes.
It also makes ropes, and has a brass
foundry and sawyard, all of which
reflect the wide range of industries
which once existed in this well-
preserved Georgian town.

🕐 Easter–beg Sep, Wed–Fri 10.30–4.30,
Sat/Sun/BHM 12–5
💷 Ad £1, SC 50p; chd free with adult
🅰 Town centre
⛟ Bewdley (Severn Valley Rlwy)
♿ 🏬

Berkeley Castle

Berkeley, Glos GL13 9BQ
☎ 0453 810332

A lot of history
here. Edward II
was foully
murdered in the
dungeons,
Shakespeare
mentions it,
Cromwell
besieged it, Queen Elizabeth
played bowls here. See the family
silver, watch butterflies from
Japan flutter by.

🕐 Apr, Tue–Sun 2–5; May–Sep,
Tue–Sat 11–5, Sun 2–5; Oct,
Sun 2–4.30
💷 Castle/Gdn: Ad £3.80,
Chd £1.90, SC £3, f/t.
Gdn: £1/50p.
Butterfly Farm: £1/50p
🅰 A38
♿(res) ☕ 🏬 🅿

Birdland

Rissington Rd, Bourton–on–the–Water,
Glos GL54 2BN
☎ 0451 820480

You can have penguins waddling
around just feet away from you.
They are joined by waterfowl and
tropical birds, many at liberty, on
this riverside garden area.

🕐 Daily: Apr–Oct 10–6;
Nov–Mar 10–4
💷 Ad £3, Chd £1.50,
SC £2.50
♿ ☕ 🏬 🅿

Birmingham Museum of Science & Industry

Newhall Street, Birmingham B3 1RZ
☎ 021 235 1661

The gallery of Light and Science is hands-on stuff. The oldest working steam engine in the world, made by James Watt, is here. There is a whole mini-museum of pens, and the locomotive hall has the coach rifled during the Great Train Robbery.

🕐 All year, Mon–Sat 11–5,
   Sun 11–5.30
💷 Adm free
🄰 Nr Telecom Tower
🚇 Snow Hill/New St 15 min
♿ 🍵 🛍

Black Country Museum

Tipton Rd, Dudley, W Midlands
☎ 021 557 9643

A whole village and more transplanted to the canal-side site by the castle. Chapel, pub, dockside work, mining and a ride on a tram are all there to be experienced, as is the real ale in the Bottle and Glass restored pub.

There are narrowboat trips along the **Dudley Canal Tunnel** to the Singing Cavern, where an audio-visual show relates mining history (☎ 021 520 5231. Mar–Nov, daily 10-5. Ad £1.90, Chd/SC £1.50).

🕐 Mar–Oct, daily 10–5;
   Nov–Feb, Wed–Sun 10–4
💷 Ad £4.95, Chd £3.40, SC £4.45, f/t
🄰 A4037
🚇 Tipton 15 min
♿ 🚶 🍵 🛍 🅿

Blenheim Palace

Woodstock, Oxfordshire OX20 1PX
☎ 0993 811091/811325 info

Visitors to Winston Churchill's birthplace (in a downstairs loo) can see the huge palace and 2,100 acres of parks and gardens, with butterfly house, adventure playground and nature trail. Motor launches, rowing on the lake and tackling the world's biggest symbolic hedge maze are optional.

🕐 Mid Mar–Oct,
   daily 10.30–5.30;
   last adm 4.45
💷 Ad £6.90, Chd £3.30,
   SC £4.90
🄰 A44
♿ 🚶 🍵 🍴 🛍 🅿

Bourton Model Village

The Old New Inn, Bourton–on–the–Water,
Glos GL54 2AF
☎ 0451 20467

Like a photographic trick, the model (one-ninth actual size in Cotswold stone) is of the very houses around you. The beautiful village of Bourton is completely re-created, including the river, the bridges, the trees, the gardens. Real church music can be heard, and right there in the middle is...a model Model Village.

🕐 Daily: summer 9.30–6.30;
   winter 10–dusk
💷 Ad £1.30, Chd 90p, SC £1.10
🄰 Centre of village
♿(res) 🍵 🍴 🅿

Bridgnorth Castle Hill Railway

Castle Terrace, Bridgnorth, Shrops
☎ 0746 763485

The best known funicular railway outside Italy. The Severn splits Bridgnorth into High Town and Low Town, one 61m higher than the other, and the 2-car railway has a gradient of 4 in 7. While you are at the top, have a look at the castle keep - one tower leans at an angle of 17°, more than the tower of Pisa.

🕐 All year, Mon–Sat 8–8, Sun 12–8
💷 Rtn fare 30p
🅰 Nr post office/High Town
▦ Bridgnorth (Severn Valley Rlwy) 10 min

Broadway Tower Country Park

Broadway, Worcs WR12 7LB
☎ 0386 852390

Don't start with the rare animals or birds, the children's farmyard or the giant chess and draughts. Delay the nature trail. Head first for the top of the tower, built in 1793, and see 12 counties of England. On a clear day.

🕐 Apr–Oct, daily 10–6
💷 Ad £2.75, Chd/SC £1.75, f/t
🅰 A44
♿ ♨ 🍴 🛍 🅿

Button Museum

Kyrle St, Ross on Wye, Hereford HR9 7DB
☎ 0989 66089

Coat buttons, glove buttons, shoe buttons, trouser buttons and buttons for places where you never thought you would need buttons. Some astonishingly expensive and decorative, others just essential.

🕐 Apr–Oct, daily 10–5
💷 Ad £1.50, SC £1.25; Chd free with adult
🅰 Town centre
♿ 🛍 🅿

Cadbury World

Linden Rd, Bournville, Birmingham B30 2LD
☎ 021 451 4180

Chocoholics will love this mixture of audio-visual history of the chocolate bean and bar, the making of the Milk Tray TV ads, and the demonstration producing individual hand-made chocolates. Ah, the smell!

🕐 Phone for details
💷 Ad £4.75, Chd £3.25, SC £4.20 (not Sat/Sun), f/t
✳ Birthday parties (021 451 4159)
🅰 M5 jnct 2/4, M6 jnct 6
▦ Bournville 10 min
♿ ♨ 🍴 🛍 🅿

Chedworth Roman Villa

Yanworth, Cheltenham GL54 3LJ
☎ 0242 890256

One of the best preserved remains
of a Roman villa found in Britain.
There are lovely mosaic floors,
central heating and *two* bath houses.
Video introduces house and history.

🕓 Mar–Oct, Tue–Sun/BH 10–5.30;
  other times/phone
💷 Ad £2.60, Chd £1.30, f/t
🅰 A40/A429, 10 miles SE of Cheltenham
♿ 🛍 🅿

Children's Farm

Ash End House Farm, Middleton,
Tamworth, Staffs B78 2BL
☎ 021 329 3240

Rare breeds, heavy horses at work,
and close contact with farm animals.
Every child receives a bucket of
food for the animals, a badge or
balloon and, when they are
available, a fresh egg warm from
the nest boxes.

🕓 All year, daily 10–5.30/dusk
💷 Ad £1.30, Chd £2.60
✳ Picnic barn, play areas
🅰 A4091 Lichfield/Tamworth
♿ ⛺ ☕ 🛍 🅿

Clearwell Caves

Nr Coleford, Glos GL16 8JR
☎ 0594 832535

This twisting labyrinth might have
started out as some natural caves,
but 2,500 years of iron mining has
created the tunnels and caverns
now on the tour. Treat it as a caving
expedition or as industrial history,
both aspects displayed en route.

🕓 Mar–Oct, daily 10–5
💷 Ad £2.80, Chd £1.70
✳ Xmas Fantasy end Nov–24 Dec
🅰 B4228
♿(res) ☕ 🛍 🅿

Corinium Museum

Park St, Cirencester, Glos GL7 2BX
☎ 0285 655611

Excellent reconstruction of a Roman
house, dining room, kitchen and
workshop where
mosaics were
made. Good
presentation of
some of the
best Roman
objects found in
Britain.

🕓 Daily: Apr–Oct,
  Mon–Sat/BH 10–5,
  Sun 2–5;
  Nov–Mar/phone
💷 Ad £1.25, Chd 75p, SC £1, f/t
🅰 Nr town centre
♿ 🛍

Cotswold Falconry Centre

Batsford Park, Moreton-in-Marsh,
Glos GL56 9QB
☎ 0386 701043

Silent, deadly flight from owls and
eagles, hawks and falcons. More
than 70 of them demonstrate their
speed and skill. Plus opportunities
to see them close up.

Also in the park is the Batsford
Arboretum, planted many years ago
by an eccentric Lord Redesdale. His
combination of oriental statues
(Buddhas, Japanese bronzes etc) and
50 acres of rare and unusual trees
has created a memorable walk
and/or picnic area.

🕐 Mar–Oct, daily 10.30–5.30;
   last flights 4.30
💷 Ad £2.50, Chd £1, SC £2
🅰 A44
⚏ Moreton-in-Marsh 1½ miles
🛦 ⛾ 🛍 🅿

Cotswold Farm Park Rare Breeds Survival Centre

Guiting Power, Cheltenham, Glos GL54 5UG
☎ 0451 850307

Claimed to be the most
comprehensive display of rare farm
breeds in Britain: lots of lovely
spotted pigs, hairy, multi-horned
sheep and busy, bright hens. Farm
trail, adventure playground and
pets' corner.

🕐 Apr–Sep, Mon–Sat 10–5 (Jul/Aug 10–6),
   Sun 10–6
💷 Ad £3, Chd £1.50, SC £2, f/t
🅰 B4077
♿ ⛾ 🛍 🅿

Cotswold Perfumery

Victoria St, Bourton-on-the-Water,
Glos GL54 2BU
☎ 0451 20698

See and smell perfumes as they are
being created. A perfume garden
with scented flowers might prepare
you for the Perfume Quiz where
you can find out how sensitive a
nose you have. There is also a little
'theatre' where you can experience
what they call 'smellyvision'.

🕐 Daily: summer 9.30–6; winter 9.30–5
💷 Ad £1.50, Chd/SC £1.20
🅰 Centre of village
♿ 🛍

Cotswold Water Park

Keynes Country Park, Shorncote,
Cirencester, Glos GL7 6DF
☎ 0285 861459

Lakes, nature reserve and country
park in 1,500 acres, with boating,
canoeing, sailing, angling,
windsurfing, paddling...and more.

🕐 All year, daily
   (Chd's beach: Jun–Sep 1–5)
💷 £2 per car Mon–Fri, £3 Sat/Sun/BH
🅰 A419, 5 miles S of Cirencester
♿ 🛦 🅿

Cotswold Wildlife Park

Burford, Oxfordshire OX18 4JW
☎ 0993 823006

The park has 200 acres to tuck in
animals (including 3 white rhinos),
insects, reptiles, and an aquarium.
There is an adventure playground
and, in summer, a narrow gauge
railway.

🕐 All year, daily 10–6/dusk
£ Ad £4.20, Chd/SC £2.70
� A361
♿ ⚲ ☕ 🛍 🅿

Cotswolds Motor Museum & Toy Collection

The Old Mill, Bourton-on-the-Water,
Glos GL54 2BY
☎ 0451 821255

The star is Brum, the little yellow
motor from the children's TV series;
then you have another 30 cars and
motorbikes from vintage to racing
machines, and a collection of toys
through the ages.

Upstairs is the **Village Life
Exhibition**, which has a complete
Edwardian village shop, bathroom,
kitchen, old radios and more.

🕐 Feb–Nov, daily 10–6
£ Ad £1.40, Chd 70p, f/t; incl Village Life
� Centre of village
♿ 🛍

Countryside Centre

Bath Rd, Haresfield, Glos GL10 3DP
☎ 0452 728338

Rescue and
conservation
is the theme
here, with
wildlife gardens
and a good
collection of owls
and birds of prey.
Nature trails and
pets' corner.

🕐 All year, daily 10–4.30
£ Ad £1.75, Chd 90p
� M5 jnct 12, B4008
♿ ☕ 🛍 🅿

Dean Heritage Centre

Camp Mill, Soudley, Cinderford,
Glos GL14 7UG
☎ 0594 822170

Woodcraft skills and charcoal-
burning in this ancient forest,
alongside a mine and mill pond.
There is an observation beehive,
and industrial history is illustrated
by a beam engine and a
waterwheel. Adventure areas and
nature trails.

🕐 Daily: Feb–Mar 10–5, Apr–Oct 10–6;
Nov–Jan Sat/Sun 10–5
£ Ad £2.60, Chd (5–16) £1.60, SC £2.10
� B4227
♿ ⚲ ☕ 🛍 🅿

Domestic Fowl Trust

Honeybourne Pastures,
Honeybourne, Evesham, Worcs WR11 5QJ
☎ 0386 833083

You can see 150 breeds of hens,
geese, ducks and turkeys, receive
advice on their history and care, or
just admire and
feed them.

🕐 All year,
Sat–Thu 10.30–5
💷 Ad £2.90, Chd £1.75, SC £2
✳ Adv playgnd
🅰 B4035, E of Evesham
♿ ☕ 🎁 🅿

Fairy Tale Gingerbread

72 Shropshire St, Market Drayton,
Shrops TF9 3DG
☎ 0630 657373

Market Drayton is the home of
gingerbread, a fact reflected in this
shop with its prize-winning range
of gingerbread novelties. Hands off!

🕐 All year, Mon–Sat 8.30–5
(not Thu/Sat pm)
💷 Adm free
🅰 Nr town centre

Hatton Locks

Canal Lane, Hatton, Warwicks CV35 7JL
☎ 0564 784634

This series of 21 locks on the Grand
Union Canal is called The Stairway
to Heaven, and you can sit and
enjoy wonderful views down the
flight to Warwick as boats
manoeuvre along the 45-metre rise
or fall.

🕐 All year
💷 Adm free
🅰 A4177, NW of Warwick
♿ 🏕 🎁 🅿

Hawkstone Park & Follies

Weston–under–Redcastle,
Shrewsbury SY4 5UY
☎ 0939 200300

A cross between an adventure
playground and a nature trail, held
in a Grade 1 historic park. The trail,
set in 100 acres of lawns, hills,
arches and cliffs, was created in the
18th century and took 2 years to
restore. Wear sensible clothes and
stout shoes.

🕐 Apr–Oct, daily 10–4 (last adm);
Nov/Dec Sat/Sun
💷 Ad £4, Chd £2, SC £3, f/t
🅰 A53, 3 miles from Hodnet
🏕 ☕ 🎁 🅿

102

Heritage Motor Centre
Gaydon, Warwicks CV35 0BJ
☎ 0926 641188

A celebration of the British motor
industry with no less than 300
historic cars, including prototypes.
Great fun is having a ride on the off-
road test circuit, or for young ones,
trying a quad bike on rough terrain.

○ Daily: Apr–Oct 10–6; Nov–Mar 10–4.30
£ Ad £5.50, Chd £3.50, SC £4.50, f/t
✳ Nature reserve, adv playgnd
/Å\ M40 jnct 12, B4100
& ♣ ¡©¡ 🛍 Ⓟ

House of the Tailor of Gloucester
9 College Court, Gloucester GL1 2NJ
☎ 0452 422856

Beatrix Potter really did base her
tale of the sewing mice on this
actual house. Now a gift shop and
exhibition of the story, with other
Potter memorabilia.

○ All year, Mon–Sat 9.30–5.30 (not BH)
£ Adm free
/Å\ City centre
✚ Gloucester City 15 min

Ironbridge Gorge
Ironbridge, Telford TF8 7AW
☎ 0952 433522/432166 (w/ends)

A World Heritage Site, Ironbridge
was at the birth of the Industrial
Revolution, creating iron rails, iron
wheels, the first cast iron bridge. It
developed fine china, amazing tile
patterns...ideas that went round the
world. A passport ticket allows you
to visit 7 museums (and stays valid
until all have been visited). All are
within easy walking distance of the
Iron Bridge, but together cover an
area of 6 square miles.

£ Passport tkt: Ad £8, Chd £5, SC £7, f/t
/Å\ M54 jnct 5/6

Museum of Iron & Darby Furnace
In 1709 Abraham Darby set up the
first coke blast furnace to smelt iron.
The furnace is still here and the
museum tells the full story. Allow
2 hours.

○ Daily: Jul–Aug 10–6; Sep–Jun 10–5
£ Ppt tkt or Ad £3, Chd £1.80, SC £2.50
& (prior notice) ☕ 🛍 Ⓟ

Blists Hill Open Air Museum
A whole small Victorian town lives
again, right down to the gas-lit
streets. The place is dominated by a
complete wrought-iron works, blast
furnace engines and railway
sidings. Allow 3 hours.

○ Daily: Sep–Jun 10–5 (Nov–Feb 10–4),
   Jul/Aug 10–6
£ Ppt tkt or Ad £6, Chd £3.80, SC £5
& (prior notice) ☕ ¡©¡ 🛍 Ⓟ

Coalport China Museum

Where fine china was first made in quantity in England. Displays of that early china, and of china being made. Allow 1 hour.

🕐 Daily: Sep–Jun 10–5, Jul/Aug 10–6
£ Ppt tkt or Ad £3, Chd £1.80, SC £2.50
& (prior notice) 🛍 🅿

Jackfield Tile Museum

In the 1880s this was one of the biggest producers of tiles in the world, and the range of patterns and colours is mind-boggling. How they were designed and produced. Allow 1½ hours.

🕐 Daily: Sep–Jun 10–5, Jul/Aug 10–6
£ Ppt tkt or Ad £3, Chd £1.80, SC £2.50
& (prior notice) 🛍 🅿

Ironbridge Tollhouse

The world's first cast-iron bridge, a great advertisement for the new technique, still standing and still admired. Tollhouse exhibition.

🕐 All year
£ Adm free
& (prior notice) 🛍 🅿

Rosehill House & Dale House

The houses of Abraham Darby and his son-in-law, restored and furnished as in 1848.

🕐 Daily: Sep–Jun 10–5, Jul/Aug 10–6
£ Ppt tkt or Ad £2, Chd £1.40, SC £1.80
& (prior notice) 🍴 🛍 🅿

Museum of the River Visitor Centre

Once a warehouse used to store iron castings before their shipment round the world, now a spectacular model of the gorge and the bridge as it was in 1796.

🕐 Daily: Sep–Jun 10–5, Jul/Aug 10–6
£ Ppt tkt or Ad £2, Chd £1.40, SC £1.80
& (prior notice) 🛍 🅿

In summer, you can see the **Tar Tunnel**, a natural deposit of bitumen in the hillside near the China Museum. You get to wear a hard hat. (Ad 80p, Chd 50p, SC 70p for non-Passport tkts). Then visit the **Teddy Bear Museum** (adm free), a less familiar part of the Ironbridge story.

Jewellery Quarter Discovery Centre

77–79 Vyse St, Hockley,
Birmingham B18 6HA
☎ 021 554 3598

Jewellery factory Smith & Pepper exactly as it was in 1914, minus the people. You can also view a modern work area where jewellers still work with gold, diamonds and precious metals.

🕐 All year, Mon–Fri 10–4, Sat 11–5
£ Ad £2, Chd/SC £1.50, f/t
🛈 Signs from city centre
🚋 Snow Hill 15 min; New St 30 min
& 🍴

Jinney Ring Craft Centre

Hanbury, Bromsgrove, Worcs B60 4BU
☎ 0527 821272

You can see people make violins
and pots and create hats for
weddings, as well as many other
crafts like needlecraft. Twelve
separate studios in an attractive
setting.

🕐 All year, Tue–Sat/BH 10.30–5,
  Sun 11.30–5.30
£ Adm free
🅰 B4091
♿ (res) ☕ 🍽 💼 Ⓟ

Jubilee Park

Symonds Yat West, Herefordshire
☎ 0600 890360

Right beside the Wye Valley Visitor
Centre, the park contains the Jubilee
Maze, among the most puzzling in
the country. A museum of mazes
has 2 hands-on exhibitions, one
using computers. More maze
puzzles in the shop.

You can calm down in the
tranquil **World of Butterflies**
which is signposted from
Jubilee Park. Huge numbers
of tropical butterflies flit free
in a giant glasshouse
(☎ 0600 890471: Open 10-
5.30; Ad £2.25, Chd £1.25,
SC £1.60).

🕐 All year, daily 11–5.30 (last adm)
£ Park: free. Maze: Ad £2.50,
  Chd £1.50, SC £2
🅰 A40, N of Monmouth
♿ ⛲ ☕ 💼 Ⓟ

Keith Harding's World of Mechanical Music

Oak House, High St, Northleach,
Glos GL54 3ET
☎ 0451 860181

You can hear a tiny mechanical bird
sing as a snuff box opens, or listen
to Rachmaninov and Gershwin play
their own compositions on a player
piano; or tune into a maharajah's
music box which has 10 bells, an
organ and another singing bird.

🕐 All year, daily 10–6; last tour 5
£ Ad £3.50, Chd £1.50, SC £2.75, f/t
🅰 Town centre
♿ 💼 Ⓟ

Kingsbury Water Park

Bodymoor Heath Lane,
Sutton Coldfield B76 0DY
☎ 0827 872660

Some 640 acres of
landscaped
countryside, pools and
30 lakes. Day
memberships for
riding,
windsurfing
and angling
(including
carp pool),
plus model
boat pond,
rare breeds
farm, nature
trails and
orienteering.

🕐 All year. Phone for details
£ Pkg £1.50
🅰 M42 jnct 9
♿ ⛲ ☕ 💼 Ⓟ

Lost Street Museum

Palma Court, 27 Brookend St,
Ross–on–Wye, Hereford
☎ 0989 562752

A kind of shopping mall from a
time machine. Real shops, from the
original front to the stock they
carried, have been reassembled
complete. The pub, plate glass
mirror and all, used to stand in
London's East End.

🕒 Feb–Nov, Mon–Sat 10–5, Sun 11–5
💷 Ad £2, Chd £1.50, SC £1.75, f/t
🅰 Town centre
♨ 🛍

Mohair Centre

Blakemore Farm, Little London,
Longhope, Glos GL17 0PH
☎ 0452 830630

If you thought that mohair came
from a mo, think again. Not only
can you see the material made and
styled, you can cuddle the goats
which produce the fleece. Feels
warm and silky - which is why the
goats wear it.

🕒 All year, Wed–Sun 10.30–5
💷 Adm free
🅰 A4136
♿ ♨ 🛍 🅿

Museum of Advertising & Packaging

The Albert Warehouse,
Gloucester Docks GL1 2EH
☎ 0452 302309

Not just bars of soap and packets of
cornflakes, but memories, social
economics, commercial and popular
history, and fun. A hundred
different kinds of beans, milk bottles
by the thousand, early TV and radio
commercials.

🕒 Summer, daily 10–6; winter,
   Tue–Sun 10–5
💷 Ad £2.95, Chd 95p, SC £1.95, f/t
🅰 City centre
🚉 Gloucester City 15 min
♿ ♨ 🛍 🅿

Museum of British Road Transport

St Agnes Lane, Hales St,
Coventry CV1 1PN
☎ 0203 832425

One of the world's best displays of
cars, motorbikes and cycles. Well
staged street scenes in period style,
a display of royalty on the road and
a reconstruction of Coventry
during the savage
Blitz attack. Audio-
visual of Thrust 2,
current land speed
record-holder.

🕒 All year, daily 10–4.30
💷 Ad £2.95, Chd/SC £1.95, f/t
🅰 City centre
🚉 Coventry 20 min
♿ ♨ 🛍

National Birds of Prey Centre
Clifford's Mesne, Newent, Glos
☎ 0531 820286

The largest private collection of birds of prey in Europe, some 200 including vultures, the comical-looking secretary bird and a special owl enclosure. Four flying displays a day (11, 12.30, 2.30, 4.15), weather permitting.

🕐 Feb–Nov, daily 10.30–5.30
£ Ad £4, Chd £2.25, f/t
🅰 B4216, S of Newent
♿ ⛲ ☕ 🛍 🅿

National Snail Farming Centre
L'Escargot Anglais, Credenhill,
Hereford HR4 7DN
☎ 0432 760218

The best bit for those with the courage or experience is the tasting. Others may prefer just to go on the guided tour to snail farming, the exhibition of British and European snails, or try the nature trail where you can identify...snails.

🕐 May–Sep, daily 11–6; Oct–Apr,
   Mon–Fri 11–5
£ Tour: Ad £1.60, Chd £1.10, SC £1.30
🅰 A480
⛲ 🛍 🅿

National Waterways Museum
Llanthony Warehouse,
Gloucester Docks GL1 2EH
☎ 0452 307009

Three floors of a giant warehouse and barges and boats at the quay tell the story of 200 years of canals and river traffic. Try on a diver's helmet, steer a narrowboat or open a lock in simulators. Blacksmiths and a huge steam dredger also on view.

🕐 Daily: summer 10–6; winter 10–5;
   last adm 1hr before
£ Ad £3.95, Chd/SC £2.95, f/t
🅰 City centre
🚌 Gloucester City 10 min
♿ ☕ 🛍 🅿

Pitt-Rivers Museum
Parks Rd, Oxford OX1 3PP
☎ 0865 270927

Collection from tribes the world over complete with carvings, but the joy is the butterfly display and the insects. Some of them are alive, and looking very well.

🕐 All year, Mon–Sat 1–4.30
£ Adm free
🅰 5 min from city centre
🚌 Oxford (bus link)
♿ 🛍

107

Puzzle Wood

Lower Perrygrove Farm, Coleford, Glos
☎ 0594 833187

In the 1800s the paths through the
site of what were Roman open cast
iron mines were arranged into a
route of puzzles set in 14 acres of
woodland. Finding your way
around is still intriguing and fun.

🕐 Easter–Oct,
   Tue–Sun 11–6;
   last adm 5
💷 Ad £1.50,
   Chd £1
🅰 B4228
▮ 🏠 🅿

Sapperton Tunnel

Sapperton, Glos GL8 8HE
☎ 0666 502797

A boat takes you along this 200-
year-old tunnel, hewn by hard men
and black powder. At 3,491 metres,
it was the longest canal tunnel in
the world, and still ranks as the
third longest.

🕐 Sun/BH 11–3 (conditions permitting)
💷 Ad £2, Chd £1
🅰 Signs from village
♿(prior notice) 🅿

Sculpture Trail

Forest Enterprise, Coleford,
Glos GL16 8BA
☎ 0594 833057

A 4-mile nature trail in the Forest of
Dean marked by sculptures designed
to make you look at the beauty
around you. Imaginative, calm,
sometimes amusing, it turns a walk
into a wonderland. Starting point:
Beechenhurst Lodge picnic site.

🕐 All year, all day
💷 Adm free
🅰 B4234
🌲 🅿

Shakespeare's Birthplace

Henley St, Stratford–upon–Avon CV37 6QW
☎ 0789 204016

The house is furnished in period,
with memorabilia of the Bard and
his family. The manure heap
outside the house, for which
Shakespeare's dad was fined, has
now gone. You can go on to see the
other Shakespeare properties: **Anne
Hathaway's Cottage**, **New
Place/Nash's House**, **Hall's Croft**
and **Mary Arden's House**.

🕐 Mar–Oct, Mon–Sat 9–5.30,
   Sun 10–5.30; Nov–Feb/phone
💷 Ad £2.60, Chd £1.20. Tkt for all 5
   sites: £7.50/£3.50/SC £7
🅰 Town centre
🚉 Stratford–upon–Avon 10 min
♿(res) 🏠

Shrewsbury Quest

Abbey Foregate, Shrewsbury SY2 6AH
☎ 0746 765576

Monk detective Brother Cadfael had
this visitor attraction dedicated to
his tales even before the TV series
was set to start. You are transported
back to 12th-century England, the
abbey of Shrewsbury, a civil war
and, hidden round the displays, are
clues to a mystery...can you solve
them?

🕐 All year, Mon–Sat 10–5, Sun 12–5
£ Ad £3.50, Chd £2, SC £2.80
🚻 Next to abbey
♯ Shrewsbury 10 min
♿ 🛗 🚽 🛍 ℗

Staffordshire Way

Rudyard, Leek, Staffs

The pretty section along Rudyard
Reservoir, which has a miniature
railway by the lakeside and some
good walking. The Kiplings courted
round here, and liked it so much
they named their boy-writer after
the place.

🕐 All year, all day
£ Adm free
🚻 A523, NW of Leek

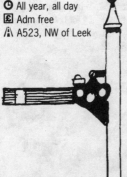

Stratford-upon-Avon Butterfly Farm

Tramway Walk, Swan's Nest Lane,
Stratford–upon–Avon CV37 7LS
☎ 0789 299288

The largest butterfly farm in
Europe, but it is the tarantulas, bird-
eating spiders and scorpions which
draw the apprehensive crowds.

🕐 Daily: summer 10–6; winter 10–dusk
£ Ad £3.25, Chd(5+) £2.25, SC £2.75, f/t
🚻 Opp RSC theatre
♯ Stratford–upon–Avon 10 min
♿ 🛍

Tamworth Castle

Holloway, Tamworth, Staffs B79 7LR
☎ 0827 63563

Figures in period settings talk you
through the 800-year history of the
fortress from the battlements to the
dungeons. You walk away
remembering the ghost of the Black
Lady in the Tower bedroom.

🕐 All year, Mon–Sat 10–5.30,
   Sun 2–5.30; last adm 4.30
£ Ad £2.90, Chd/SC £1.45
🚻 Town centre
♯ Tamworth 7 min
🛍 ℗

Warwick Castle

Warwick CV34 4QU
☎ 0926 408000

History starting with William the
Conqueror, 60 acres of grounds
landscaped by Capability Brown, a
dungeon with torture chamber, and
smashing displays of life as it was
within the ramparts. An audio-
visual brings to life battle
preparations in 1471, and there is a
Madame Tussaud's staging of a
royal weekend party in 1898.

🕒 Daily: Apr–Sep 10–6 (Aug Sat/Sun
10–7); Oct–Mar 10–5
£ Ad £7.75, Chd (4–16) £4.75,
SC £5.50, f/t
🅰 M40 jnct 15
🚻 Warwick 15 min
⛺ ☕ 🍴 👜 🅿

Waterfowl Sanctuary

Wigginton Heath, Hook Norton,
Banbury, Oxfordshire
☎ 0608 730252

 Young people
meet and hug
young
animals. Over
the season the
sanctuary has
ducklings,
goslings, chicks, as
well as baa-lambs and bunnies.

🕒 All year, daily 10.30–dusk
£ Ad £2, Chd £1
🅰 A361, SW of Banbury
♿ ⛺ 🅿

Wernlas Collection

Onibury, Ludlow, Shrops SY7 9BL
☎ 0584 77318

Everyone knows about Rhode
Island Reds, but what about black
and gold Vorwerks? And when did
you last see a Cochin? The most
extensive collection of large fowls in
the UK, plus pigs, cattle and a
seaweed-eating sheep.

🕒 All year, Tue–Sun/BH 10.30–5.30
(summer daily)
£ Ad £2.75, Chd (4–16) £1.40, SC £2.40
🅰 A49
⛺ ☕ 👜 🅿

West Midlands Safari
& Leisure Park

Spring Grove, Bewdley, Worcs DY12 1LF
☎ 0299 402114

Take the train through reserves
roamed by lions, rhinos, giraffes
and monkeys to test the fearsome
roller coaster or to walk the plank
to the Pirate Ship ride. Gentler
amusements include sea lions and
pets' corner.

🕒 Apr–Oct, daily 10–5 (last adm)
£ £3.99 per head + £4 for unlimited rides
🅰 A456
♿ ⛺ ☕ 🍴 👜 🅿

Westonbirt Arboretum

Nr Tetbury, Glos
☎ 0666 880220

The 600 acres contain trees you
never knew existed; azaleas and
rhododendron in spring and maples
in autumn create an astonishing
blaze of colour. Every tree named,
and a meadow untouched by man
for over 100 years.

🕐 All year, daily 10–8/dusk
£ Ad £2.50, Chd £1, SC £1.50
🅰 A433
♿ ⛺ ☕ 🛍 🅿

Wildfowl & Wetlands Trust Centre

Slimbridge, Glos GL2 7BT
☎ 0453 890333

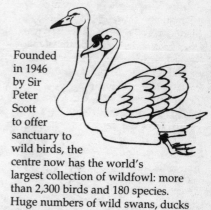

Founded
in 1946
by Sir
Peter
Scott
to offer
sanctuary to
wild birds, the
centre now has the world's
largest collection of wildfowl: more
than 2,300 birds and 180 species.
Huge numbers of wild swans, ducks
and geese come in autumn.

🕐 All year, daily 9.30–5/dusk
£ Ad £4.50, Chd £2.25, SC £3.40, f/t
🅰 M5 jnct 13, A38
♿ ☕ 🍽 🛍 🅿

Cheshire
Greater Manchester
Lancashire
Merseyside

Alderley Edge
Nr Macclesfield, Cheshire
☎ 0625 584412

The great 183-metre sandstone ridge
overlooks the Cheshire Plain.
Readers of Alan Garner's book *The
Weirdstone of Brisingamen* will know
about the Edge and the Bronze Age
relics. For others, it is a dramatic
way-marked walk.

🕐 All year, all day
£ Adm free
🅰 A34, B5087
⛺ 🅿 NT

Anderton Boat Lift
Winnington Lane, Anderton,
Northwich, Cheshire
☎ 0606 862862

A Victorian engineering wonder
which lifted whole boats and
cargoes of salt from the River
Weaver up to the Trent and Mersey
Canal. Being renovated as the
centrepiece of a new heritage site.

🕐 All year
£ Adm free
🅰 A533
🅿

Animal World

Moss Park, Moss Way, Bolton, Lancs
☎ 0204 846157

Updated so that children can have
more contact with the farm animals.
There's more room for free flying
birds too, and a brand new
waterfall. The playground has a
safety surface.

🕐 Apr–Oct, daily 10–6; Nov–Mar 10–4
💷 Adm free
🅰 Off Northern Ring Rd
☕ 🅿

Anything To Declare?

Merseyside Maritime Museum,
Albert Dock, Liverpool
☎ 051 207 0001

This new Customs & Excise
museum is all about smuggling.
Find out how to spot suspect
travellers at airports, help search a
car ferry for contraband and see
how drug smugglers are caught.
Ticket includes admission to
Maritime Museum and
Museum of Liverpool Life.

🕐 All year, daily 10–5.30
(last adm 4.30)
💷 Ad £2.50, Chd/SC £1.30, f/t
✳ Albert Dock facilities
🅰 Follow Albert Dock signs
⌗ Lime Street (bus link)
♿ ☕ 🍴 🅿

Beatles Story, The

Britannia Vaults, Albert Dock,
Liverpool L3 4AA
☎ 051 709 1963

An 18-part tour of the rise and rise
of the Fab Four, re-creating the
Cavern Club, the first taste of fame,
Beatlemania and all those chart-
topping hits.

🕐 All year, daily 10–6 (later Jul/Aug)
💷 Ad £3.95, Chd/SC £2.45, f/t
✳ Albert Dock facilities
🅰 Follow Albert Dock signs
⌗ Lime Street (bus link)
♿ ☕ 🍴 🅿

Blackpool Pleasure Beach

Revolution House, 525 Ocean Blvd,
Blackpool FY4 1EZ
☎ 0253 341033

Dare you try The Big One, claimed
to be the tallest (72m) and fastest
(87mph) roller coaster in the world?
Some 145 attractions, including
fantasy theme rides, haunted
and horror houses,
ice-skating and
magic shows,
and a
circus.

🕐 Late Mar–beg Nov, daily 10–6;
winter Sat/Sun 2–11
💷 £13 per head (inc rides)
🅰 Nr South Pier
⌗ Blackpool S, 5 min
♿ ☕ 🍴 🅿

Blackpool Sea Life Centre
The Promenade, Blackpool FY1 5AA
☎ 0253 22445

A walk through a transparent
tunnel, where visitors get a close-up
(but luckily not hands-on!) view of
Europe's largest display of tropical
sharks - and more, in a whole world
under the waves.

🕐 Daily: summer 10–9; winter 10–5
💷 Ad £4.45, Chd £2.95, SC £3.35
🅰 On Golden Mile
🚉 Blackpool N, 10 min
♿ ☕ 🛍 🅿

Blackpool Tower & Tower World
The Promenade, Blackpool FY1 4BJ
☎ 0253 22242

Not just a landmark. There are 7
levels of activities, with the famous
ballroom, a circus, a dark ride
through time, and Jungle Jim's
Adventure Playground. The view is
pretty good, too.

🕐 Easter–May Sun–Fri 10–6,
   Sat 10–11pm; Jun–beg Nov,
   daily 10–11pm; Nov–Mar/phone
💷 Ad £5.95, Chd/SC £4.95;
   (Aug–Nov) £7.95/£4.95
✳ Tkt covers all attractions
🅰 You can see it for miles
🚉 Blackpool N, 10 min
♿ 🍴 🅿

Blackpool Zoo Park
East Park Drive, Blackpool FY3 8PP
☎ 0253 765027

The enclosures, for around 500
beasts and birds, are landscaped
both for the animals' comfort and
for good viewing. Sea lions are fed
at 11 and 3, penguins at 2.30. Also a
miniature railway.

🕐 Daily: summer 10–5.30;
   winter 10–4.30
💷 Ad £3.80, Chd/SC £1.90, f/t
🅰 M55 jnct 4, A583
♿ 🏕 ☕ 🍴 🛍 🅿

Boat Museum
Ellesmere Port, S Wirral L65 4EF
☎ 051 355 5017

An amazing variety of canal boats
from a tiny weed-cutter to one 300-
tonner. Climb aboard and see how
some were lived in. Plus working
smithy and restored Victorian
cottages.

🕐 Apr–Oct, daily 10–5; Nov–Mar,
   Sat–Wed 11–4
💷 Ad £4.50, Chd £3, SC £3.50, f/t
✳ Boat trips
🅰 M53 jnct 9
🚉 Ellesmere Port 10 min
♿ ☕ 🛍 🅿

British Commercial Vehicle Museum

King St, Leyland, Preston PR5 1LE
☎ 0772 451011

They start with horse-drawn coal carts and move steadily on through the years with more than 40 working motors - buses, fire engines, steam wagons and even the famous Popemobile.

🕑 Apr–Sep, Tue–Sun 10–5;
　Oct–Nov Sat/Sun/BH 10–5
💷 Ad £3, Chd £1.50
🅰 M6 jnct 28
🚉 Leyland 10 min
♿ ☕ 🅿

British Lawnmower Museum

106–114 Shakespeare St,
Southport PR8 5AJ
☎ 0704 535369

More than 100 mowers spanning 160 years, from Shanks' Pony to some of the fastest mowers in the world.

🕑 All year, Mon–Sat 9–5.30
💷 Ad £1, Chd 50p, SC £1
🅰 E of town centre
🚉 Southport 15 min
🅿

Brookside Miniature Railway

Brookside Garden Centre, Macclesfield Rd,
Poynton SK12 1BY
☎ 0625 872919

The little train, running on either steam or diesel, has its own station, working signals and a waiting room. Passengers are trundled for half a mile through a large garden centre, so it is pretty too.

🕑 Apr–Sep, Wed/Sun 11.30–5
　(+Tue/Thu Jul/Aug); Oct–Mar Sun
💷 20p per ride
🅰 A523
♿ 🍽 🅿

Bubbles Leisure Park

Marine Rd, Morecambe, Lancs LA4 4EJ
☎ 0524 419419

Never mind the weather, you can get wet in here. The indoor pool has a 61m chute, wild waves, water cannon and lots of bubbles. The outdoor pool is also heated, has waves and a beach. Live shows during summer.

🕑 Summer,
　daily 10–6.40;
　winter/phone
💷 Ad £3.50,
　Chd/SC £2.50
🅰 M6 jnct 34,
　A589
♿ ☕ 🅿

Camelot Theme Park

Charnock Richard, Chorley,
Preston PR7 5LP
☎ 0257 453044/452100 info

The Beast and the Tower
of Terror are just 2 of the
white-knuckle coaster
rides. Knights joust in
front of the
fairytale-style
castle; there's
a medieval
village, flying
falcons, a
Sooty show
and a themed
picnic area.

🕐 Jun–beg Sep,
daily from 10–5/6/7
(varies); Sep/Oct/
Mar–May/phone
£ Ad/Chd(4+) £9.99,
SC £4.75, f/t
ⓘ M6 jnct 27/28, M61 jnct 8
♿ ⛲ ☕ 🎁 Ⓟ

Catalyst

Mersey Rd, Widnes, Cheshire WA8 0DF
☎ 051 420 1121

The lift to the Observatory is all
glass, floor to ceiling, and rises 30m
above the river. Catalyst is all
about the tricky things
chemistry can do, including
Scientific - 30 different hands-
on ways of exploring the world
of chemicals.

🕐 All year, Tue–Sun 10–5
£ Ad £2.50, Chd £1.75, SC £2, f/t
ⓘ M56 jnct 12, M62 jnct 7
♿ ⛲ ☕ 🎁 Ⓟ

Cavern, The

Mathew St, Liverpool L2 6RE
☎ 051 236 9091

Replica of the original Cavern
Club from where the Beatles
launched themselves to
international mega-stardom.
Makes you wonder why
they knocked it down in the
first place. Discos in the
evening.

🕐 Phone for times/price
ⓘ Cavern Walk Shopping Centre
▦ Lime Street 10 min
♿ ☕

Cheshire Workshops Candle Makers

Burwardsley, Chester CH3 9PF
☎ 0829 70401

Careful dipping and shaping are
followed by skilful use of what
looks like a scalpel to produce
attractive and multi-coloured
candles. Almost a pity to light them.
At weekends children can have a go.

🕐 All year, daily 10–5
£ Adm free
ⓘ Signs from A41
♿ 🍴 🎁 Ⓟ

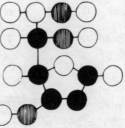

Chester Zoo
Upton–by–Chester, CH2 1LH
☎ 0244 380280/info 0839 406184

Britain's largest garden zoo, with an
island full of chimps and a pool full
of penguins, as well as orang-utans,
elephants, a huge collection of birds
and an aquarium. Much of the zoo
can be seen from an overhead
monorail system with a
synchronised sound system.

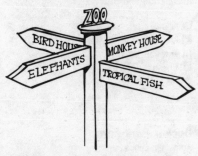

🕐 All year, daily 10–6.30; last adm 5
£ Ad £6.50, Chd/SC £4
✱ Children's farm, brass rubbing
Ⓐ A41, N of Chester
⊞ Bache 20 min
♿ 🍴 ☕ 🍽 🛍 🅿

Chocolate House
1 Glenfield Park, Philip Rd,
Blackburn BB1 5PF
☎ 0254 581019

Tasty demonstrations of the art of
producing hand-made chocolates.
You have to book in advance.

🕐 All year, Mon–Fri 9–5 (+Sat 6 wks
before Easter/Xmas)
£ £3.25 per head
Ⓐ A6119, N Blackburn ring road
♿ 🛍 🅿

Coronation Rock Co
11 Cherry Tree Road North,
Blackpool FY4 4NY
☎ 0253 762366

You can see from a specially built
viewing gallery how they put
BLACKPOOL in Blackpool rock,
and other sweet things.

🕐 All year, Mon–Thu 10–3, Fri 10–2
£ Adm free
Ⓐ M55 jnct 4, A583
♿ 🛍 🅿

Croxteth Hall & Country Park
Muirhead Ave East, Croxteth, Liverpool
☎ 051 228 5311

The home of the Earls of Sefton, set
in 500 acres, has been turned into a
keyhole on life in the Edwardian
era. The house is staging a
houseparty and you can see in
specially displayed layouts how it is
all put together, from preparing
guest rooms to cooking dinner both
upstairs and downstairs.
The grounds have farm
animals, woodland walks,
a miniature railway and
adventure playground.

🕐 Park: all year,
daily 9–6.
Hall: Easter–Oct 11–5
£ Ad £2.50, Chd/SC
£1.25p
Ⓐ M57 jnct 4,
A580
♿ 🍴 ☕ 🍽 🅿

Cyberdrome Crystal Maze

The Sandcastle,
South Promenade, Blackpool
☎ 0253 408100

You go in as a team with 2-6 players
to try challenges in any one of 22
computer-led games to be played
against the clock, some physical,
some mental. Based on the
Channel 4 TV show.

🕐 Jul–Nov, daily 10–8; Dec–Jun
  Sat/Sun 12–6
💷 Pk/Off Pk: £3.99/£2.99
⚠ Nr South Pier
🚉 Blackpool S, 10 min
♿ ☕ Ⓟ

Deva Roman Experience

Pierpoint Lane, Bridge St,
Chester CH1 2BJ
☎ 0244 343407

Start your visit to Roman Britain by
stepping aboard a galley and going
back in time to Fort Deva, where
you can walk through a typical
street in Roman Chester,
experiencing sights, sounds and
smells. You can also see an
archaeological dig.

🕐 All year, daily 9–5.30
💷 Ad £3.80, Chd £1.90, SC £3
⚠ Town centre
🚉 Chester 10 min
♿ 🛍 Ⓟ

Delamere Forest Visitor Centre

Linmere, Delamere, Northwich,
Cheshire CW8 2JD
☎ 0606 882167

Lovely forest where the Centre,
sensibly, gives you a lot of tree
information and route guides
before setting you off on some
noted walks.

🕐 All year, Mon–Fri 10.30–12.30/1–4.15,
  Sat/Sun 10.30–4.45
💷 Adm free
⚠ B5152, nr rlwy stn
🚉 Delamere 10 min
♿ 🚻 ☕ 🛍 Ⓟ

Docker Park Farm

Arkholme, Lancs
☎ 052 42 21331

A working farm with a range of
accessible livestock. You can feed
the baby animals or the trout in the
lake, or take a tractor-trailer ride to
see farm life.

🕐 Daily: Mar (lambing)/Easter–Oct 10.30–5;
  Feb h/term 10.30–4
💷 Ad £2.50, Chd £2
⚠ B6254, S of
  Kirby Lonsdale
♿ ☕ 🛍 Ⓟ

East Lancashire Railway

Bolton St Station, Bolton St, Bury, Lancs
☎ 061 705 5111/764 7790

The 17-mile route between Bury and
Rawenstall was called Golden
Valley because of the wealth
produced by the cotton mills. Fine
steam trains and well-maintained
stations.

🕐 All year, Sat/Sun 9–6 (+ some BH)
£ Rtn: Ad £5, Chd £2.50
⚠ Signs from town centre
♿ ☕ Ⓟ

Frontierland Western Theme Park

Morecambe Bay, Lancs LA4 4DG
☎ 0524 410024

A choice of around 30 rides from
white-knuckle thrillers to
much gentler children's
rides. There are live
shows in the Crazy
Horse saloon and an
indoor fun house.

🕐 All year, daily; phone
re times
£ Ad £6.99, Chd £3.99
⚠ A589
♿ ☕ 🍴 🛍 Ⓟ

Fylde Country Life Museum

Pilling, Lancs
☎ 0995 603113

Life in the 1930s: inside the home
and at the local post office and
telephone exchange. Then
the years and displays
move on to World War II
and the Home Guard.
Elsewhere, clog-making and
hot-metal printing.

🕐 Apr–Oct; phone re times
£ Ad £2, Chd £1
⚠ A6, W of Garstang
♿ ☕ Ⓟ

🎬 Granada Studios Tour

Water St, Manchester M60 9EA
☎ 061 832 9090/4999 info

Visit Coronation Street, the sets for
Sherlock Holmes, and listen to a
comedy debate in the House of
Commons. See how TV shows are
made, and learn about the different
techniques. Go to the cinema where
the seats move with the action.
Allow 3-5 hours.

🕐 Apr–Sep, Tue–Sun/BH 9.45–7
(last adm 4); Oct–Mar/phone
£ From: Ad £10.99, Chd £7.99;
SC £8.99 (Jan–Mar)
⚠ Signs/all major routes
🚇 Salford/Deansgate
5 min
♿ ☕ 🍴 🛍 Ⓟ

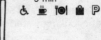

Gulliver's World

Old Hall, Warrington WA5 5YZ
☎ 0925 444888

Gulliver's travels this time take him
to Alice's Wonderland,
Western World, Circus
World and Dinosaur
World. The
target age
range is
14 and

under, so the rides are exciting but
not frantic.

🕐 Easter–mid Sep, daily 10.30–5;
    mid Sep–Oct Sat/Sun + h/term
💷 Ad/Chd £4.50, SC £3.95;
    Chd under 3ft free
🅰 M62 jnct 9, M6 jnct 22
♿ ☕ 🍴 🎁 Ⓟ

Hillside Ornamental Fowl

Damson Lane, Mobberley,
Knutsford, Cheshire
☎ 0565 873282

This landscaped
setting is stuffed with more
birds than you can imagine,
including ibis, pelicans, flamingoes,
toucans, penguins and some pretty
dramatic-looking waterfowl.

🕐 Apr–Oct, Sat/Sun/Wed/BH 11.30–5
💷 Ad £2.50, Chd £1.50
🅰 M6 jnct 19, B5085
🚸 Ⓟ

Historic Warships

Corn Warehouse Quay, East Float Dock,
Wallasey, Merseyside
☎ 051 650 1573

Frigate HMS *Plymouth* and
submarine HMS *Onyx*, both
veterans of the Falklands, can be
explored above and below decks.
Nearby is the third historic ship, the
Mersey Lightship, now retired.

🕐 Daily: Apr–Sep 10–5 (9pm summer hols);
    Oct–Mar 10–4
💷 Ad £4, Chd/SC £2, f/t
🅰 M53 jnct 1, A41
☕ Ⓟ

Ingleborough Show Cave

Ingleborough, Lancaster LA2 8EE
☎ 0524 251242

A showpiece entrance to part of a
huge cave system. Your tour takes
you to the start of the Gaping Gill
system, through ½km of silent,
echoing chambers and damp
passages lined with stalagmites.

🕐 Mar–Oct, daily 10.30–5.30
💷 Ad £3.50, Chd £1.75
🅰 Off A65 at Clapham
♿ ☕ Ⓟ

🚩 Jodrell Bank Science Centre & Arboretum

Lower Withington, Macclesfield SK11 9DL
☎ 0477 71339

The Centre has an exhibition of
space exploration and satellites with
hands-on displays; the Planetarium,
a tour of the Solar System. You
come back to earth with trails in a
35-acre tree show which explains
how trees are vital to the
environment and world survival.

🕐 Late Mar–Oct, daily 10.30–5.30;
　Nov–Feb Sat/Sun 11–4.30
💷 Ad £3.50, Chd £1.90, SC £2.50, f/t
🅰 M6 jnct 18, A535
  ♿ 🚻 ☕ 🅿

Judge's Lodgings Museum

Church St, Lancaster LA1 1UA
☎ 0524 32808

Once the home of Tudor witch
hunter Thomas Clavell. Now the
attraction for children is the famous
doll collection, a Victorian
schoolroom and Edwardian day
and night nurseries.

🕐 Easter–Jun/Oct, Mon–Sat 2–5; Jul–Sep,
　Mon–Fri 10–1/2–5, Sat/Sun 2–5
💷 Ad £1, Chd 40p, f/t
🅰 Town centre
🚉 Lancaster 5 min
☕ 🏪

Knowsley Safari Park

Prescot, Merseyside L34 4AN
☎ 051 430 9009

Drive through the largest herd of
African elephants in Europe. Part of
a 5-mile drive which also takes in
rhinos, lions, tigers, wildebeest,
camels and zebras. Performing sea
lions, a pets' corner, reptile house
and amusement park.

🕐 Mar–Oct, daily 10–5.30 (last adm 4)
💷 £8 per car. Sea lions: Ad £1.30,
　Chd 90p
🅰 M57 jnct 2
♿ 🚻 ☕ 🏪 🅿

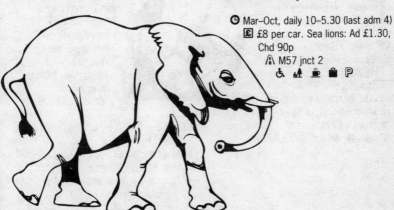

Louis Tussauds Waxworks

87–89 Central Promenade, Blackpool
☎ 0253 25953

The famous waxworks is constantly
updating its figures of the famous
and infamous. Will Gazza still
appear for England? There is a
chilling Chamber of Horrors and an
optional 'Anatomy Exhibition'.

🕐 Apr–Nov, daily 10–6;
   Dec–Mar Sat/Sun 10–6
💷 Ad £3, Chd £1.50, SC £2
🅰 Nr Central Pier
⊞ Blackpool N or S, 10 min
♿ ☕ ℗

Macclesfield Riverside Park

Beechwood Mews, Tytherington,
Macclesfield
☎ 0625 511086

There are marked paths through
wildflower meadows, woodland
and wetland, passing through the
area where a herd of rare longhorn
cattle breed. The 70 acres run beside
the river from Macclesfield to
Prestbury.

🕐 All year, daily 9–4
💷 Adm free
✳ Visitor centre
🅰 A538
♿ 🌲 ℗

Lyme Park

Disley, Stockport SK12 2NX
☎ 0663 762023/766492 info

The biggest house in Cheshire,
home of the Legh family for 600
years. Furniture from down the
ages, paintings, and a unique clock
collection. The vast park has herds
of deer and great views. The
gardens have lakes, an
orangery and adventure
playground.

🕐 Phone for details
💷 £3 per car.
   Hse/Gdn: Ad £2.50,
   Chd £1.25;
   Gdn: £1/50p; f/t
🅰 A6, 7 miles SE of Stockport
⊞ Disley 10 min
♿ ☕ 🍴 ℗ NT

Manchester United FC Museum & Tour Centre

Old Trafford, Manchester
M16 0RA
☎ 061 877 4002

Plenty of trophies in the museum,
and a back room tour of the
ground, dressing rooms
and training facilities
(not match days).
Magic for fans who
can even sit on the
manager's seat.
Wise to book.
[**Liverpool FC** also
offer tours:
☎ 051 263 2361.]

🕐 Tue–Sun 9.30–4 (or kick–off match days).
   Tours: hourly 10–2
💷 Mus/tour: Ad £4.95, Chd/SC £2.95.
   Mus: £2.95/£1.95; f/t
✳ Tours every ½hr in sch hols
🅰 Signs/all major routes
♿ ☕ ℗

Mersey Ferries

Victoria Pl, Seacombe, Wallasey,
Wirrall L44 6QY
☎ 051 630 1030

(Ferries: Liverpool Pierhead,
Woodside and Seacombe)

Hong Kong has ferries, New York has ferries, but the song is about *this* ferry. Apart from the shuttle service, the ferries take 50-minute cruises, enlivened by the captain's tales of the waterfront. You can break off at **Seacombe** to visit the **Aquarium**, or at Woodside. Ships leave Liverpool every hour on the hour, Seacombe 20 past the hour and Woodside at half past.

🕐 Ferries: daily 7–7. Cruises: 10–3 (10–6 Sat/Sun). Aquarium: daily 10–6
£ Ferries: Ad £2.90, Chd £1.50, f/t. Aquarium: £1.30/70p, f/t
/i\ Signs/embarkation points
♿ ☕ Ⓟ

Museum of Childhood

Church St, Ribchester, Lancs PR3 3YE
☎ 0254 878520

Not just toys, but very unusual toys, like Professor Tomlin's Flea Circus. The dolls' house and doll collection are famous. And there is Punch and Judy.

🕐 All year, Tue–Sun 10.30–5
£ Ad £2.45, Chd £1.75
/i\ M6 jnct 31, A59
♿ ☕ 🛍 Ⓟ

Museum of Science & Industry

Liverpool Rd, Castlefield, Manchester
☎ 061 832 2244/1830 info

Set in the oldest passenger railway station in the world. Now that Stephenson's *Rocket* no longer calls, there are 14 galleries covering 7 acres of scientific wonders for you to play with (though perhaps not the Victorian sewer).

🕐 All year, daily 10–5
£ Ad £3.50, Chd £1.50
/i\ Next to Granada TV
⊞ Salford/Deansgate 5 min
♿ ☕ 🛍 Ⓟ

Paradise Silk Mill

Park Lane, Macclesfield SK11 6TJ
☎ 0625 618228

Macclesfield was the centre of Britain's silk industry, and this restored factory with its 26 looms shows how it was done. The design and cutting rooms etc are set out 30s style - when the mill flourished. Look in at **The Silk Museum** in Roe Street [☎ 0625 613210; Mon-Sat 11-5, Sun 1-5] which will fill you in on the silkworm's path from grub to glory.

🕐 Summer, Tue–Sun 1–5; winter/phone
£ Ad £2, Chd £1.30, f/t
/i\ A523, A537
⊞ Macclesfield 5 min
♿ ☕ 🍴 🛍 Ⓟ

Pilkington Glass Museum

Prescot Rd, St Helens,
Merseyside WA10 3TT
☎ 0744 692014

Traces 4,000 years of glass-making.
Some rare and many unusual glass
objects, and you can use a working
periscope to see across the lake.

🕐 All Year, Mon–Fri 10–5, Sat/Sun/BH
2–4.30
£ Adm free
🅰 A58, 1 mile from town centre
♿ ☕ 🅿

🍦 Pleasure Island

Riverside Drive, Otterspool,
Liverpool L17 7HJ
☎ 051 728 7766

Huge indoor centre on site of
Festival gardens. Disco-type roller-
skating arena, 10-pin bowling alley
and the world's biggest indoor
adventure playground. Younger
children have a soft play area, and
there is a flying saucer-shaped
science area with a lot of interactive
features.

🕐 All year, daily 9am–midnight
£ Ad £5.50, Chd £4.50
🅰 5 min from city centre
🚇 St Michael's 5 min
♿ 🍴 ☕ 🍽 🅿

Port Sunlight Heritage Centre

95 Greendale Rd, Port Sunlight L62 4XE
☎ 051 644 6466

The man who created Lux soap
wanted to be kinder to workers and
the 130-acre garden village of Port
Sunlight, built in 1888, was the
result. The Centre has the how and
the why.

🕐 Apr–Oct, daily 10–4; Nov–Mar,
Mon–Fri 10–4
£ Adult 20p, Chd free
🅰 M53 jnct 5, A41
🚇 Port Sunlight (opp)
♿ 🅿

Quarry Bank Mill

Styal, Cheshire SK9 4LA
☎ 0625 527468

The water-powered cotton mill (the
only one in the world) demonstrates
weaving and spinning, and there
are galleries showing the life of
millworkers. The Apprentice House
reveals how child apprentices lived
and worked (and worked) around
1830. The factory, set in a 275-acre
park, has a timed ticket system for
guided tours.

🕐 Mill: Apr–Sep, daily 11–6;
Oct–Mar 11–5. App Hse/phone
£ Mill/App Hse: Ad £4.50, Chd £3.20, f/t.
App Hse: £3/£2.30
🅰 M56 jnct 5, B5166
🚇 Styal (not Sun)
♿ ☕ 🍽 🎁 🅿 NT

Royal Liver Building
Pierhead, Liverpool
☎ 051 236 2748

There are 483 steps from the basement to the bird at the top of Liverpool's most famous building. That's like 22 double-decker buses, whack. The 1-hour tour must be booked in advance.

🕐 Apr–Sep, Mon–Fri 2pm
£ Adm free
⊞ James St (opp)

Sabden Treacle Mines
Lower House Mill, The Holme, Sabden, Clitheroe BB7 9DZ
☎ 0282 775279

A world of soft toys comes alive. They make boggarts here, and boggarts eat treacle and work in the local treacle mines. You can discover more about their very unusual lifestyle in their own, specially created model village.

🕐 All year, Mon–Fri 9–5, Sat 9–4, Sun 12–4
£ Ad 50p, Chd (with adult) free
⚠ A59, S of Clitheroe
♿ 🛍 Ⓟ

Salt Museum
162 London Rd, Northwich, Cheshire CW9 8AB
☎ 0606 41331

A celebration of salt and the huge network of local mines where the precious substance is pumped up as brine. Science, history, a sprinkling of chemistry and the fascinating tales of the Salt Barons.

🕐 All year, Tue–Fri 10–5, Sat/Sun 2–5 (Aug, daily 10–5)
£ Ad £1, Chd 50p
⚠ Nr town centre
⊞ Northwich 1½ miles
☕ 🛍 Ⓟ

Sandcastle, The
South Promenade, Blackpool FY4 1BB
☎ 0253 343602/404013 info

Getting wet down the 91m giant slide, or hurtling through the Barracuda water chute or splashing around in the Sleepy Lagoon, which has a water mushroom and bubblers for the very young. Up above, a high-level adventure playground.

🕐 Apr–May, Mon–Fri 10–3, Sat/Sun 10–6; Jun–Nov, daily 10–6 (7pm Aug)
£ £4.50 per head
⚠ Nr South Pier
⊞ Blackpool S, 5 min
♿ ☕ Ⓟ

South Asian Gallery

Central Museum & Art Gallery, Museum St,
Blackburn BB1 7AJ
☎ 0254 667130

The culture in Britain and South
Asia of the Asians who have settled
in Blackburn. Story told in mixture
of tape recordings and ancient and
modern arts and textiles.

🕒 All year, Tue–Sat 9.45–4.45
💷 Adm free
🅰 Town centre
🚉 Blackburn 5 min
♿ (res)

Sovereign Cruises

Town Quay, Northwich, Cheshire
☎ 0606 76204

A 2½-hour river trip through
industrial history. The cruise takes
in the famous Anderton Boat Lift
[qv], passes Victorian swing bridges
and busy shipyards, as well as the
factories created by the salt mining
which sparked the whole thing off.

🕒 Apr–Oct; phone for details
💷 Ad £5, Chd £3
🅰 Nr town swing bridge
🚉 Northwich 25 min
♿ (res) ☕

Speke Hall

The Walk, Liverpool L24 1XD
☎ 051 427 7231

What is 500 years old, has hiding
places for priests, a room designed
so that you can hear secret
conversations, and looks like a giant
liquorice allsort? Speke Hall, one of
the finest black-and-white Tudor
houses in the country.

🕒 Easter–Oct: Tue–Sun 1–5.30
   (not Good Fri)
💷 Hse/Gdn: £3.40, f/t. Gdn: £1
🅰 A561, S of Liverpool
♿ ☕ 🛍 🅿

Stapeley Water Gardens

Stapeley, Nantwich,
Cheshire CW5 7LH
☎ 0270 623868

Piranhas, sharks and moray eels
share the 1-acre tropical house with
parrots and giant water lilies.
Elsewhere there is a
collection of bygones
including a Churchill
tank, steam roller and
toy trains.

🕒 Summer: Mon–Fri 9–6,
   Sat 10–6, Sun/BH 10–7.
   Winter/phone
💷 Trop Oasis/Yesteryear:
   Ad £2.90, Chd £1.45
🅰 A51, A530
♿ ☕ 🛍 🅿

Stockley Farm

Smithy Farmhouse,
Arley, Northwich,
Cheshire CW9 6LZ
☎ 0565 777323

The milking
gallery can
handle 200
Friesians,
and you can
see all
the
action, then
help feed
baby
animals,
have a ride
on the
tractor or, perhaps best of all,
bounce in the hay. Special play area.

🕐 End Mar–beg Oct, Wed/Sat/Sun/BH
   12–5.30; Aug, Tue–Sun
£ Ad £2.50, Chd(3+) £1.50, f/t
🚗 M56 jnct 9, A49
♿ ♨ ♨ 💼 Ⓟ

Tatton Park

Knutsford, Cheshire WA16 6QN
☎ 0565 654822/750250 info

The mansion is set in 1,000 acres of
deer forest, with 50 acres of gardens,
an 18th-century farm being run 1930s-
style, a medieval hall and lakes big
enough to take a sailing centre. Cycle
hire, riding, carriage rides, fishing.

🕐 Phone for times/individual
   attraction prices
£ All–in: Ad £6, Chd £4.20, f/t
🚗 M6 jnct 19, M56 jnct 7
🚉 Knutsford 2 miles
♿ ♨ 🍴 Ⓟ NT

Toy & Teddy Bear Museum

373 Clifton Drive North,
Lytham St Annes, Lancs FY8 2PA
☎ 0253 713705

Comfortably small collection of 200
dolls, 50 dolls' houses, working toy
train layouts, Meccano, Teddy bears,
books and games.

🕐 Whit–Oct, Wed–Mon 11–5;
   Nov–May, Sun 11–5 (sch hols, daily)
£ Ad £1.60, Chd £1.20
🚗 Nr town centre
🚉 St Annes 10 min
♿ Ⓟ

Western Approaches

1 Rumford St, Liverpool L2 3FZ
☎ 051 227 2008

Re-creation of World War II
'bunker' from where the Royal
Navy directed the close-run
campaign against U-boats attacking
Atlantic supply convoys.

🕐 Daily: May–Sep 9–6; Oct–Apr 10–5
£ Ad £3.99, Chd £3.49, f/t
🚗 Behind town hall
🚉 Lime St 10 min
Ⓟ

Wigan Pier

Wigan, Lancs WN3 4EU
☎ 0942 323666/44888 info

Professional actors help bring alive
Lancashire life in 1900. Visitors can
talk to mill girls, suffragettes,
soldiers off to the Boer War, and
even sit in a very strict classroom.
Palace of Varieties shows. Free
waterbus criss-crosses the complex.

🕐 Easter–Sep, Mon–Thu 10–5,
  Sat/Sun 11–5. Winter/phone
💷 Ad £4.10, Chd £3.10
🛣 M6 jnct 24/25/26, M61 jnct 5/6
🚇 Wigan 10 min
♿ ☕ 🍴 Ⓟ

Witton Country Park

Preston Old Rd, Blackburn BB2 2TP
☎ 0254 55423

A 480-acre estate. Children's corner
and mammal centre has delights
like the edible dormouse, ferrets,
pigmy shrew. Agricultural museum,
footpaths, horse trail and more.

🕐 Apr–Oct, Mon–Sat 1–5, Sun/BH 11–5;
  Nov–Mar, Thu–Sun 1–5
💷 Adm free
🛣 1 mile from city centre
🚇 Cherry Tree 15 min
♿ ☕ ☕ 🏠 Ⓟ

Wildfowl & Wetlands Centre

Martin Mere, Burscough, Ormskirk,
Lancs L40 0TA
☎ 0704 895181

Swans, geese and
ducks from all over
the world, seen
from 9 roomy
hides. In the
waterfowl
gardens, many
of the birds (not
the flamingoes) will
eat from your hand.
Bring binoculars and
camera.

🕐 Summer, daily 9.30–5.30;
  winter 9.30–dusk
💷 Ad £3.95, Chd £2, SC £2.95, f/t
✳ Brass rubbing, art gallery
🛣 A59, N of Ormskirk
♿ ☕ ☕ 🍴 Ⓟ

Antrim
Armagh
Down
Fermanagh
Londonderry
Tyrone

Altmore Open Farm

32 Altmore Rd, Pomeroy, Co Tyrone
☎ 0868 758977

Sheep farm high in the Sperrin
mountains, with 2 working
waterwheels, a collection of rare
breed farm animals and farm tours,
plus pony trekking in summer.
Pitch and putt course, and boat
fishing.

🕓 All year, daily 9–dusk
💷 £1 per car; activities extra
🅰 3 miles S of Pomeroy
♿ ☕ 🅿

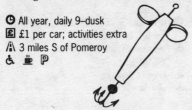

Argory, The

Derrycaw Rd, Moy, Dungannon,
Co Tyrone BT71 6NA
☎ 086 87 84753

The name means 'Hill of the
Garden' and it is a beautiful spot.
The house seems to have stopped
time. The acetylene gas plant might
still be lighting the chandeliers, cues
on the billiard table are ready to be
picked up, and the dining table is set
for dinner. Fine walks in 300 acres of
woodland. Adventure playground.

🕓 2–6: Easter daily; Jul/Aug, Fri–Wed;
   Apr/May/Jun/Sep, Sat/Sun/BH.
   Last tour 5.15
💷 Ad £2.20, Chd £1.10
🅰 M1 jnct 13/14
♿ ⚓ ☕ 🛍 🅿 NT

Ark Open Farm

296 Bangor Rd, Newtownards,
Co Down BT23 3PH
☎ 0247 812672/820445

Your chance to see Irish Moiled
cattle and other rare breeds, as well
as pot-bellied pigs, Nigerian pygmy
goats and pilgrim geese. There is a
pets' corner, and pony rides.

🕐 Mid Mar–Oct, Mon–Sat 10–5.30,
   Sun 2–6
💷 Ad £1.75, Chd(3+) £1, SC £1.20
✳ BBQ sites
🅰 A21
♿ 🚻 ☕ Ⓟ

Ballycopeland Windmill

Millisle, Co Down
☎ 0247 861413

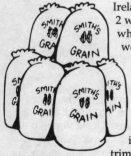

Ireland has only
2 windmills left
which can still
work, and this
18th-century
tower mill
was actively
grinding
corn until
1915. Now it
is just kept in
trim, but there is
a working model, corn by the
sackload and a flour-making
exhibition.

🕐 Easter–Sep, Tue–Sat 10–7, Sun 2–7;
   Oct–Mar, Sat 10–4, Sun 2–4
💷 Ad 75p, Chd (under 10)/SC 35p
🅰 B172, 1 mile W of Millisle
Ⓟ

Belfast Zoo & Castle

Antrim Rd, Belfast BT36 7PN
☎ 0232 776277

What will you like best? The
spectacled bears and gorillas, or the
penguins and sea lions which you
can watch
underwater?
There is a lot
to see in this
mountain
park perched
above the city.
The castle has
a heritage
centre
overlooking fine gardens.

🕐 Daily: Apr–Sep 10–5;
   Oct–Mar 10–3.30 (2.30 Fri)
💷 Ad £4.10, Chd(4+) £2.05, SC free.
   Cheaper Oct–Mar
🅰 4 miles N of city
♿ ☕ 🍴 🛍 Ⓟ

Benburb Valley Heritage Centre

Milltown Rd, Benburb, Co Tyrone BT71 7LZ
☎ 0861 549752

Walk in the woods along to the site
of the old Ulster Canal before seeing
the restored linen mill with its
Victorian steam engine and
Edwardian water turbine.

🕐 Park: daily 9–dusk. Centre: Easter–Sep,
   Tue–Sat 10–5, Sun 2–7
💷 Park: free; Centre: Ad £2.50,
   Chd/SC £1.50
🅰 Signs in Benburb
♿ 🚻 ☕ Ⓟ

Carnfunnock Country Park

Drains Bay, Coast Rd, Larne, Co Antrim
☎ 0574 270541/260088

Handsome parkland with an
adventure playground, pitch and
putt course and a fun maze cut to
the shape of a map of Northern
Ireland. There is also an old lime
kiln and an ice house.

🕐 Park: all year. Centre: Easter–Oct,
    daily 10–dusk; Nov–Xmas Sat/Sun
💷 Park: free. Maze: Ad £1, Chd 50p
✳ BBQ area
🅰 A2, 3½ miles N of Larne
♿ 🛝 ☕ 🅿

Carrick-a-rede Rope Bridge

Larrybane, Ballycastle, Co Antrim
☎ 02657 62024 (TIC)

This ingenious swinging rope
bridge spans, with a drop of 24m,
the 18m chasm between Carrick-a-
rede Island and the mainland (the
name means 'Rock on the road').
Exciting for the active, the bridge is
a 15-minute cliff-top walk from the
car park, and there is a salmon
fishery on the island.

🕐 Centre: Easter/May–Aug, daily 11–6;
    Sep, Sat/Sun 11–5. Bridge: May–Sep
💷 Car park £1.50
🅰 A2, 5 miles W of Ballycastle
🅿

Carrickfergus Gasworks

Irish Quarter West, Carrickfergus,
Co Antrim BT38 9DG
☎ 0960 366455 (TIC)

This was one of the last coal-fired
gasworks to survive in Ireland,
pumping out gas till 1964. You can
see how it was all done in an audio-
visual display, as well as a
surprising range of gas-fired
appliances like hairdryers and
footwarmers.

🕐 Phone for details
💷 Ad £1, Chd 50p
🅰 Signs from town centre
🚻 Carrickfergus 5 min
♿ 🅿

Carrothers Family Heritage Museum

Carrybridge Rd, Tamlaght,
Co Fermanagh BT74 4NN
☎ 0365 87278

Spanning the
generations, the
collection has
everything
from fossils
to letters
home
from
World
War I.

🕐 Apr–Oct, Mon–Sat 11–9
    (Nov–Mar/phone)
💷 Ad £1.50, Chd (5–12) 50p
🅰 A4, 1 mile W of Lisbellaw
♿ 🅿

Castle Espie Centre

Wildfowl & Wetlands Trust, 78 Ballydrain Rd,
Comber, Co Down BT23 6EA
☎ 0247 874146

You can see Ireland's largest
collection of geese, swans and ducks
from concealed hides, or visit the
waterfowl gardens after a woodland
walk. Nature centre and gallery
specialising in bird paintings.

🕘 All year, Mon–Sat 10.30–5,
   Sun 11.30–5
💷 Ad £2.50, Chd £1.25, SC £1.85, f/t
🅰 A22, 3 miles S of Comber
♿ 🍴 🏪 🅿

🌂 Castle Ward

Strangford, Downpatrick,
Co Down BT30 7LS
☎ 0396 881204

The toys and dressing up in the
castle's Victorian pastimes
centre will appeal most to the
young, but the 700-acre estate
has a working corn mill,
sawmill, a wildfowl collection,
Victorian laundry, and a
theatre where visiting players
stage entertainments.

🕘 Days/times vary. Phone
   for details
💷 Ad £2.50, Chd £1.25. Grnds only:
   £3.50 per car (Nov–Mar £1.50)
✳ Braille guide, deaf loops
🅰 A25, 1½ miles W of Strangford
♿ 🅰 🍴 🏪 🅿 NT

Castlewellan Forest Park

Main St, Castlewellan, Co Down
☎ 039 67 78664

They started planting trees here 250
years ago and are still planting. The
result is a grand drive, walks past
noble, colourful trees. Tropical birds
in a conservatory visitor centre, and
a 3-mile sculpture trail round the
lake.

🕘 All year, daily 10–dusk
💷 £2.50 per car
🅰 A25/A50
♿ 🍴 🅿

Causeway Safari Park

28 Benvarden Rd, Ballymoney,
Co Antrim BT53 8AF
☎ 026 57 41474

Lions roam free
and thrive
here. They
are the most
numerous of
the foreign
beasts on
view.
There is a
mini-zoo
and
farmyard
area, as
well as an amusement park with a
miniature railway.

🕘 Apr/May/Sep, Sat/Sun 10–6.30;
   Easter/Jun–Aug, daily 10–6.30
💷 Ad/Chd £3.50 (inc rides for Chd)
🅰 B67, N of Ballymoney
🅰 🍴 🏪 🅿

Causeway School Museum
Causeway Head, Co Antrim BT57 8SU
☎ 026 57 31777

A real old school where you can sit
at real old desks and blot exercise
books with real old ink pens. At
playtime you can skip, play marbles
or whip tops.

🕐 Jul–Aug, daily 11–4.30;
   other times/phone
💷 Ad 75p, Chd/SC 50p, f/t
🚻 Next to Giant's Causeway Centre
♿ 🅿

Coalisland Corn Mill
Limeside, Coalisland, Co Tyrone
☎ 086 87 48532

Start of a big industrial archaeology
complex. Already there is a restored
corn mill and a weaving factory
museum, backed up by audio-
visual displays and
spoken histories.

🕐 Apr–Oct, Mon–Fri
   10–8, Sat 10–6,
   Sun 12–6; Nov–Mar,
   Mon–Fri 10–6
💷 Ad £1.50, Chd 80p,
   SC £1.20
🚻 A45 Dungannon road
♿ 🍴 🎁 🅿

Down County Museum
The Mall, Downpatrick, Co Down BT30 6AH
☎ 0396 615218

Imaginative use of the old jail. One
cell block is more or less intact, with
life-size model prisoners. St Patrick
display and local Bronze Age finds
also on show.

🕐 Jul–mid Sep, Mon–Fri 11–5,
   Sat/Sun 2–5; Mid Sep–Jun,
   Tue–Fri/BH 11–5, Sat 2–5
💷 Adm free
🚻 Signs in town centre
🍴 🎁 🅿

Dunluce Centre
Dunluce Ave, Portrush,
Co Antrim BT56 8BF
☎ 0265 824444

Fun park with the big attraction
being the turbo thrill-ride, but with
a Myths and Legends audio show
and a computer quiz also on offer.
Viewing tower to see all the action.

🕐 All year. Days/times vary.
   Phone for details
💷 All-in: £4 (£3.50/low season),
   or per ride
🚻 Signs in town centre
🚉 Portrush 2 min
♿ 🍴 🎁 🅿

Exploris

The Rope Walk, Castle St,
Portaferry,
Co Down BT22 1NZ
☎ 024 77 28062

The latest in aquarium
style, all designed to show
the underwater life in the Irish
Sea (including sharks) and in
nearby Strangford Lough (eels,
trout). Hands-on, doing things
approach.

🕐 All year, Mon–Sat 10–6, Sun 1–6
£ Ad £3, Chd(5+)/SC £2, f/t
✳ Playgnd, tennis etc
/!\ Signs in town
 ♿ 🛗 ☕ Ⓟ

Foyle Valley Railway Centre

Foyle Rd, Londonderry BT48 6QS
☎ 0504 265234

Once, no fewer than 4 railway
companies served Londonderry.
You can see some of their locos
and ride on one of the early
diesel railcars. Look out for
the Pup, a car fitted with a
Ford engine which used to
stop on the line when
anyone hailed it.

🕐 All year, Tue–Sat 10–5
  (+Sun 2–6, May–Sep)
£ Railcar: Ad £2, Chd/SC £1
  (under 5s, 50p), f/t
/!\ Nr Craigavon Bridge
▦ Londonderry 10 min
♿

Giant's Causeway

Bushmills, Co Antrim BT57 8SU
☎ 026 57 31582

Massive, elaborate hexagonal pillars
of rock created millions of years ago
as volcanic rock cooled slowly.
Dramatic enough to become a
World Heritage Site and certainly
unforgettable. *Girona*, the treasure
ship of the Spanish Armada, sank
within sight of the rocks.

🕐 All year, all day
£ Adm free; pkg £2
✳ Minibus with wheelchair hoist
  mid Mar–Oct (other times/phone)
/!\ B146, 2 miles N of Bushmills
 ♿ ☕ Ⓟ NT

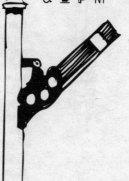

Giant's Causeway Centre

44A Causeway Rd, Bushmills,
Co Antrim BT57 8SU
☎ 026 57 31855

Discover the geological
explanations for the gigantic basalt
columns, learn more of the history
of the wrecked treasure galleon,
and don't miss the replica of the
strange hydro-electric tram which
used to run from Portrush to the
Causeway.

🕐 Jul/Aug, daily 10–7 (closes earlier rest
of year)
£ 25–min audio-visual show: Ad £1,
Chd 50p, f/t
⚠ B146, 2 miles N of Bushmills
♿ ☕ 🅿

Gortin Glen Forest Park

Omagh, Co Tyrone
☎ 066 26 48217

Five-mile drive through magnificent
forest with frequent lay-bys to
admire fine views. Sika deer
enclosure and wildfowl area.
Nature trails and visitor centre.

🕐 All year, daily 9–dusk
£ Car £2 (£1 coin lifts unmanned barrier)
⚠ B48, 7 miles N of Omagh
♿ ⛺ ☕ 🅿

Harland & Wolff Shipyard Tours

Bookings: Public Affairs Office, Harland &
Wolff, Queen's Island, Belfast

Regular tours of the shipyard, but
must be booked well in advance.
They built the *Titanic* here.

Hilltop Open Farm

Dunn's Farm, 51 Beragh Hill Rd, Ballyarnet,
Londonderry BT48 8LY
☎ 0504 354556

There are rare
breeds of sheep, pigs and Highland
cattle, and every day between 3.30
and 4 you can bottle-feed the baby
animals. They have pony and cart
rides, too.

🕐 Mar–Aug, daily 1–6; Sep–Feb Sun only
(other times/phone)
£ Ad £1.40, Chd/SC £1.20
⚠ A2, signs
♿ ⛺ ☕ 🛍 🅿

135

Irish Linen Centre
Market Square, Lisburn,
Co Antrim BT28 1AG
☎ 0846 663377 (TIC)

Opens in September 1994. Re-creation of the industry that made Northern Ireland world famous. Weaving shop with handlooms, audio-visual of whole process including beetling, the last touch which gave smoothness.

🕐 Phone for details
💷 Ad £2.50, Chd/SC £1.50, f/t
🅰 Town centre
🚉 Lisburn 5 min
🍴 🎒

Knight Ride & Heritage Plaza
Antrim St, Carrickfergus,
Co Antrim BT38 7DG
☎ 0960 366455

Trendy journey through time on a monorail, sweeping through a multi-media history of the area from AD531 right up to modern times. Can be combined with a visit to the 12th-century Carrickfergus Castle.

🕐 Apr–Sep, Mon–Fri 10–8, Sat 10–6, Sun 12–6; Oct–Mar, daily 10–4.30
💷 Ad £2, Chd/SC £1. Cmbd tkt with Castle: £3.60/£1.80; f/t
🅰 Town centre
🚉 Carrickfergus 5 min
♿ 🍴 🎒 🅿

Leslie Hill Heritage Farm Park
Macfin Rd, Ballymoney, Co Antrim BT53 6QL
☎ 026 56 66803

See the collection of grand carriages, then have a donkey ride around this handsome 18th-century estate, passing deer, guinea fowl and rare breeds; or take a nature trail around the lakes.

🕐 Jun, Sat/Sun 2–6; Jul–Aug, Mon–Sat 11–6, Sun 2–6; Apr/May/Sep, Sun/BH 2–6
💷 Ad £2.10, Chd/SC £1.40, f/t
✳ Museum, playgnd
🅰 A26, 1 mile W of Ballymoney
🍴 🎒 🅿

Lough Neagh Discovery Centre
Oxford Island, Craigavon,
Co Armagh BT66 6NJ
☎ 0762 322205

The largest lake in the UK is formed by no fewer than 6 rivers converging. Ideal conditions for eels, for they catch 10 tons of them in the lough every day. Audio-visuals with all the facts, and some hands-on exhibits. There are also bird hides and 5 miles of nature walks to try.

🕐 Daily: May–Aug 10–9; Apr/Sep 10–7.30; Oct–Mar 10–5; last adm 1hr before
💷 Adm free. Exhib: Ad £2, Chd £1.30, SC £1.50, f/t
✳ Boat trips for birdwatchers
🅰 M1 jnct 10
♿ 🍴 🎒 🅿

Loughside Open Dairy Farm

17 Island Rd Lower, Ballycarry,
Co Antrim BT38 9HB
☎ 0960 353312

Perhaps having vixens in the pets'
corner is why there is also a bird
sanctuary. Working farm: the
Highland cattle, fallow deer, ponies
and Jacob sheep are there for the
visitors. Adventure playground
with miniature train.

🕐 Mar–Oct, daily 12–7; Nov–Feb, Sat/Sun
£ Ad £1.80, Chd(3+)/SC £1.20, f/t
🅰 B90, N of Carrickfergus
♿ ☕ 🅿

🌸 Marble Arch Caves

Marlbank Scenic Loop, Florencecourt,
Co Fermanagh BT92 1EW
☎ 0365 348855

These eerie caverns, 49m below the
Cuilcagh mountains, were found by
a Frenchman in 1895. The 75-minute
tour starts
with a boat
trip across a
silent,
darkened
lake.
Impressive
formations of
stalagmites
and stalactites.
Geology
exhibition and
audio-visual presentation.

🕐 Mid Mar–Sep, daily from 11 (closing
times vary)
£ Ad £4, Chd £2, SC £3, f/t
🅰 A4/A32, 12 miles SW of Enniskillen
♿ ☕ 🎒 🅿

North Down Heritage Centre

Castle Park Ave, Bangor, Co Down
☎ 0247 271200

This is music country, and they
have an audio-visual show
featuring Viking music as well as
pipes and lyre. After you have seen
the observation beehive, there are
swords dating from 500BC. But the
toy display could be favourite.

🕐 Sep–Jun, Tue–Sat 10.30–4.30,
Sun 2–4.30; Jul–Aug,
Mon–Sat 10.30–5.30, Sun 2–5.30
£ Adm free
🅰 Nr town centre
🚉 Bangor 3 min
♿ 🍴 🅿

Palace Stables Heritage Centre

Friary Rd, Armagh BT60 4EL
☎ 0861 522722

Reconstruction of the life in a day of
the year 1776 at the palace of the
Archbishop. The stables still have
horses, you can walk through an
ancient tunnel to see the impressive
ice house, and
take a carriage
ride. Craft
demonstrations
and walks in the
grounds. Can be
combined with St
Patrick's Trian [qv].

🕐 Apr–Sep, Mon–Sat 10–7, Sun 1–7;
Oct–Mar, Mon–Sat 10–5, Sun 2–5
£ Ad £2.50, Chd £1.50, SC £2.
Cmbd tkt with St Patrick's Trian:
£5/£2.70/£4; f/t
🅰 Signs from town centre
♿ ☕ 🎒 🅿

137

Parkanaur Forest Park

Dungannon, Co Tyrone
☎ 0868 758256/767432

Through the trees you may glimpse
white fallow deer: the herd is
descended from a pair given as a
gift from Elizabeth I to her god-
daughter. The nature trail passes
under huge beech trees round a
Victorian garden. Stop at the
wishing well.

🕐 All year, daily 8–dusk
£ Car £2 (£1 coin lifts unmanned barrier)
🅰 Off A4, 4 miles W of Dungannon
🅿

Patterson's Spade Mill

Antrim Rd,
Templepatrick,
Co Antrim BT39 0AP
☎ 0238 510721

The Irish spade helped create
the British Empire, digging
canals, railways and trenches, and
here is where they made it. The
water-driven spade mill is the last of
its kind, and you can see spade-
making demonstrated.

🕐 Jun–Aug, Wed–Mon 2–6; Apr/May/Sep,
   Sat/Sun/BH 2–6
£ Ad £2.50, Chd £1.25
🅰 A6, 2 miles S of Templepatrick
♿ 🅿 NT

Portrush Countryside Centre

Bath Rd, Portrush, Co Antrim
☎ 0265 823600

The Centre has a wildlife exhibition
but the highlight is a big touch tank
where you can identify and handle
rockpool creatures.

🕐 Jun–Sep, Wed–Mon 12–8
   (other times/phone)
£ Adm free
🅰 Signs in town
🚻 Portrush 10 min
♿ 🅿

Quoile Countryside Centre

5 Quay Rd, Downpatrick,
Co Down BT30 7JB
☎ 0396 615520

The Centre uses models,
marked trails and visits
to a fishing jetty to show how
flood control barriers changed
water in the estuary from salt to
fresh - and how the environment
has benefited. Next to ruins of 16th-
century Quoile Castle.

🕐 Apr–Sep, daily 11–5; Oct–Mar,
   Sat/Sun 1–5
£ Adm free
🅰 A25, N of
   Downpatrick
♿ 🅿

Rathlin Island Bird Sanctuary

c/o TIC, 7 Mary St, Ballycastle,
Co Antrim BT54 6QH
☎ 026 57 62024 (TIC)/63935
(Sanctuary)

Tens of thousands of birds,
up to 175 species, live and
nest on the sheer, 107m-
high cliffs. At times,
there is a whole tide of
razorbills, kittiwakes
and guillemots on the 7-
mile-long island. The
'upside-down' lighthouse
has its lens at its base. Rathlin
Island is where Scots king Robert
the Bruce hid in a cave and met the
famous spider.

🕐 All year, daily. Phone for details
£ Sanctuary: free. Ferry rtn: Ad £5.40,
   Chd £2.70, SC £4.30
✳ Minibus trips on island
🅰 Ballycastle quayside
♿(prior notice) 🅿

Seaforde Tropical Butterfly House

Seaforde Nursery, Seaforde,
Co Down BT30 8PG
☎ 0396 811225

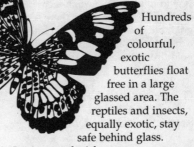

Hundreds
of
colourful,
exotic
butterflies float
free in a large
glassed area. The
reptiles and insects,
equally exotic, stay
safe behind glass.
Intricate and tricky maze.

🕐 Easter–Sep,
   Mon–Sat 10–5, Sun 2–6
£ Ad £2, Chd/SC £1.20.
   Maze: £2/£1.20.
   All–in: £3.50/£2
🅰 A24, 20 miles S of Belfast
♿ ☕ 🎁 🅿

St Patrick's Trian

40 English St, Armagh BT61 7BA
☎ 0861 527808

Armagh remembers Jonathan Swift,
creator of *Gulliver's Travels*, and its
own history, in a new centre with
audio-visual presentation.
   Can be combined with visit to
Palace Stables Heritage Centre [*qv*].

🕐 Apr–Sep, Mon–Sat 10–7, Sun 12–7;
   Oct–Mar, Mon–Sat 10–5, Sun 2–5
£ Ad £3, Chd £1.50, SC £2.
   Cmbd tkt with Palace Stables:
   £5/£2.70/£4; f/t
🅰 Signs in city centre
♿ ☕ 🎁 🅿

Shane's Castle Railway

Randalstown Rd, Antrim BT41 4NS
☎ 0849 463380

The narrow gauge steam train
travels along the shores of Lough
Neagh into a nature reserve with
bird hides for better viewing. After
that there are guided tours of the
deer park and rare breed area.

🕐 Apr–Sep. Phone for times/prices
🅰 M22 jnct 2, A6
♿ ☕ 🅿

Sperrin Heritage Centre

274 Glenelly Rd, Cranagh, Gortin,
Co Tyrone BT79 8LF
☎ 06626 48142

The scenery is spectacular and there is gold in the hills. A high-tech exhibition tells the story: there *is* gold, but chemical extraction is too expensive. Still, panning for fools' gold (iron pyrites) in a special stream is fun.

🕐 Easter–Sep, Mon–Fri 11–6,
   Sat 11.30–6, Sun 2–7
£ Ad £1.80, Chd/SC 80p, f/t.
   Pan hire: 65p/35p
🅰 B47, 9 miles E of Plumbridge
 ♿ 🚼 🛍 🅿

Streamvale Open Dairy Farm

38 Ballyhanwood Rd, Belfast BT5 7SN
☎ 0232 483244

Feed the animals, including bottle-feeding lambs, and watch the dairy herd being milked. Small animals are fed at noon and 4pm, milking is at 3.30. In between there are nature trails and pony rides.

🕐 Easter/Jul–Aug, daily 10.30–6;
   Jun, 12–6.
   Other times/phone
£ Ad £2.50,
   Chd/SC £1.50,
   f/t
🅰 Nr Dundonald
   Ice Bowl
 ♿ 🧒 🚼 🅿

Talnotry Cottage Bird Garden

2 Crumlin Rd, Crumlin,
Co Antrim BT29 4AD
☎ 0849 422900

A Georgian walled garden has been turned into a refuge for sick and injured birds of all kinds. Most are released to the wild when they are well, but many different species have stayed on to be seen by human visitors.

🕐 All year. Phone for details
£ Ad £2, Chd £1
🅰 A52
🚉 Crumlin 10 min
 ♿ 🚼 🅿

Tannaghmore Gardens & Farm

Silverwood, Craigavon,
Co Armagh BT66 6LL
☎ 0762 343244

They have a cow which is smaller than some pigs, and a sheep with 4 horns. The rose garden is normal.
   Watersports and fishing.

🕐 Daily. Gdn from dawn,
   farm from 10am.
   Closes 1hr before dusk
£ Adm free
🅰 M1 jnct 10
🚉 Lurgan 20 min
 ♿ 🧒 🅿

Tropical Ravine & Palm House

Botanic Gardens, Stranmillis Rd, Belfast
☎ 0232 324902

Grand Victorian glass and plant
extravaganza which is the 1889
equivalent of modern rainforest
simulations. Exotic ferns flourish in a
sunken glen: you watch from a
balcony. Giant Palm House next door.
The Arts Council **Sculpture Park**
(☎ 0232 381591) is just down the
road. It is open all the time and they
encourage touching, even climbing
on, the modern wood, steel and
bronze creations.

🕐 Apr–Sep, Mon–Fri 10–5,
   Sat/Sun/BH 2–5; Oct–Mar, Mon–Fri
   10–4, Sat/Sun/BH 2–4. Closed lunch
🅴 Adm free
🄰 Signs from city centre
♯ Botanic Park 5 min
♿

Ulster-American Folk Park

Camphill, Omagh, Co Tyrone
BT78 5QY
☎ 0662 243292/3

The theme is emigration to the New
World. Tiny cottages people were
forced to leave lead to a busy
quayside with a full-size replica of a
sailing brig carrying emigrants.
Then there is the other side: life in
pioneer America with log cabins
(with real pigs) up to small
mansions. Americans can trace their
ancestors on computer.

🕐 Apr–Sep, Mon–Sat 11–6.30,
   Sun/BH 11.30–7; Oct–Easter,
   Mon–Fri 10.30–5. Last adm 1½hr before
🅴 Ad £3, Chd/SC £1.50
🄰 A5, 3 miles N of Omagh
♿ ☕ 🎒 🅿

Ulster Folk & Transport Museum

Cultra, Holywood, Co Down BT18 0EU
☎ 0232 428428

A village of rescued houses,
watermills, a church and more,
furnished in period. Samples from
the railway era, including the
biggest loco ever made in Ireland,
donkey carts, schooners and planes.
Top it off with a carriage ride.

🕐 All year. Days/times vary. Phone for
   details
🅴 Ad £3, Chd/SC £2, f/t. ♿free
🄰 A2
♯ Cultra, adjacent
♿ ☕ 🎒 🅿

🏺 Ulster History Park

Cullion, Omagh, Co Tyrone
☎ 06626 48188

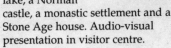

They are rebuilding,
using the same
methods and
materials, life
in Ulster from
8000BC right
up to the 17th
century. Already
they have a crannog
fort set in its own
lake, a Norman
castle, a monastic settlement and a
Stone Age house. Audio-visual
presentation in visitor centre.

🕐 Apr–Sep, Mon–Sat 10.30–6.30,
   Sun 11.30–7; Oct–Mar, Mon–Fri
   10.30–5. Last adm 1½hr before
🅴 Ad £2.50, Chd/SC £1.50
🄰 B48, N of Omagh
♿ ⛲ ☕ 🅿

Watertop Open Farm

Ballyvoy, Ballycastle, Co Antrim BT54 6RL
☎ 02657 62576/63785

If you have never seen a sheep
being sheared, now is your chance.
The shearing takes place
surrounded by lots of activities:
pony trekking, farm tours, boating,
fishing. All watched by the
ornamental birds.

🕐 Easter/Jul–Aug, daily
   10–5.30. Other times/phone
£ Ad £1, Chd 60p;
   trekking/fishing extra
✳ BBQ site
⚠ A2, 6 miles SE of Ballycastle
♿ ♨ ☕ 🏠 🅿

Wellbrook Beetling Mill

20 Wellbrook Rd, Corkhill, Cookstown,
Co Tyrone BT80 9RY
☎ 064 87 51735/51715

Beetling is the final stage in linen
manufacture when the cloth is
hammered to produce a sheen, and
this is a water-powered 18th-
century hammer mill with the
original machinery in working
order. There are good wooded
walks along the Ballinderry river
and by the mill race.

🕐 2–6: Easter, daily; Jul/Aug, Wed–Mon;
   Apr–Jun/Sep, Sat/Sun/BH
£ Ad £1.40, Chd 70p
⚠ A505, 4 miles W of Cookstown
🏠 🅿 NT

Cleveland
Durham
Northumberland
Tyne & Wear

Alnwick Castle

Alnwick, Northumb NE66 1NQ
☎ 0665 510777

The second largest inhabited castle
in England. It housed the warlike
Percys in the 14th century, hence
the armoury and dungeon; later
generations bought the
Canalettos, Titians and
Meissen china. Great
chandeliers.

🕓 Easter–mid Oct,
   daily 11–5 (last adm 4)
💷 Ad £4, Chd £2.20,
   SC £3.50, f/t
✳ Access to Hulme Park
🅰 A1068
♿ (res) ☕ 🎁 🅿

Bamburgh Castle

Bamburgh, Northumb NE69 7DF
☎ 0668 214208/214515

Sits on a basalt crag overlooking the
North Sea. Still lived in, and the
   exhibits reflect the warlike
      Border history it has seen.
         Lots of good armour and
            tapestries, plus an
               interesting Victorian
               scullery.

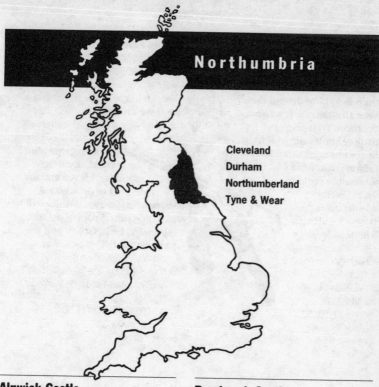

🕓 April–Oct,
   daily 12–5
💷 Ad £2.50, Chd £1.20,
   SC £2
🅰 A1, B1342
♿ ☕ 🎁 🅿

Berwick-upon-Tweed Barracks

The Parade, Berwick–upon–Tweed TD15 1DE
☎ 0289 304493

Built in 1717 to defend the
English against a Scottish
invasion. Well-staged
display shows the rough
life of the British
infantryman from
Redcoat to regular.
Ticket includes
admission to
Berwick Borough
Museum [qv].

🕐 Apr–Oct, daily 10–6;
    Nov–Mar,
    Wed–Sun 10–4
💷 Ad £2.20,
    Chd £1.10, SC £1.65
🅰 Town centre
🚉 Berwick–on–Tweed 5 min
♿(res) 💼 🅿 EH

Berwick Borough Museum

Ravensdowne Barracks,
Berwick–upon–Tweed TD15 1DQ
☎ 0289 330933

You walk through the door-sized
mouth of a 'dragon' to view objects
through distorting mirrors, or
glimpse the wonders of fibre optics.
You also get to see some very fine
art given by millionaire shipbuilder
Sir William Burrell, and find out
about local history.

🕐 Easter–Sep, daily 10–6; Oct–Mar,
    Tue–Sun 10–4
💷 As for Berwick Barracks [qv]
🅰 Town centre
🚉 Berwick–on–Tweed 5 min
♿ (res) 💼 🅿

Bowes Museum

Barnard Castle, Co Durham DL12 8NP
☎ 0833 690606

The highlight is the silver swan
near the children's
                    gallery. It
                 'swims' through
                a precious metal
                pond, under a
            spinning glass fountain.
        Designed to deck grand
     banqueting tables. Adults will like
the French and Spanish paintings,
especially the El Greco, and the
parterre garden.

🕐 May–Sep, Mon–Sat 10–5.30, Sun 2–5;
    Apr/Oct, Mon–Sat 10–5, Sun 2–5.
    Nov–Mar/phone
💷 Ad £2.50, Chd/SC £1.50
🅰 W of market place
♿ ☕ 💼 🅿

Bowes Railway Centre

Springwell Village,
Washington, Tyne & Wear NE9 7QL
☎ 091 416 1847

The world's only standard gauge
rope-hauled railway. Built in 1826
by George Stephenson, it eventually
reached 15 miles long and was used
to pull coal to the docks. You can
see it demonstrated, ride on steam
trains and watch them being
restored.

🕐 All year, Mon–Sat 9–4
💷 Ad £2.50, Chd/SC £1.50, f/t
🅰 N of town centre
♿ ☕ 🅿

Castle Eden Dene National Nature Reserve

Oakerside Dene Lodge,
Stanhope Chase, Peterlee SR8 1NJ
☎ 091 586 0004

On a sunny day you can walk in dappled woodland shade on any of the 12 miles of footpaths in this 500-acre reserve.

🕐 All year, daily 8–dusk
💷 Adm free
🅰 S of Peterlee
♿ 🅿

Chesters Fort

Chollerford, Humshaugh,
Hexham NE46 4EP
☎ 0434 681379

Here, at the key defensive position where Hadrian's Wall crossed the Tyne, is the best-preserved Roman cavalry fort in the country. See the bath house, with its underfloor heating.

🕐 Daily:
   Apr–Oct 10–6; Nov–Mar 10–4
💷 Ad £2, Chd £1, SC £1.50
🅰 B6318
🚌 Hexham (bus link)
♿ 🍵 🎁 🅿 EH

Chillingham Castle

Chillingham, Northumb NE66 5NJ
☎ 06685 359

Earl Grey, who invented bergamot-flavoured tea, came from the family who have owned Chillingham since the 13th century. Huge, beamed halls and grim dungeons, against a backdrop of large grounds and gardens. Look for the Wild White cattle, survivors of herds which once roamed the forests of northen Britain.

🕐 Easter/May–Sep, Wed–Mon 1.30–5
💷 Ad £3.30, Chd £2.20, SC £2.70
🅰 B6346, NW of Alnwick
🧺 🍵 🎁 🅿

Cragside

Rothbury, Morpeth, Northumb NE65 7PX
☎ 0669 20333/20266

The first house in the world to be lit by hydro-electricity. The system included man-made lakes and they planted millions of trees and laid 40 miles of paths and drives. Marked 1½-mile walk round water-power system.

🕐 Apr–Oct Tue-Sun. Hse: 1–5.30
   (last adm 4.45). Gdn: 10.30–5.30;
   Grnds: 10.30–7 (+ Nov–mid Dec)
💷 All–in: Ad/Chd £5.50;
   Grnds/Gdn £3.40; f/t
✱ Chd's guides, adv playgnd
🅰 B6341, 13 miles SW of Alnwick
♿ 🧺 🍵 🍽 🎁 🅿 NT

Darlington Railway Centre & Museum
North Road Station, Darlington DL3 6ST
☎ 0325 460532

The 1842 station has Locomotion No 1, the engine which opened the Stockton &

Darlington Railway in 1825. Part of a collection of engines, plus displays, model railway, and steam rides on selected dates.

🕐 All year, daily 9.30–5
£ Ad £1.70, Chd 85p, SC £1.25
🅰 N of town centre
🚃 North Rd
♿ ☕ 🎁 🅿

Durham Cathedral
Durham DH1 3EQ
☎ 091 386 2367

The 900-year-old cathedral has housed saints like Cuthbert and The Venerable Bede, and sinners like the Civil War troops who stabled their horses there. Don't miss the rich robes and relics in the treasury.

🕐 Daily: May–Sep 7am–8pm; Oct–Apr 7–6
£ Adm free. Treasury: Ad £1, Chd 20p
🅰 City centre
🚃 Durham 10 min
♿ 🍴 🎁 🅿

Earl Grey's Monument
Grey St, Newcastle–upon–Tyne
☎ 091 261 0691 (TIC)

Climb up inside the Greek column (164 steps, 41m high), which commemorates most people being allowed to vote. Great views over the city. Look closely at the statue of Grey - the head was replaced after being hit by lightning in 1941.

Apart from being responsible for the vote-giving Reform Bill of 1832, Earl Grey's government can claim credit for abolishing slavery throughout the British Empire. So he deserves his monument.

🕐 Easter–beg Oct, Sat/BH 11.30–4.30
£ Ad 40p, Chd (with Ad)/SC 25p
🅰 City centre
🚃 Newcastle Central 5 min

Earle Hill Household & Farming Museum
Langleford Rd, Wooler,
Northumb NE71 6RH
☎ 0668 281243

Unusual and personal collection mapping out life in a farming family over the years: from christening robes to toys, tools and farm records.

🕐 May–Oct, Fri/BH 1–6
  (other times by appt)
£ Ad £1.50, Chd 50p
🅰 A697
🅿

🦜 Farne Islands
Northumberland
☎ 0665 721099/720651 (Warden)

Home to about 55,000 pairs of
breeding birds. In the summer
you can spot puffins, eider
ducks, guillemots,
kittiwakes etc. Also a
grey seal colony. A
small chapel
commemorates St
Cuthbert, who died on
Inner Farne. You pay
warden on landing.

🕐 Daily: April/Aug/Sep 10.30–6.
   May–Jul: Staple Is 10.30–1.30;
   Inner Farne 1.30–5.
£ May–Jul £3.50, other times £2.70
   (excl boat)
/A\ Boats from Seahouses
♿ (res) NT

Fishing Experience Centre
Neville House, Fish Quay,
N Shields NE30 1HE
☎ 091 296 5449/0937 541030

The first part uses charts, video
and aquaria to tell
you about the North
Sea and the fish in
it. Then you go on to
a trawler deck, see
how nets are handled, boats
steered, catches landed, and
have lifeboat drill.

🕐 Apr–Oct, Wed–Fri 10–4.30,
   Sat/Sun/BH 10–5.30
£ Ad £2.10, Chd £1.50, SC £1.80, f/t
/A\ River front
🚇 N Shields (metro) 10 min
♿ ☕ 🎁 Ⓟ

Grace Darling Museum
Radcliffe Rd, Bamburgh NE69 7AE
☎ 0665 720037

In 1838, young Grace and her father
           rowed out in a wild storm
               to rescue survivors
             from SS *Forfarshire*,
            driven aground on
           the Farne Islands.
           Original relics,
           including the actual
           boat used.

🕐 Easter–Sep, daily 11–6
£ Adm free
/A\ Signs in Bamburgh
♿ 🎁 Ⓟ

Grindon Museum
Grindon Lane, Sunderland SR9 8HW
☎ 091 514 1235

Carefully preserved, fully furnished
Edwardian home and shop
interiors. You can step inside and
find yourself in a 1900s post office,
chemist shop, dentist's surgery etc.

🕐 All year, Mon–Wed/Fri
   9.30–5; Sat 9–4.
   Closed lunch+BH
£ Adm free
   /A\ A183
       Ⓟ

Hall Hill Farm

Lanchester, Co Durham DH7 0TA
☎ 0388 730300

Working farm in lovely countryside,
where visitors are given every
chance to get close to the animals,
particularly the lambs. Farm trailer
rides, woodland and riverside walks.

🕐 Apr–Oct, Sun/BH 1–5
  (Easter/summer hols, Sun–Fri 1–5)
💷 Ad £2.50, Chd £1.25
✳ Santa visits/Dec
🅰 B6296, 4 miles from Lanchester
♿(res) 🍴 🅿

Hamsterley Forest

Redford, Hamsterley Forest,
Bishop Auckland DL13 3NL
☎ 0388 488312

Some 2,500 hectares with a 4-mile
marked forest drive. Cycling, pony
trekking, orienteering, and a
summer arts programme where
actors perform plays, musicians
make instruments from forest
wood, and children over 10 are
invited to bring a hammer and
handsaw and make a sculpture.

🕐 All year. Centre: Easter–Oct,
  Mon–Fri 10–4, Sat/Sun 11–5
💷 Adm free. Forest Drive: £1.50 per car
🅰 Off A68; entrance at Bedburn
♿ 🛝 🍴 🛍 🅿

Hancock Museum

Claremont Rd, University Precinct,
Newcastle–upon–Tyne NE2 4PT
☎ 091 222 7418

Great collection of birds, mammals,
insects, fossils, in the North East's
biggest natural history museum.
Lots of trails to follow.

🕐 All year, Mon–Sat 10–5, Sun 2–5
💷 Ad £1.80, Chd £1, SC £1
🅰 Follow University signs
🚉 Newcastle Central 10 min
♿(res) 🛝 🛍 🅿

Hardwick Hall Country Park

Sedgefield, Co Durham
☎ 091 383 3594 (County Hall)

County-maintained park based on
parkland landscaped for 18th-
century mansion which still has
follies and a serpentine lake. Nature
walks, water birds (and bird hides),
play equipment for children.

🕐 All year, daily 8.30–5
💷 Adm free
🅰 W of A177 Sedgefield Bypass
♿ 🅿

Hartlepool Historic Ships

Jackson Dock, The Marina, Hartlepool
☎ 0429 223193/266522

HMS *Trincomalee*, built in Bombay
in 1817 and now being restored, is
the only surviving frigate in her
class. Across the dock is the paddle
steamer *Wingfield Castle*, once a
ferry, now the visitor centre.

🕐 All year, Mon–Fri 1–4.30,
   Sat/Sun/BH 10.30–4.30
£ Ad £2.50, Chd/SC £1.50
🅰 A689
♿ 🅿

Hartley Wood Glassblowing

Portobello Lane, Monkwearmouth,
Sunderland SR6 0DN
☎ 091 567 2506

Craft glassblowing. You can see
glass coloured and molten from the
furnace, blown and shaped. Exhibits
and video on the art of glass-
making.

🕐 All year, Mon–Fri 9–5
£ Ad £1, Chd 50p, SC 75p
🅰 A183, 'Glass Trail' signs
♿ 🅿

House of Hardy

Willowburn, Alnwick NE66 2PG
☎ 0665 602771

The rods and reels produced here
are the Rolls-Royces of the fly-
fishing world. Phone for a factory
tour.

🕐 All year, Mon–Fri 9–5, Sat 10–5,
   Sun (Mar–Oct) 1.30–5
£ Adm free
🅰 Signs from town centre
♿ 🅿

Kielder Forest

Forest Enterprise, Eals Burn,
Bellingham, Northumb NE48 2AJ
☎ 0434 220242

A man-made forest of 125,000 acres,
mostly conifers, with a 12-mile
forest drive. Walks, bike trails, a
viewpoint where you can watch
eagles circle below, and the visitor
centre was once the Duke of
Northumberland's hunting lodge.

🕐 All year, dawn–dusk.
   Centre: Easter–Oct, 10–5
£ Forest Drive: £1 per car
✳ Play area, cycle hire
🅰 Begins at Bellingham/B6320
♿ 🅿

Kielder Water

Operations Centre, Hexham NE48 1BX
☎ 0434 240398

Landscaped reservoir covering 2,684
acres, now a magnet for holiday
fishermen and
sailors. The
27½-mile
shoreline
lets walkers
and cyclists
in on the
views and
nature trails.
Cruises (5 times a day)
take 75 minutes. Water-skiing,
windsurfing, rowing, and more.

🕐 All year, dawn–dusk. Centre: May–Sep
    10–6; other times/phone
💷 Varies/activities
🅰 B6320
♿ ♨ ☕ 🍴 🅿

Killhope Lead Mining Centre

Cowshill, St John's Chapel,
Bishop Auckland DL13 1AR
☎ 0388 537505

The huge 10m waterwheel powered
the crusher in this Victorian lead
mine, the best-preserved in the
country. A woodland trail takes you
to places where the miners lived,
and you can 'pan' for lead.

🕐 Apr–Oct, daily 10.30–5; Nov,
    Sun 10.30–5
💷 Ad £2, Chd/SC £1, f/t
🅰 A689, 2½ miles W of Cowshill
♿ ☕ 🎁 🅿

Lindisfarne Castle

Holy Island, Berwick–upon–Tweed
TD15 2SH
☎ 0289 89244

A 16th-century castle restored by
architect Sir Edwin Lutyens and with
a famous garden. It is not possible to
cross to the island from 2 hours
before until 3½ hours after high tide.
Don't worry if you are stranded - St
Coombes Open Farm [qv] and the
priory are worth seeing too.

🕐 Apr–Oct, Sat–Thu 1–5.30 (last adm 5)
💷 Ad/Chd £3.40
✳ Braille guide
🅰 Across causeway
☕ 🅿 NT

Marine Life Centre & Fishing Museum

4 Main St, Seahouses,
Northumb NE68 7RG
☎ 0665 721257

Tanks holding
North Sea
fish, crabs
and
lobsters,
with
displays of
old-time
fishing,
baiting,
mending nets,
smoking kippers and making
barrels. Then, as it is today, with an
electronic wheelhouse on a trawler.

🕐 Daily: May–Sep 10–6, Apr/Oct 10–5
💷 Ad £1.50, Chd(6+)/SC £1
🅰 Harbour
♿(res) 🎁 🅿

Metroland

39 Garden Walk, MetroCentre,
Gateshead NE11 9YZ
☎ 091 493 2048

Europe's biggest indoor theme
park within a shopping
complex. It has roller coasters,
a ferris wheel, dodgems, plus a
soft play area for young ones.
There is also live entertainment
with stage shows and karaoke
sessions. Whew!

🕐 All year, Mon–Wed 12–8,
Thu–Sat 10–9, Sun 12–6
💷 Adm/rides: Over 1.2m £4.95,
Under 1.2m £3.95 (after 6pm £3 per
head); Adm only: Ad £1
✳ Tkts allow re–entry
🅰 A1(M)
▦ MetroCentre
♿ 🚇 🍴 🅿

Monkwearmouth Station Museum

North Bridge St, Monkwearmouth,
Sunderland SR5 1AP
☎ 091 567 7075

Built when the railway king George
Hudson became the local MP, this
handsome station retains a booking
office in full working order, a
restored platform and displays of
locos in a siding. Must be the only
museum where current trains run
through.

🕐 All year, Tue–Fri 10–5.30,
Sat 10–4.30, Sun 2–5
💷 Adm free
🅰 A1018, N of town centre
▦ Sunderland 10 min
♿ 🅿

Morpeth Chantry Bagpipe Museum

The Chantry, Bridge St, Morpeth NE61 1PJ
☎ 0670 519466

The keening sound of the
Northumbrian pipes floats through
this converted 13th-century chapel,
where you can see and listen to the
history and development of the
bagpipes and their music. A wail of
a time.

Have a look at **Morpeth Clock
Tower**, one of only 8 non-church
bell towers in Britain. The clock has
only one hand, and they still ring
the curfew every night (☎ 0670
519664 for details).

🕐 Jan–Feb, Mon–Sat 9.30–5;
Mar–Dec, Mon–Sat 9.30–5.30
💷 Ad £1.50, Chd/SC 50p, f/t
✳ Deaf loop
🅰 Nr town centre
▦ Morpeth 10 min
🛍 🅿

Newburn Hall Motor Museum

Townfield Gardens, Newburn,
Newcastle–upon–Tyne NE15 8PY
☎ 091 264 2977

Star cars,
motorbikes and
things like old-
fashioned petrol
pumps, some of
which have
featured in films
and on TV.

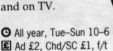

🕐 All year, Tue–Sun 10–6
💷 Ad £2, Chd/SC £1, f/t
🛣 A695
♿ ☕ Ⓟ

Newcastle Discovery

Blandford House, Blandford Sq,
Newcastle–upon–Tyne NE1 4JA
☎ 091 232 6789

An exciting modern museum
complex with hands-on science
exhibits and lights and mirrors to
dazzle and baffle, plus a walk-
through city history of the 20th
century from Newcastle United to
shipbuilding. Children can try on
old-fashioned shoes and clothes on
the way round.

🕐 All year, Mon–Sat 10–5
💷 Adm free
🛣 City centre
🚉 Newcastle Central 5 min
♿ ☕ Ⓟ

North of England Open Air Museum

Beamish, Tyne & Wear DH9 0RG
☎ 0207 231811

A re-created town from around
1913, brought to life and peopled by
inhabitants dressed in the styles of
the times. The town is joined by a
colliery village and a farm, and the
railway station has trains. A visit
lasts around 5 hours, the memory
lingers much longer.

🕐 Apr–Oct, daily 10–5
(6pm summer hols);
Nov–Mar (not Mon/Fri) 10–4;
last adm 2hr before
💷 Summer: Ad £6.99,
Chd/SC £3.99;
Winter: £2.99/£1.99
✳ In winter, only Town & Tramway areas
🛣 A693
♿ ☕ 🍴 🛍 Ⓟ

Rising Sun Country Park

Whitley Rd, Benton, Newcastle–upon–Tyne
NE12 9SS
☎ 091 266 7733

Farm, woodland, and nature reserve
on a great pond - 400 acres in all.
Organised events during summer.
The visitor centre has a special
tactile exhibition for the poorly
sighted, and a bird hide adapted for
wheelchair users.

🕒 Park: all year, dawn–dusk.
   Centre: Mon–Fri 9–5
💷 Adm free
🅰 A193
♿ ♨ ☕ 🛍 🅿

St Coombes Open Farm

Lindisfarne, Holy Island
☎ 0289 89294

The farm specialises in rare breeds,
and visitors can feed or come close
to a variety of birds and beasts. [See
Lindisfarne Castle]

🕒 Easter–Oct, daily 10–6
💷 Ad £1.20, Chd/SC 60p, ♿(free)
🅰 Only one road on island
♿ 🛍 🅿

Saltburn Smugglers Heritage Centre

Ship Inn, Saltburn–by–the–Sea,
Cleveland TS12 1HF
☎ 0287 625252

Set in old fishermen's cottages
alongside the local inn, this sight,
sound and smell re-creation of the
days and deeds of Black John
Andrew, King of the Smugglers, is a
drop of the good stuff.

While you are in this Victorian
seaside resort, see the **Saltburn
Inclined Tramway**. This water-
balanced tram links the upper town
to the beach and promenade daily
[June–mid Sep 10-1 & 2-7; ☎ 0287
622528 for details].

🕒 Easter–Sep, daily 10–6;
   Oct–Mar, Sat/Sun 10.30–4
💷 Ad £1.50, Chd £1, f/t
🅰 On sea front
🚉 Saltburn-by-the-Sea 10 min
♿ ☕ 🍽 🛍 🅿

🌴 Transporter Bridge

Ferry Rd, Middlesborough
☎ 0642 247563

The only one in the country. When
the central section of the bridge is
filled up with 9 cars (or 200 people),
it slides across on a gantry to the
other side of the River Tees. Then it
goes back again.

🕒 All year, Mon–Sat 5am–11pm,
   Sun 2pm–11pm
💷 Car 57p, M'cycle 27p, On foot 25p
🅰 Signs from town centre
♿

Vindolanda Fort & Museum
Chesterholm, Bardon Mill,
Hexham NE47 7JN
☎ 0434 344277

Active archaeological site on
Hadrian's Wall. Major
discoveries, including
reports, notes, even
menus written on
wood, have
revealed a lot about
life with the
Roman garrison. Video of
excavations.

🕐 Site: all year. Mus: mid Feb–Nov,
 daily from 10 (close varies)
£ Ad £3, Chd £1.75, SC £2.25, f/t
🅰 Btwn A69 & B6318
♿ 🧸 ☕ 🏠 🅿 EH

Wet 'n' Wild
Rotary Way, N Shields,
Tyne & Wear NE29 6DA
☎ 091 296 1333/1444 info

Not the place to go for a
quiet swim. You can
test your nerve as
you plunge
down the UK's
first double-
twister flume, or
ride the breakers
in the ocean wave pool,
or go for a spin on the
Calamity Canyon raft ride. It's all
fast, furious and frothy in this
indoor waterpark.

🕐 All year, daily 10am–10.30pm
£ Ad £5.95, Chd/SC £3.50
✳ Swimming accessories on sale
🅰 1 mile from N entrance to the Tyne
 Tunnel
⊖ Percy Main (bus link)
♿ (res) ☕ 🅿

Scotland-Central, Lowlands & Borders

Borders

Dumfries & Galloway

Central

Fife

Lothian

Strathclyde (S)

Tayside

Almond Valley Heritage Centre

Millfield, Kirkton North, Livingston,
Lothian EH54 7AR
☎ 0506 414957

A new industry area remembers the
past with a friendly working farm
with animals to meet, a watermill
and 'mining' for oil in shale.

Narrow gauge
railway, nature
trail, and horse-
drawn cart rides.

🕘 Jan–Dec,
   daily 10–5
💷 Ad £1.50,
   Chd(5+)/SC 75p
🅰 A705
♿ ⛺ ☕ 🎁 🅿

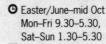

Atholl Country Collection

Blair Atholl, Perthshire PH18 5SG
☎ 0796 481232

Re-creation of an entire village with
figures including a smith, vet and
gamekeeper, post office, school and
church. Imaginative way to show
how people lived in the past.

🕘 Easter/June–mid Oct
   Mon–Fri 9.30–5.30,
   Sat–Sun 1.30–5.30
💷 Ad £1.50, Chd 75p
🅰 A9
🚉 Blair Atholl 5 min
♿ ☕ 🅿

Auchingarrich Wildlife Centre

Glascorrie Rd, Comrie,
Perthshire PH6 2JS
☎ 0764 679469

Say hello to Rosie, the 298kg pig who shares 100 acres with Highland cattle, deer and goats, and 100 species of waterfowl on 17 ponds. Visitors can handle young chicks and try out a child-sized 'rabbit burrow'.

🕓 All year, daily 10–dusk
£ Ad £3.25, Chd £2.25, f/t
✳ BBQ sites
🅰 B827
🔥 ☕ 🎁 Ⓟ

Bannockburn Heritage Centre

Bannockburn, Stirling FK7 0LJ
☎ 0786 812664

Perhaps it is rubbing it in a bit for the Scots to ask visitors from over the border to share the experience of their most famous victory over the English, but this lavish audio-visual presentation of the battle in 1314 *was* opened by the Queen.

🕓 Apr–Oct, daily 10–5.30
£ Ad £1.90, Chd/SC 80p
✳ Brass rubbing
🅰 M9 jnct 9, A91
♿ 🎁 Ⓟ NTS

Barras, The

Gallowgate, Glasgow G40 2SB
☎ 041 552 7258 (Wed–Sun 10–4)

The locals claim it is the biggest and best street market west of Cairo. More than 800 stalls, all under cover (with a bit of spillage).

🕓 All year, Sat–Sun 9–5
£ Adm free
🅰 Signs from Glasgow Cross
🚉 Glasgow Central 10 min
☕

Barrie's Birthplace

9 Brechin Rd, Kirriemuir, Angus DD8 4BX
☎ 0575 572646

The creator of Peter Pan is remembered in style in the house where he was born. See the little wash house, inspiration for the Wendy House, plus life-size figures, stage sets, manuscripts and a dancing light, like Tinkerbell, as a guide.

The play *Peter Pan* grew out of stories Barrie made up for 5 young orphaned brothers, whom he looked after following their parents' death. In 2004 Peter Pan will reach his century - but he won't look a day older.

🕓 Easter/May–Sep, Mon–Sat 11–5.30,
   Sun 1.30–5.30; 1–23 Oct,
   Sat 11–5.30, Sun 1.30–5.30
£ Ad £1.80, Chd/SC 90p
🅰 A926, A928
♿ ☕ Ⓟ NTS

Biggar Gasworks Museum

Gasworks Rd, Biggar, Strathclyde
☎ 031 225 7534 info

The only surviving gasworks
in Scotland. See how they used
coal gas to illuminate and heat
a nation before gas came from
the North Sea.

🕐 Jun–Sep, daily 2–5
£ Adm free
🅰 Nr town war memorial
♿ Ⓟ

Biggar Puppet Theatre

Broughton Rd, Biggar,
Strathclyde ML12 6HA
☎ 0899 20631 (box office 20521)

Complete 100-seat miniature
Victorian theatre offering full
puppet plays and demonstrations.
Backstage tour and museum.

🕐 All year. Times vary/phone
£ Ad £4, Chd £3. Tour/Mus:
  Ad £1.50, Chd £1
🅰 B7016
♿ ⛺ ☕ Ⓟ

Blackshaw Farm Park

West Kilbride, N Ayrshire
☎ 0563 34257

See sheep clipped and
sheared, cows milked,
calves fed. That's before
or after you try grass
sledging, or 4-wheel all-
terrain motorbikes, or
just have a ride on a
tractor.

🕐 Easter–mid Aug, daily 10.30–5;
  mid Aug–Sep Sat–Mon
£ Ad £3, Chd £2.40, f/t
🅰 B781
♿ Ⓟ

Blair Drummond Safari & Leisure Park

Nr Stirling, Perthshire FK9 4UR
☎ 0786 841456

Stay in the car and drive through
wild animal reserves, take to a boat
to see chimpanzees on an island.
Sea lion displays, meet-and-greet
pet farm, cable slide across lake,
adventure playground.

🕐 Beg Apr–beg Oct 10–5.30
  (last adm 4.30)
£ Ad £5.50, Chd (3–14)
  £3.50
✳ BBQ sites;
  transport for
  non-drivers
🅰 M9 jnct 10, A84
♿ ⛺ ☕ 🍽 Ⓟ

Blowplain Open Farm

Balmaclellan, Castle Douglas DG7 3TY
☎ 064 42206

Hill farm with dramatic-looking Belted Galloway cows. Feed the lambs in spring and wander among strolling pheasants and peacocks.

🕒 Easter–Oct, Sun–Fri;
   tour 2pm
💷 Ad £1.50, Chd/SC 75p
🅰 A712
♿ 🅿

Bo'ness & Kinneil Railway

Union St, Bo'ness, W Lothian EH51 9AQ
☎ 0506 822298

Bo'ness has Scotland's largest collection of steam rolling stock, engines and railway buildings. Birkhill, the other end of the 3½-mile train route, has guided tours of a rarity - a fireclay mine, above and below ground.

🕒 Times vary/phone
💷 Ad £3.20,
   Chd (5–15) £1.60. Train/Tour:
   £4.90/£2.50; f/t
✳ Santa train
   (Nov/Dec)
🅰 M9 jnct 3/5, A904
♿ 🚬 📷 🅿

Bowhill House & Country Park

West of Selkirk, Scottish Borders
☎ 0750 20732/22326

The house, apart from pictures by artists like Canaletto, Van Dyck and Raeburn, has a collection of painted miniatures and a Victorian kitchen. The park has mountain bike trekking, an adventure playground, riding centre and nature trails.

🕒 Park: May–Aug. Hse: July.
   Phone for details
💷 Park: £1. Hse: Ad £3.50, Chd £1,
   SC £2
🅰 A708, W of Selkirk
♿ 🍴 🅿

Brodick Castle

Brodick, Isle of Arran KA27 8HY
☎ 0770 302202

Built on the site of a
Viking fortress, owned
by a string of dukes, the
rich interior is now
supplemented by
adventure
playgrounds. Ranger-
led woodland walks
and a naturalist centre.

🕐 Castle: May–Sep daily
  1–5, Oct Sat/Sun.
  Park: 9.30–dusk
💷 Ad £4, Chd/SC £2. Park only: £2/£1
🅰 2 miles N of Brodick Pier
♿ 🍴 🎁 🅿 NTS

Cruising on Loch Katrine

SS Sir Walter Scott, Trossachs Pier,
Loch Katrine, Callander
☎ 041 355 5333

One of the most beautiful of
  Scotland's lochs, seen from
  aboard the *Sir Walter Scott*, a
  Clyde-built steamship. Hour-
  long cruises, much better than
  driving.

🕐 End Mar–beg Oct,
  Sun–Fri 11/1.45/3.15, Sat 2/3.30
💷 Ad £3.25, Chd £1.90,
  SC £1.90, f/t
🅰 A821
♿ ☕ 🅿

Clatteringshaws Forest Wildlife Centre

New Galloway, Dumfries & Galloway
☎ 0556 503626

Forest wildlife with
a herd of red deer
and grazing wild
goats. Ranger-
guided tours.

🕐 Apr–beg Oct,
  daily 10–5
💷 Adm free
🅰 A712, 6 miles W of New Galloway
⛺ ☕ 🅿

Culzean Castle & Country Park

Maybole, Ayrshire KA19 8LE
☎ 06556 274/269 info

This impressive Adam house has
masses of American connections,
especially with Eisenhower and
Kennedy. The park, a huge 563
acres, has lots to see, including deer,
swans, wildlife walks and
  adventure playground.

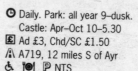

🕐 Daily. Park: all year 9–dusk.
  Castle: Apr–Oct 10–5.30
💷 Ad £3, Chd/SC £1.50
🅰 A719, 12 miles S of Ayr
♿ 🍴 🅿 NTS

Dalkeith Park

Main St, Dalkeith, Lothian
☎ 031 663 5684/665 3277

Interesting architecture and
woodland walks, and some huge
working Clydesdale horses. There
are other farm animals plus an
adventure playground and nature
trails.

🕐 Easter–Oct , daily 10–6
£ Ad/Chd £1.50, SC £1, f/t
✳ Ranger service
🅰 A68, entrance
   off High St
♿ 🧸 🏠 ℗

Denny Ship Model Experiment Tank

Castle St, Dumbarton G82 1QS
☎ 0389 63444

Worth a small detour to see how
they designed the shapes of the
great Clyde-built liners like the
Queen Mary and *QE2*. This is the
oldest surviving model experiment
tank. Making the wax model forms
hasn't changed
since 1883.

🕐 All year,
   Mon–Sat 10–4
£ Ad £1, Chd/SC
   50p, f/t
🅰 Town centre
   🚉 Dumbarton
   Central 5 min
      ☕ ℗

🍦 Deep Sea World

Forthside Tce, N Queensferry,
Fife TY11 1JR
☎ 0383 411411

Set under the Firth of Forth. Visitors
walk through transparent tunnels
among thousands of fish. Claims to
be the largest fish display in
northern hemisphere.

🕐 Easter–late Oct, daily 9.30–6
   (8pm Jul/Aug); late Oct–Mar, Mon–Fri
   10–4, Sat/Sun 9–6
£ Ad £4.50, Chd/SC £3.25, f/t
🅰 Forth Rd Bridge, N exit
🚉 N Queensferry 5 min
🍴 🏠 ℗

Discovery Point

Discovery Quay, Tay Bridge,
Dundee DD1 4XA
☎ 0382 201245

Captain Scott's Antarctic
exploration ship comes home to the
city where it was built. The hull,
almost a metre thick in places, was
built from wood which doesn't
float. You can still taste the salt in
her beams, and her building and
voyage are relived in a dramatic
video presentation.

🕐 Easter–Oct, Mon–Sat 10–5,
   Sun 11–5; Nov–Mar 10–4, Sun 11–4
£ Ad £4, Chd/SC £2.90, f/t
🅰 N end of Tay Bridge
🚉 Dundee (opp)
♿ ☕ ℗

Doune Motor Museum

Doune, Stirlingshire FK16 6HD
☎ 0786 841203

The Earl of Moray's castle
just up the road has been
knocked about over the
years, but his collection of
cars, including vintage
Bentleys, Aston Martins
and the second oldest Rolls-
Royce in the world, is in
beautiful condition.

🕐 Apr–Oct, daily 10–5
💲 Ad £2.75, Chd/SC £1.50
/Å\ A84
♿ 🍴 🅿

Edinburgh Butterfly & Insect World

Melville Garden Centre, Dalkeith Rd,
Midlothian EH18 1AZ
☎ 031 663 4932

A slice of tropical rainforest
with exotic butterflies
fluttering free among
waterfalls and exotic
plants. Spiders,
scorpions and other
creepy crawlies in
abundance, with a honey bee
exhibit and a bird of prey centre
close by.

🕐 Daily: Late Mar–late Oct, 10–5.30;
late Oct–beg Jan, 10–4
💲 Ad £3.25, Chd(5+) £1.90,
SC £2.55, f/t
/Å\ A7, 5 miles S of Edinburgh
♿ ⚙ 🍴 🛍 🅿

Edinburgh Castle

Castlehill, Edinburgh
☎ 031 244 3101

One of the world's great castles.
Started in 12th century but a fortress
ever since people started fighting.
Still garrisoned, it houses the
Scottish crown jewels and masses of
military exhibits. Famous Tattoo
held here every year during
Edinburgh Festival.

Don't miss the **Camera Obscura**
(☎ 031 226 3709) in the tower next
to the castle. Revolving mirror and
lenses give amazing bird's-eye
views of the city.

🕐 Apr–Sep, daily 9.30–6 (last adm 5.15)
💲 Ad £5, Chd £1, SC £3
/Å\ Above city
🚉 Edinburgh Waverley 5 min
♿ 🍴 🅿 EH

Edinburgh Zoo

Corstorphine Rd, Edinburgh EH12 6TS
☎ 031 334 9171

Some 1,500 mammals, birds and reptiles including endangered species. World's largest penguin enclosure with underwater viewing. Penguins parade every day at 2pm from April to September.

🕐 All year, Mon–Sat 9–5,
   Sun 9.30–5.30
💷 Ad £5.10, Chd £2.70,
   SC £3.20, f/t
🅰 A8
♿ 🍴 🛝
🛍 🅿

Gladstone's Land

477b Lawnmarket, Edinburgh EH1 2NT
☎ 031 226 5856

How the very rich lived 350 years ago. Narrow 6-storey building with authentic feel right down to the shop which displays 17th-century best buys.

🕐 Apr–late Oct, Mon–Sat 10–5, Sun 2–5
💷 Ad £2.50, Chd/SC £1.30
🅰 On Royal Mile
🚉 Edinburgh Waverley 5 min
🛍 NTS

Glasgow Art Gallery & Museum

Kelvingrove Park, Glasgow G3 8AG
☎ 041 357 3929

The place is packed not just with art but with hundreds of model boats, real Red Indian costumes and huge dinosaur models.

🕐 All year, Mon–Sat 10–5, Sun 11–5
💷 Adm free
🅰 Signs from city centre
🚉 Partick 10 min
⊖ Kelvinhall 10 min
♿ 🍴 🛍 🅿

Glasgow Museum of Education

Scotland St School, 225 Scotland St,
Glasgow G5 8QB
☎ 041 429 1202

It takes imagination to make education this interesting. There are classrooms through the ages - Victorian, World War II, 1950s and 1960s - and a cookery room from Edwardian times. Set in a school designed by famous architect Charles Rennie Mackintosh.

🕐 All year, Mon–Sat 10–5, Sun 2–5
💷 Adm free
🅰 1st exit S off Kingston Bridge
⊖ Shields Rd (opp)
♿ 🛝 🛍 🅿

Glasgow Museum of Transport

Kelvin Hall, 1 Bunhouse Rd,
Glasgow G3 8DP
☎ 041 357 3929

Cars, motor-bikes,
fire engines, steam
trains...and a
whole Glasgow street
c1938 with a kind of
traffic jam of double-
decker trams, buses, lorries
etc. A transport of delight.

🕐 All year, Mon–Sat 10–5,
Sun 11–5
💷 Adm free
🅰 Signs from city centre
⊖ Kelvinhall 10 min
♿ ☕

Heatherbank Museum of Social Work

163 Mugdock Rd, Milngavie, Glasgow
☎ 041 956 5923

Glasgow is packed with off-the-wall
attractions including this child-
orientated exhibition of juvenile
justice. It has videos, hands-on
activities, even rap songs about crime.

Other off beat places to see in
Glasgow are a grove of fossil trees
in **Victoria Park**; the **Amazing
Kibble Palace**, a giant greenhouse
with Britain's best collection of
orchids; and the **Necropolis**, a huge
cemetery with astonishing marble
memorials.

🕐 All year, Sun–Fri 2–5
💷 Donation
🅰 N Glasgow
🚉 Milngavie 15 min
♿ ☕ 🛍 🅿

Jedforest Deer & Farm Park

Mervinslaw, Camptown, Jedburgh TD8 6PL
☎ 08354 364

Apart from the red deer, this
working farm has rare breeds of
animals and birds, some of which
you can get close to. Plus fishing,
horse riding and tractor safari rides.

🕐 Daily: May–Aug 10–5.30,
Sep/Oct 11–4.30
💷 Ad £2.30, Chd £1.40
✳ BBQ site; farmed venison sold
🅰 A68, 5 miles S of
Jedburgh
♿ ⛺ ☕ 🛍 🅿

Kelburn Country Centre

South Offices, Fairlie, Ayrshire KA29 OBE
☎ 0475 568685/568554

Try the Royal Marine-built Commando course, or the wooden stockade play park. Plus pets' corner, children's rides, waterfall pool...and castle lived in by Earls of Glasgow.

🕒 Apr–late Oct,
daily 10–6.
Rest of year, grnds
only 11–5
£ Ad £3.50,
Chd/SC £2 +
Castle £1.50/£1
✳ Riding centre extra
⚠ A78, S of Largs
⊞ Largs (free bus Jul/Aug)
♿ ☕ 🍴 Ⓟ

Kerr's Miniature Railway

West Links Park, Arbroath, Tayside
☎ 0241 879249

Mini steam and diesel trains run alongside main London/Aberdeen line. You can wave to the passengers.

🕒 Apr–Sep, Sat/Sun 2–5,
Sch hols daily 2–5
£ 50p per head
⚠ Signs in town
⊞ Arbroath 1 mile
♿ Ⓟ

New Lanark Visitor Centre

New Lanark Mills, Lanark ML11 9DB
☎ 0555 661345

New Lanark was a model town designed in 1785 to provide ideal conditions for workers. Today it is being revitalised with lots of working machinery, restored houses and a high-tech exhibition with a theme park-style 'dark ride' with sights, sounds and smells.

🕒 All year, daily 11–5
£ Ad £2.75, Chd/SC
£1.75, f/t
⚠ S of Lanark
♿ ☕ 🛍 Ⓟ

Paddle Steamer Waverley

Waverley Excursions,
Waverley Terminal, Glasgow G3 8HA
☎ 041 221 8152

The last sea-going paddle steamer in the world, built for service on the Clyde. Excursion cruises to Ayr and Clyde Coast ports. The gleaming brass and the huge, churning paddle-wheel are unforgettable.

🕒 Phone for timetable
£ Vary
⚠ Signs from city centre
♿ ☕ 🛍 Ⓟ

Palace of Holyrood House

Canongate, Edinburgh EH8 8DX
☎ 031 556 7371/1096 info

The Queen actually stays here when she is in Edinburgh. So did Bonnie Prince Charlie, and most British royalty. Romantics will love the Mary Queen of Scots connection. Brass plaque marks the place where her lover, Rizzio, was stabbed to death before her eyes.

🕐 Apr–Oct, Mon–Sat 9.30–5.15,
　 Sun 10.30–4.30; Mar/Nov/Dec
　 9.30–3.45 (not Sun)
💷 Ad £3, Chd (5–16) £1.50,
　 SC £2.50, f/t
✳ Closed royal visits/state occasions
🄰 At foot of Royal Mile
⚏ Edinburgh Waverley 15 min
♿ ☕ 🅿

Palacerigg Country Park

Cumbernauld, Strathclyde G67 3HU
☎ 0236 720047

Deer, badgers, stoats, bison, lynx and rare wildcats. There are also pony treks, nature trails, a children's farm and a golf course.

🕐 Daily: summer 10–6;
　 winter 10–4.30
💷 Adm free
✳ BBQ sites
🄰 B803, SE of
　 Cumbernauld
♿ ⛺ ☕ 🅿

People's Palace

Glasgow Green, Glasgow G40 1AT
☎ 041 554 0223

How women got the vote. Famous Scots comedians. Toys in Victorian Glasgow and famous Glasgow murderers. A museum with a difference.

🕐 All year, Mon–Sat 10–5, Sun 11–5
💷 Adm free
🄰 Signs from city centre
⊖ St Enoch 10 min
⚏ Bridgeton Cross 5 min
♿ ☕ 🅿

Robert Smail's Printing Works

7/9 High St, Innerleithen EH44 6HA
☎ 0896 830206

Step back in time to the pre-computer age. See type set by hand, pictures etched in acid and then printed on Victorian machines. WPs might be faster but this is romantic.

🕐 Apr–late Oct, Mon–Sat 10–1 & 2–5,
　 Sun 2–5; (last adm 12 & 4)
💷 Adult £2, Chd/SC £1
🄰 Signs in town
♿ (res) ⚓ NTS

St Mungo Museum of Religious Life & Art

2 Castle St, Glasgow G4 0RH
☎ 041 553 2557

Looks at all the world's religions in terms of the beautiful things they have produced. Range covers Buddhists, Sikhs, Christians, Jews and Hindus and Muslims, and includes Egyptian mummy musk of 500BC as well as Salvador Dali painting.

🕐 All year, Mon–Sat 10–5, Sun 11–5
💷 Adm free
🛣 City centre
♿ ☕ 🎁 ℗

Scottish Maritime Museum

Laird Forge Bldgs, Gottries Rd, Irvine, Ayrshire KA12 8QE
☎ 0294 278283

Apart from a trip on the museum's ferry, you can clamber aboard a lifeboat, a trawler and, a special delight, a puffer - the workhorse boat that carried goods and people to highlands and islands.

🕐 Apr–Oct, daily 10–5
💷 Ad £1.75,
   Chd/SC 90p, f/t
🛣 Signs to Irvine Harbour
🚉 Irvine 2 min
♿ ☕ 🎁 ℗

Shaw's Sweet Factory

Fulton Rd, Wester Gourdie
Industrial Estate, Dundee DD2 4SW
☎ 0382 610369

Old-fashioned boiled sweets have a magical smell, and to see how they put the stripe in 'bulls' eyes' and stretch and pull the sugar is fun. Teeth will have to be brushed vigorously afterwards.

🕐 May–Sep, Mon–Fri 11.30–4;
   Oct–Apr, Wed only 1.30–4
💷 Ad/Chd 50p
🛣 Signs from Kingsway dual carriageway
♿ ☕ 🎁 ℗

🧸 Teddy Melrose

Teddy Bear Museum, The Wynd, Melrose TD6 9PA
☎ 089682 2464

Claims to be the most comprehensive collection of British bears. Winnie the Pooh, Paddington, Rupert and Bully Bear all to the fore, plus history of other famous Teds.

🕐 All year, daily 10–5
💷 Ad £1, Chd free with
   adult (or with bear)
✳ Braille guide
🛣 Town centre
♿ ☕ 🎁 ℗

Tenement House

145 Buccleuch St, Glasgow G3 6QN
☎ 041 333 0183

A surprise hit as one of Scotland's
most popular attractions. Left
undisturbed for more than 50 years,
the tiny 2-room dwelling still has
original box beds, stove, and coal
bunker inside. Phone ahead - you
can't get many in at one time.

🕐 Apr–late Oct, daily 1.30–5
£ Ad £2, Chd/SC £1
🅰 Signs from Charing X
▦ Charing X 5 min
⊖ Cowcaddens 5 min
NTS

Thirlestane Castle

Lauder, Scottish Borders TD2 6RU
☎ 0578 722430

The haunted castle with its many
towers has a touch of Snow White
to it. The nursery *wing* has a big
collection of historic toys: young
visitors can use 'dressing up chest'
and play with replica toys. Good
exhibitions, large open grounds.

🕐 Jul–Aug, Sun-Fri; Easter/May/Jun/Sep,
   Mon/Wed/Thur/Sun. Castle 2–5; Grnds
   12–6 (last adm 4.30)
£ Ad/Chd £3.50, f/t. Grnds only: £1
🅰 A68

Time Capsule Monklands

Buchanan St, Coatbridge,
Lanarks ML5 1EK
☎ 0236 441444

This up-to-date leisure centre
specialises in water and ice effects
with pools featuring waves,
bubblers, slides, whirlpools and
rapids. Then there is the ice rink
with a huge disco/video wall,
snow and even woolly
mammoths.

🕐 All year, daily 10–10
£ Pool or Rink:
   Ad £3.35, Chd
   £2.60. Cmbd tkt:
   £4.35/£3.10.
   Skate hire £1
🅰 M8 jnct 8
▦ C'bridge
Sunnysides/Central 5 min
♿ ☕ 🍽 🛍 🅿

Traquair House

Innerleithen, Peebleshire EH44 6QW
☎ 0896 830323/830785

They say 27 Scottish monarchs have
visited Traquair House, so why not
you? Continuously lived in for 1,000
years. Apart from royal relics, they
have a working brewery, a maze,
woodland and riverside walks, and
you can look at the (still closed)
Bear Gates, not to be opened until a
Stuart ascends the Scottish throne
again.

🕐 Easter/May–Sep, daily 1.30–5.30;
   Jul–Aug 10.30–5.30
£ Ad £3.50, Chd £1.50, SC £3, f/t
🅰 B709, 8 miles SE of Pebbles
♿(res) ☕ 🍽 🛍 🅿

Trimontium Exhibition

Ormiston Institute, The Square, Melrose
☎ 0896 822463

A chance to dress up and become a Roman legionary. The show recalls the nearby border outpost of Trimontium. Replica of smithy and pottery, mock-ups of armour and weapons.

🕐 Apr–Oct, daily 10.30–4.30
💷 Ad £1, Chd/SC 50p
🚹 Town centre
🛍 🅿

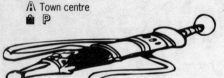

Tweedhope Sheepdogs

Moffat Fisheries, Hammerlands, Moffat, Dumfries
☎ 0683 21471

You can cuddle a sheepdog puppy, stroke lambs, watch sheepdogs at work. Very happy hands-on visit.

🕐 Mar–Oct, Mon–Fri, demos 11 & 3. Winter/phone
💷 Ad £2, Chd £1
🚹 A708, outskirts of Moffat
☕ 🅿

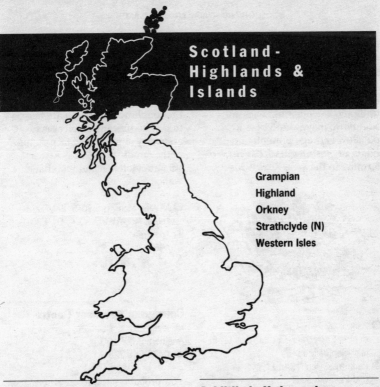

Grampian
Highland
Orkney
Strathclyde (N)
Western Isles

Aberdeen Fishmarket

Off Market St, Aberdeen
☎ 0224 897744

Every morning, hundreds of tons of
fish are unloaded, displayed and
auctioned off in great bustle. You
will see fish you never knew existed
in great gleaming piles, but only if
you get up early, as most of the
action happens between 7 and 8 am

🕐 All year, Mon–Fri
£ Adm free
🅰 City centre
▦ Aberdeen 5 min
♿ ☕ 🅿

Achiltibuie Hydroponicum

Achiltibuie, Highland IV26 2YG
☎ 0854 622202

An amazing garden which grows
plants without soil. Not just
vegetables, but flowers and fruits,
even lemons and figs. Guided tours.
  Stop off at **Achiltibuie
Smokehouse** (☎ 0854 622353), 5
miles down the road, and see them
make kippers and smoked salmon.
Very tasty trip.

🕐 Easter–Sep, daily.
  Guided tours only: 10/12/2/5
£ Ad £3.50, Chd (5–16) £2
🅰 A835, 25 miles N of Ullapool
♿ ☕ 🛍 🅿

Aden Country Park

Mintlaw, Aberdeenshire
☎ 0771 622857

Active 230 acres of wildlife, nature trails and orienteering, with an adventure playground plus a polished heritage presentation (videoed, costumed) of 200 years of farming in the area. Real 1950s-style farm.

🕐 Park: daily 7am–10pm.
Centre: Easter/Apr–Oct Sat/Sun 12–5;
May–Sep daily 11–5
£ Park: free. Centre: Ad £1,
Chd free with adult
🅰 A950, A92
♿ 🚻 🍴 🅿

Balmoral Castle

Ballater, Aberdeenshire
☎ 03397 42334/5

The Royals' favourite Scottish holiday spot. Visitors see only a tiny bit - a collection of carriages, royal travel displays etc - but there are country walks, pony trekking and pony cart rides.

🕐 May–mid Aug,
Mon–Sat 10–5
£ Ad £2, SC £1.50, Chd free
🅰 A93, 8 miles W of Ballater
♿ 🍵 🏠 🅿

Baxters of Speyside

Fochabers, Grampian IV32 7LD
☎ 0343 820393

Discover the secret of cock-a-leekie, find out how they persuade haggis to go into tins and smell seas of raspberry jam. Guided factory tour of the famous food firm. Also a Victorian kitchen and woodland walks.

🕐 All year, Mon–Fri 9.30–5, Sat/Sun 10–5.
Tours: Mon–Thur 9.30–4, Fri 9.30–2
£ Adm free
🅰 A96
♿ 🚻 🍴 🏠 🅿

Cairngorm Reindeer Centre

Reindeer House, Glenmore,
Aviemore PH22 1QU
☎ 0479 861 228

You probably wondered where Santa sent them on holiday. Britain's only reindeer roam free in the Cairngorms. Daily visits to herd at 11am, weather permitting; also 2.30pm in high season.

🕐 All year
£ Ad £3, Chd/SC £2
🅰 A9, 6 miles E of Aviemore
🅿

Caithness Glass

Airport Industrial Estate, Wick,
Caithness, KW1 5BT
☎ 0955 2286

Watch experts turn a mixture of
sands into a complex and beautiful
paperweight or decorative piece of
glass. Galleries upstairs and
down give a good view.

🕐 All year,
Mon–Sat 9–5, Sun
(Easter–Xmas) 11–5
💷 Adm free
✳ Glass–making
Mon–Fri only
⚠ A9, N end
of Wick
♿ 🍴 🎁 🅿

Cloverleaf Fibre Stud

Mill of Kinnairdy, Bridge of Marnoch,
Huntly, Grampian
☎ 0466 780879

The small farm
breeds llamas,
alpacas,
guanacos and
goats
producing
cashmere and
mohair. You can also see
them milk sheep.

🕐 Daily tours 11am/1pm/3pm.
Shop 10.30–5.30
💷 Ad £2, Chd/SC £1
⚠ A97, 3 miles S of Aberchirder
♿ 🎁 🅿

Codona's Amusement Park

Beach Boulevard, Aberdeen
☎ 0224 581909

Massive
fairground, with
everything from 2
colours of
candyfloss to
dodgems and
major fun
rides. Take
home a
goldfish.

🕐 2–10pm: Apr–Sep Sat/Sun;
Easter/summer hols daily
💷 Adm free; rides vary
⚠ On sea front
🚊 Aberdeen 20 min
☕ 🅿

Culloden Visitor Centre

Culloden Moor, Inverness
IV1 2ED
☎ 0463 790607

Bonnie Prince Charlie's
last fling. His Highland
army was brutally crushed
here in 1746, in the last major battle
fought in Britain. Graphic account
in video, battle relics, graves.

🕐 Site: all year. Centre: Apr–Oct 9–6;
Feb–Mar/Nov–Dec 10–4
💷 Centre: Ad £1.80, Chd/SC 90p
⚠ B9006, 5 miles E of Inverness
♿ 🦽 🍴 🎁 🅿 NTS

Dee Valley Confectioners

Station Square, Ballater, Aberdeen
☎ 03397 55499

Watch them make old-fashioned
sweets in traditional ways. It takes
about 30 minutes from the sugar
and spice to the all things nice.

🕐 All year, Mon–Thu 9–5
£ Adm free
🅰 Nr town centre
🚌 Ballater
♿ 🎒 🅿

European Sheep & Wool Centre

Drimsynie Leisure Complex,
Lochgoilhead, Strathclyde
☎ 03013 247

See one Scottish
dog control a gaggle
of geese while daring
no less than 19
different breeds of
sheep to move
from their places.
All part of the
show. Year-
round leisure
centre with curling,
skating, pony
trekking etc.

🕐 All year:
    shows 11am/1pm/3pm
    (Sat/Sun 1/3)
£ Ad £3, Chd £1.50
🅰 A83, B839
♿ ☕ 🍴 🎒 🅿

Fort George

Nr Ardersier, Inverness
☎ 0667 462777

Built after Culloden to repel
rebellious Highlanders. Scan the
mile of ramparts around
reconstructed 18th-century barracks.
Display of muskets and pikes.

🕐 Apr–Sep, Mon–Sat 9.30–6, Sun 2–6;
    Oct–Mar, Mon–Sat 9.30–4, Sun 2–4
£ Ad £2.50, Chd £1, SC £1.50
🅰 A96, B9039, B9092
♿ ☕ 🅿 EH

Fyvie Castle

Fyvie, Turriff AB53 8JS
☎ 0651 891266

A very grand house,
owned by just 5
families in 500
years. After you
have had a last
look at the suits
of armour
there's a cool,
slightly creepy
ice house, a kind
of ancient tennis
court, a bird hide
and lochside
walks.

🕐 Castle: Easter/May/Jun/Sep,
    daily 1.30–5.30; Jul/Aug 11–5.30;
    Oct/phone. Gdn: all year, 9.30–dusk
£ Castle: Ad £3.50, Chd/SC £1.80.
    Gdn: donation
🅰 A947, 8 miles SE of Turriff
♿ 🧺 ☕ 🅿 NTS

Giant MacAskill Museum

Dunvegan, Isle of Skye
☎ 047022 296

Tiny, but it can hold a life-size
model of the tallest Scotsman ever
(and at 2.36m the tallest 'true'
giant). Wall panels offer tall tales
about his feats of strength.

🕐 Easter–Oct, daily 9.30–5
£ Ad £1, Chd free
🅰 Centre of Dunvegan
♿ 🅿

Glamis Castle

Glamis, Angus DD8 1RQ
☎ 0307 840242/840393

A royal residence since 1372, the
Queen Mother was brought up
here, Princess Margaret was born
here and Shakespeare set *Macbeth*
here. You don't see all the nooks
and crannies, but what is on view is
pretty impressive.

🕐 Apr–Oct, daily 10.30–5.30;
last tour 4.45
£ Ad £4.20, Chd £2.30, SC £3.30, f/t
✻ Adv playgnd
🅰 A928
⛺ ☕ 🍴 🛍 🅿

Glenaray Fish Farm

Inveraray, Argyll
☎ 0499 2233

Disarmingly honest, the owners of
these 10 ponds, 2 fishing lakes and a
smokehouse
advertise:
'Watch them!
Feed them!
Catch them!
Eat them!'.
There is also a fish
hospital, a play area
and pets' corner. Rods
for hire.

🕐 Apr–Oct, daily 10–6
£ Ad £1.30, Chd/SC 70p
🅰 A819, N of Inveraray
♿ ⛺ ☕ 🅿

Glencoe

Visitor Centre, Ballachulish, Argyll
PA39 4HX
☎ 08552 307

Scotland at its most beautiful and
tragic. Audio-visual history of how
on a snowy night in 1692 a group of
Campbells murdered the
Macdonalds who had given them
shelter. In summer the glen shelters
golden eagles, deer and wildcats,
and sheer crags challenge expert
climbers.

🕐 Centre: Apr–mid
May/beg Sep–mid Oct, daily 10–5;
mid May–beg Sep 9.30–6
£ Ad 50p, Chd 25p
✻ Ranger service
🅰 A82, 17 miles S of Ft William
♿ ⛺ ☕ 🛍 🅿 NTS

Glencoe Chairlift
By Kingshouse, Lochaber
☎ 08556 226

The winter ski lift
swoops summer
visitors 640m above
the breathtaking
scenery of Glencoe
and the moors. See
how many mountains
you can count.

🕐 Late May–Sep, daily 10–5
   (Oct weather permitting)
💷 Ad £3.50, Chd (6–18) £2.20, f/t
🅰 Off A82 at Kingshouse
♿ 🍴 🅿

Glengoulandie Deer Park
Aberfeldy, Perthshire PH16 5NL
☎ 0887 830261/830306

Drive or walk through the park,
which has herds of red deer,
Highland cattle and rare sheep
roaming free on the slopes of
(mostly) snow-capped, 1083m-high
Schiehallion.

🕐 May–Oct,
   daily 9–1hr before dusk
💷 £3 per car
🅰 B846, NW of
Aberfeldy
⛺ 🛍 🅿

Grampian Transport Museum
Alford, Aberdeenshire AB33 8AD
☎ 09755 62292

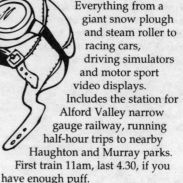

Everything from a
giant snow plough
and steam roller to
racing cars,
driving simulators
and motor sport
video displays.
Includes the station for
Alford Valley narrow
gauge railway, running
half-hour trips to nearby
Haughton and Murray parks.
First train 11am, last 4.30, if you
have enough puff.

🕐 End Mar–Oct, daily 10–5
💷 Ad £2.50, Chd 80p, SC £1.80, f/t
✳ Summer events
🅰 Town centre
♿ 🅿

Haddo House & Country Park
Tarves, Ellon AB41 0ER
☎ 0651 851489

Very grand Adam-style house with
a lot to see, but the pleasure is
enhanced by the parks, with
woodland and lake walks, bird
hides, adventure
playground and nature
displays.

🕐 Easter/May/Jun/Sep–mid Oct,
   daily 1.30–5.30; Jul/Aug, 11–5.30.
   Park: all year, 9.30–dusk
💷 Park: free. Hse: Ad £3.50,
   Chd/SC £1.80
🅰 B999, 4 miles N of Pitmedden
♿ ⛺ 🍴 🛍 🅿 NTS

Highland Museum of Childhood

Old Station, Strathpeffer
☎ 0997 421031

Growing up in the Highlands through the centuries. Digging peat and school life seem to have been the easy bit. Lots of activities, including quizzes.

🕐 Jun–Sep Mon–Fri 9–5, Sat 10–5, Sun 1–5. Mar–May/Oct–Dec: phone
💷 Ad £1.25, Chd/SC £1, f/t
🅰 Town centre
♿ 🛍 🅿

Highland Wildlife Park

Kincraig, Highland
☎ 0540 651270

Scotland's Royal Zoological Society has collected together Scottish mammals past and present. Drive through herds of bison and deer to see areas showing eagles, wolves, wildcats and the rare capercaillie.

🕐 Daily: Easter/May 10–4, June–Aug 10–5, Sep–Nov 10–4
💷 Driver only £5.20; Driver+1 £9.70; up to 4 people £11.70
🅰 A9, N of Kingussie
🍴 ☕ 🅿

Holmisdale House Toy Museum

Glendale, Skye
☎ 047081 240

You can not only see yesterday's toys, you can play with them. What a good idea.

🕐 All year, Mon–Sat 10–6
💷 Ad £1.50, Chd 50p
🅰 8 miles W of Dunvegan
♿ 🛍 🅿

Inveraray Castle

Inveraray, Argyll
☎ 0499 2203

Still the home of the Duke of Argyll, Chief of the Clan Campbell, the castle looks like a cake made in Disneyland. Worth seeing for the masses of armour and the lavish decorations.

🕐 Apr–Jun/ Sep/Oct, Mon–Sat (ex Fri) 10–1 & 2–5.30, Sun 1–5.30; July/Aug, Mon–Sat 10–5.30, Sun 1–5.30
💷 Ad £3.50, Chd £1.75, SC £2.50, f/t
🅰 A83
♿ ☕ 🛍 🅿

Inveraray Jail
Church Square, Inveraray, Argyll
☎ 0499 2381

Scarily authentic. Guides dress like warders, lifelike figures sew herring nets as punishment, 1820s trials are restaged. Visitors can try out cells. Well staged, with soundtracks and even smells adding to the shivers as the doors shut.

🕐 Apr–Oct, daily 9.30–6; Nov–Mar 10–5; (last adm 5/4)
£ Ad £3.85, Chd £2, SC £2.50, f/t
/🅰\ Town centre
💼 ℗

Inverawe Smokery
Bridge of Awe, by Taynuilt, Strathclyde
☎ 08662 446

Traditional kippering and salmon-smoking. You can watch fish cured and smoked here in special smoke boxes.
Play area.

🕐 All year, Mon–Fri 9–4.30
£ Ad 50p, Chd free
/🅰\ A85, SE of Taynuilt
♿ ☕ 💼 ℗

Jonah's Journey
Rosemount Place, Aberdeen
☎ 0224 647614

Find out about life in biblical times. Children can dress up, visit a nomad's tent, grind grain, draw water from a well.

🕐 Jun–Sep, Mon–Sat 10–4; Oct–May 10–2. Sun by appt
£ Ad £1, Chd £2
/🅰\ Nr city centre
🚇 Aberdeen 15 min
♿ ☕ ℗

Kingspark Llama Farm
Berriedale, Caithness
☎ 05935 202

The open plan farm breeds llamas and you can mingle with them (there are often baby llamas) or take them for a walk along the beach. Meanwhile, back at the ranch, you can see raccoons, chipmunks and hairy goats. Don't offend the llamas: when they are angry they spit.

🕐 All year, daily dawn–dusk
£ Ad £1, Chd 50p
/🅰\ A9, 9 miles N of Helmsdale
♿ ℗

Kylerhea Otter Haven
Kylerhea, Skye

Park the car, take
binoculars and
walk quietly.
This is a
hide from
which
you can
observe
sea
otters
diving
and
playing
off the
beach below. Above, there are often
golden and sea eagles.

🕐 All day, all year
💷 Adm free
🅰 Off unclassified Glen Arroch road
♿ 🅿

Landmark Highland Heritage
Carrbridge, Grampian PH23 3AJ
☎ 0479 841613

You have a choice. Either the 3-
screen video of Highland history,
triumphs, feuds and all, or the net
walkway high in the trees, the
giant slide at the adventure
playground and a steam-powered
sawmill.

🕐 Daily: Apr–Jun 9.30–6; July/Aug
   9.30–8; Sep/Oct 9.30–5.30;
   Nov–Mar 9.30–5
💷 Ad £4.15–£4.75, Chd £2.75–£3.10
🅰 Old A9, 6 miles N of Aviemore
🚌 Carrbridge 15 min
♿ 🍴 🍽 🍴 🅿

Loch Etive Cruises
Taynuilt Pier, Taynuilt, Strathclyde PA35 1JQ
☎ 086 62 430

Three hours cruising on this 20-
mile-long sea loch. Take binoculars
and a camera for the seal colony
   you will pass, or for the
   buzzards, cormorants or deer on
   Buachaille Etive Mor.

🕐 Phone for details
💷 Ad £6, Chd (5–12) £3, f/t
✳ Evening cruises (Jun/Jul)
🅰 A85
🚌 Taynuilt 10 min
♿ 🍴 🅿

Loch Ness & the Monster Exhibitions
Drumnadrochit, Inverness

Nessie the monster is big business
at the **Original Loch Ness Visitor
Centre** (☎ 0456 450342), which has
a film on the history and latest
developments in the hunt, plus
cruises with monster-spotting sonar
equipment.
   Or you might prefer the **Official
Loch Ness Monster Exhibition**
(☎ 0456 450573) with its 40-minute
audio-visual show of the hunt,
display of equipment actually used
by hunters and 'life-size' Nessie
model on a wee 'loch' outside. Of
course there is always the 6-passenger
submarine (☎ 0285 760762) if you
want to see for yourself.

Original
🕐 Daily: Jun–Oct 9–9; Oct–May 9–5
💷 Ad £3, Chd/SC £2.50, f/t
🅰 A82
♿ 🍴 🛍 🅿

Official

🕐 Daily: summer 9.30–9.30;
   mid season 9.30–5.30; winter 10–4
💷 Ad £4, Chd (7–16) £2.50, SC £3, f/t
🛆 A82
♿ ☕ 🍴 🛍 🅿

Mallaig Marine World

The Harbour, Mallaig PH41 4PX
☎ 0687 2292

Mallaig once had a huge fishing
fleet, and apart from aquaria with
big fish, small fish and all that lives
on the bottom, there is an
interesting look at the life of
fisherfolk.

🕐 Daily: Jun–Sep 9–9; Oct–May 9–5
💷 Ad £2.50, Chd £1.50, SC £2, f/t
✳ Marine biologist on hand
🛆 On the pier
▦ Mallaig 1 min
♿ 🅿

Mull & West Highland Railway

Old Pier Station, Craignure,
Isle of Mull PA65 6AY
☎ 06802 494

This narrow gauge steam train
takes 20 minutes to puff the 1¼
miles up to Torosay Castle. You
could walk it faster, but it wouldn't
be as much fun. Torosay is more a
comfortable big house than a stately
home.

🕐 Easter–mid Oct; phone re times
💷 Rtn/Single: Ad £2.25/£1.50,
   Chd £1.50/£1, f/t
✳ Dogs free
🛆 Car ferry:
   Lochaline–Fishnish/Oban–Craignure
♿ ☕ 🅿

Nairn Leisure Park

Marine Road, Nairn IV12 4EA
☎ 0667 453061

After treetop climbs on an aerial
runway, defending an adventure
fort or tackling a woodland
suspension bridge, step
indoors to swim, play
games, even have a
Turkish bath.

🕐 Indoor: all year
   Mon–Fri
   8am–9pm,
   Sat/Sun 9–5.
   Outdoor:
   Easter–Sep,
   daily 11–6 (9pm
   Jul/Aug)
💷 Vary/facilities
🛆 On beach road
▦ Nairn 10 min
♿ ☕ 🅿

178

Nevis Range

Torlundy, Inverness
☎ 0397 705825

Eighty closed gondolas designed for
winter skiers lift summer visitors for
breathtaking views, more than 610m
up, beside Ben Nevis. There is a bar
at the top, and mountain bike hire.

🕐 Jan–Oct, daily 10–5
£ Rtn: Ad £5, Chd £3.50, SC £4.50, f/t
🅰 A82, 6 miles N of Ft William
♿ ☕ 🍴 🅿

North East Falconry
Visitor Centre

Broadland, Cairnie, Aberdeenshire
☎ 0466 87344

Controlled grace and power from
around 40 birds of prey. There are
eagles, falcons and owls, plus
falconers to describe the action
during regular flying
demonstrations.

🕐 Apr–Oct, daily 10–6
£ Ad £3.50, Chd/SC £2
🅰 A96, 3 miles NW of Huntly
♿ ☕ 🅿

Rothiemurchus Estate
Visitor Centre

Rothiemurchus, Aviemore, Highland
☎ 0479 810858

In Cairngorm Nature Reserve.
Landrover tours and guided walk,
plus Highland cattle, deer, hawking
demonstrations, fishing, clay pigeon
shooting. Very impressive forest.

🕐 All year, daily 9–5
£ Vary/facilities
🅰 B970, S of Aviemore
♿ ☕ 🛍 🅿

Satrosphere

19 Justice Mill Lane, Aberdeen AB1 2EQ
☎ 0224 213232

Have fun with the wonders of
science. Children (and grown-ups)
can discover technology secrets in
almost 100 hands-on experiments,
from why the earth spins to why ice
floats.

🕐 Sch hols: Mon–Sat 10–5, Sun 1.30–5.
 Term: W/days (not Tue) 10–4,
 Sat 10–5, Sun 1.30–5
£ Ad £3, Chd/SC £1.50, f/t
✳ Special events/displays
🅰 City centre
🚋 Aberdeen 10 min
♿ ☕ 🛍 🅿

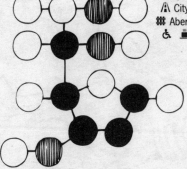

Scottish Centre for Falconry

Turfhills, Kinross
☎ 0577 862010

See the birds in the aviary and flying free, then watch them hunting. Early summer visitors can see hatching out and rearing of chicks on closed circuit TV.

🕐 Mar–Dec,
daily 10.30–5.30
💷 Ad £3, Chd/SC
£2, f/t
🚻 M90 jnct 6
♿ ☕ 🛍
Ⓟ

Skara Brae

Nr Kirkwall, Mainland, Orkney
☎ 0856 84815

Not just one of the sights of Scotland but of Europe, this Stone Age village was covered by a sandstorm for 4,500 years. You can still see stone beds, tables, cupboards.

🕐 Apr–Sep, Mon–Sat 9.30–6.30,
Sun 11.30–6.30; Oct–Mar 9.30–4.30,
Sun 2–4.30
💷 Ad £2.50, Chd £1, SC £1.50
✳ Cmbd tkt available for 4 Orkney
monuments
🚻 B9056, 19 miles NW of Kirkwall
♿ Ⓟ EH

Skye Serpentarium

The Old Mill, Harrapool, Broadford, Skye
☎ 0471 822209

You can see the world's snakes, lizards and frogs in re-created natural habitats, and handle some of them if you want. Supervision and information.

🕐 Easter–Oct, Mon–Sat 10–5 (+Sun Jul/Aug)
💷 Ad £2, Chd/SC £1, f/t
✳ Baby snakes for sale
🚻 A850
♿ 🛍 Ⓟ

Sea Life Centre

Barcaldine, Oban, Argyll
☎ 0631 72386

From shrimps to sharks, and all British. Seal nursery with appealing pups on the Centre's sea loch shore.

🕐 Daily: Jul–Aug 9–7; Sep–Jun 9–6
💷 Ad £4.35, Chd £2.95,
SC £3.25
🚻 A828, 10 miles N
of Oban
♿ 🍴 🛍
Ⓟ

Storybook Glen

Kirkton of Maryculter, Aberdeen
☎ 0224 732941

The Old Woman Who Lived In A
Shoe has the shoe in 20 acres of
gardens here and her neighbours
(100 or so) include Snow White,
Goldilocks and Jack and the
Beanstalk, all life-size in fibreglass.
Lots of fun for the young.

🕐 Mar–Oct, daily 10–6; Nov–Feb,
   Sat/Sun 11–4
£ Ad £3, Chd £1.50, SC £2
🅰 B9077, 5 miles SW of Aberdeen
♿ ⦿ Ⓟ

Strathspey Railway

Aviemore Speyside Station,
Dalfaber Rd, Aviemore
☎ 0479 810725

Once part of the main line to
Inverness, these 10 or so miles to
the turntable at Boat of Garten were
saved by steam enthusiasts. Boat of
Garten (a pretty place) has display
of rolling stock and
memorabilia.

🕐 Apr–Oct;
   phone for details
£ Vary;
   under 5s free
🅰 A9, B970
🚉 Aviemore
♿ ☕ Ⓟ

Timespan Heritage Centre

Dunrobin St, Helmsdale, Sutherland
KW10 6JS
☎ 04312 327

Enterprising and effective high-tech
visuals and models cover Viking
visits, witch burning, Highland
clearances, the Highland Gold Rush
(brief but exciting) and other
historic highs up to the finding of
North Sea Oil.

🕐 Easter–Oct, Mon–Sat 10–5,
   Sun 2–5 (6pm Jul/Aug)
£ Ad £2.75, Chd (4–14) £1.65,
   SC £2.20, f/t
🅰 Town centre
🚉 Helmsdale 5 min
♿ 💼 Ⓟ

Treasures of the Earth

Corpach, Fort William, Highland
☎ 0397 772283

Large, well-staged display of
diamonds, rubies, emeralds, right
through to rock crystal and
polished granite. Good fossils and a
creative 'mining' sequence.

🕐 Daily: Jul–Sep 9.30–7; Oct–Jun
   (not 3–31 Jan) 10–5
£ Ad £2.50, Chd £1.50
🅰 A830, 4 miles N of Fort William
♿ 💼 Ⓟ

♟ Waltzing Waters

Balavil Brae, Newtonmore, Highland
PH21 1DR
☎ 0540 673752

Electronic treatment of an old
music-hall delight. The waters are
jet fountains which change colour
and height in time to music,
whether classic, show or pop.
Shows every hour on the hour and
at 8.30pm (summer).

🕐 Daily: late Feb–Oct 10–5;
Nov–5 Jan 10–4
💷 Ad £3.50,
Chd (4–16) £1,
SC £3
🅰 A86
🚉 Newtonmore
10 min
♿ ☕ 🎁 🅿

World in Miniature

North Pier, Oban, Argyll
☎ 085 26 272

Whole houses of rooms, carved,
decorated and curtained, equipped
with tools and tiny furniture. All
meticulously made to one-twelfth
actual size. Magic to the very young.

🕐 Apr–Oct, Mon–Sat 10–5, Sun 2–5
💷 Ad £1.50, Chd/SC £1, f/t
🅰 Under red clock tower
🚉 Oban 2 min
♿ (res)

Kent
Surrey
E Sussex
W Sussex

Amberley Museum

Amberley, Arundel, W Sussex BN18 9LT
☎ 0798 831370

A museum about working. Watch
craftsmen produce wheels, see an
old-fashioned telephone exchange,
a vintage wireless exhibition and a
host of other working attractions.
You can even travel by workers'
train or bus.

🕐 Late Mar–late Oct, Wed–Sun/BH 10–6;
  daily/sch hols
💷 Ad £4.50, Chd (5–16) £2.10,
  SC £3.60, f/t
✳ Summer events
⚠ B2139/opp rlwy stn
⊞ Amberley
♿ ⚑ ☕ Ⓟ

Archbishops' Palace & Heritage Centre

Mill St, Maidstone ME15 6YE
☎ 0622 663006

Costumed tableaux of medieval
Archbishop Courtenay and his
retinue and a reconstructed cell
housing John Ball, leader of the
14th-century Peasants' Revolt. Plus
a fascinating collection of state and
private carriages including
miniature royal ones used by
Queen Victoria's children.

🕐 All year, daily 10.30–4 (last adm)
💷 Plce: free. Centre: Ad £2.95,
  Chd/SC £1.95, ♿free
⚠ Town centre
⊞ Maidstone E or W, 10 min
♿ ⚑ ☕ 🛍

Arundel Castle

Arundel, W Sussex BN18 9AB
☎ 0903 883136

Norman stronghold, home of the
Dukes of Norfolk. Stuffed with
famous paintings and great sets of
armour. Open-air theatre in August.

🕓 Apr–late Oct, Sun–Fri 11–5
💷 Ad £4.50, Chd (5–15) £3.50, SC £4
🅰 A27
♯ Arundel 5 min
♿ ☕ 🍽 🛍 ℗

Badsell Park Farm

Crittenden Rd, Matfield, Tonbridge, Kent
☎ 0892 832549

Working farm with a lot of extras,
including a pets' corner, pony and
tractor rides, butterfly house, nature
trail, outdoor and indoor play
centres.

🕓 All year, daily 10–5.30
💷 Ad £4, Chd (3–16) £2.50, SC £3, f/t
✳ PYO fruit
🅰 A228, N of Pembury
♿ ⛲ ☕ 🛍 ℗

Basingstoke Canal Centre

Mytchett Place Rd, Mytchett,
Camberley, Surrey
☎ 0252 370073

Narrowboats, barges and canal craft
with towpaths, tunnels and locks -
exhibition spanning 200 years of
canal history. Good pets' area and
nature trails. Boat trips and
boat/canoe hire.

🕓 Easter–Oct, Tue–Sun 10.30–5;
   Nov–Mar (exhib only) Mon–Fri
💷 Ad £1.50, Chd(6+)/SC £1
✳ Waterside events, painting courses
🅰 A321 Frimley/Farnborough
♿ ⛲ 🛍 ℗

Bentley Wildfowl & Motor Museum

Halland, Lewes, E Sussex BN8 5AF
☎ 0825 840573

Based on the biggest private
collection of wildfowl in Britain
(more than 1,000 birds) with
collection of Edwardian motors,
most still roadworthy. Miniature
steam railway on summer Sundays.
Woodland walk, adventure
playground.

🕓 Apr–Oct, daily 10.30–4.30;
   Nov–Mar/phone
💷 Ad £3.60, Chd (4–15) £2,
   SC £2.80, f/t
✳ Special events
🅰 A22, B2192
♿ ⛲ ☕ 🛍 ℗

Bexhill Museum of Costume
Manor Gardens, Upper Sea Rd,
Bexhill–on–Sea, E Sussex
☎ 0424 210045

How people from chambermaids to generals have dressed up through the centuries. Contemporary dolls, toys and furniture help complete the picture.

🕐 Jun–Aug, Mon–Fri 10.30–5, Sat/Sun 2–5.30; Apr/May/Sep/Oct: phone
£ Ad £1, Chd 50p, SC 75p
🅰 Old town
⌗ Bexhill–on–Sea 5 min
♿ Ⓟ

Bignor Roman Villa
Bignor, Pulborough, W Sussex RH20 1PH
☎ 07987 259

The Romans lived well here as this villa shows. Archaeologists uncovered richly decorated mosaics (including the longest in Britain), underfloor central heating and lots more.

🕐 Mar–May/Oct Tue–Sun/BH 10–5; Jun–Sep, daily 10–6
£ Ad £2.50, Chd £1.25, SC £1.65
🅰 A285, A29
♿ ⛲ 🍽 🛍 Ⓟ

Birdworld & Underwaterworld
Holt Pound, Farnham, Surrey GU10 4LD
☎ 0420 22140

Flamingoes, emus, penguins, pelicans and toucans are just some of the 1,000 or so birds. Indoor tropical walk. Aquarium with rarities like mud fish and blind cave fish. Nature trail, play area.

🕐 Daily: summer 9.30–6; winter 9.30–4
£ Ad £3.85, Chd (3–14) £2.10, SC £2.95, f/t
🅰 A325, S of Farnham
♿ ⛲ 🍽 Ⓟ

Blean Bird Park
Honey Hill, Blean, Canterbury CT2 9JR
☎ 0227 471666

Parrots flying around you and talking to themselves; cockatoos and macaws. The parrots don't get to try the woodland walk or the play area though.

🕐 Mar–Nov, daily 10–5
£ Ad £2.75, Chd £1.75, SC £2.50
🅰 A290
♿ ⛲ 🍽 🛍 Ⓟ

Bluebell Railway

Sheffield Park Stn, Sheffield Park,
Uckfield TN22 3QL
☎ 0825 723777/722370 t/table

Most elaborate steam set-up in
Southern England. Large collection
of locos and Golden Arrow Pullman
dining-car at weekends.

🕐 Daily: May–Sep (+Oct h/term);
   other times/phone
💷 Sample rtn fare: Ad £7, Chd(3+) £3.50,
   SC £6, f/t
✳ Santa train/Dec
🅰 A275
♿ � 🍽 🛍 🅿

Booth Museum of Natural History

194 Dyke Rd, Brighton BN1 5AA
☎ 0273 552586

Obsessive Victorian collectors left
this irreplaceable collection of stuffed
birds, butterflies and dinosaur bones.
The whale bones make you realise
just how big they are.

🕐 All year, Fri–Wed 10–5, Sun 2–5
💷 Adm free
🅰 Nr town centre
🚉 Brighton 20 min
♿ 🛍 🅿

Brambles Wildlife Park

Wealden Forest Park, Herne Common,
Herne, Kent
☎ 0227 712379

Rarer British breeds, from owls to
fierce Scottish
wildcats. They
also have
wallabies,
buzzards and
raccoons on
the 26
acres.
Under-5s
play area
and a
'walk-in
rabbit
world'.

🕐 Late Mar–late Oct, daily 10–5
💷 Ad £2.20, Chd(2+) £1.40, SC £1.80
🅰 A291
⛺ ☕ 🅿

Brighton Museum & Art Gallery

Church St, Brighton BN1 1UE
☎ 0273 603005

Good quality museum
fare, but special is the
Closet of Curiosities,
which includes a 'real'
stuffed mermaid, and the china
cat which purrs 'thank you' when
you feed it money.

🕐 All year, Mon/Tue/Thu–Sat 10–5,
   Sun 2–5
💷 Adm free
🅰 Nr Royal Pavilion
🚉 Brighton 10 min
♿(res) ☕ 🛍

Brighton Sealife Centre
Marine Parade, Brighton BN2 1TB
☎ 0273 604234

Lavish displays of the secrets of the undersea world. Whale and dolphin exhibition and the underwater shark tunnel are among the favourites.

🕐 Summer, daily 10–6; winter/phone
£ Ad £4.50, Chd £3.25, SC £3.75
🅰 On sea front
▦ Brighton 15 min
♿ ☕

Brogdale Horticultural Trust
Brogdale Farm, Brogdale Rd,
Faversham ME13 8XZ
☎ 0795 535286

The National Fruit Collection where they have 4,000 varieties of tree fruits: apples, plums, pears, cherries and more. Scrumping is frowned upon.

🕐 Easter–Dec Wed–Sun/BH 10–5; other times/phone
£ Ad £2, Chd 50p, SC £1.50
🅰 M2 jnct 6
▦ Faversham 1½ miles
⛺ ☕ 🛍 🅿

🍦 Brooklands Museum
Brooklands Rd, Weybridge,
Surrey KT13 0QN
☎ 0932 857381

Brooklands and its banked racing car track put the roar into the Roaring 20s. On view are many of the famous cars, the workshops and old press box. The aircraft collection includes a Harrier jump jet, a Wellington bomber found in Loch Ness, and a display about The Dambusters' 'bouncing bomb'.

🕐 Tue–Sun/BH: summer 10–5, winter 10–4
£ Ad £4.50, Chd(5+) £2.50, SC £3.50, f/t
🅰 M25 jnct 10/11
▦ Weybridge 15 min
⛺ ☕ 🛍 🅿

Butlin's Southcoast World
Bognor Regis, W Sussex PO21 1JJ
☎ 0243 822445

Boating, roller skating, tropical
swimming with waves, slides,
flumes and still more. Then there
are the films and stage shows and a
big funfair. It goes on and on.

🕐 Easter–Oct, daily 10–9.30
(last adm 4/5); winter/phone
£ £3–£6.99 per head (varies/season);
under 2s free
🅰 On sea front
⊞ Bognor 10 min
♿ ⬛ 🍴 🎒 ℗

Buckley's Yesterday's World
89–90 High St, Battle, E Sussex
☎ 0424 775378

Amazing 'time machine' collection
enlivened by videos, sounds and
smells. Apart from Victorian shops,
there is a photographer's studio, a
penny arcade, and a royalty room
with a talking model of Queen
Victoria. Garden, miniature golf,
children's play village.

Pop across the road to see **Battle
Abbey**, the site of the Battle of
Hastings in 1066.[EH]

🕐 All year, daily 10–6 (last adm 5)
£ Ad £3.75, Chd(5+) £2.50,
SC £3.25, f/t
🅰 Opp Battle Abbey
⊞ Battle 5 min
♿(res) ⬛
☕ ℗

Capstone Farm Country Park
Capstone Road, Capstone, Kent ME7 3JG
☎ 0634 812196

This close to the urban sprawl, you
would not expect 250 acres of
nature walks, way-marked trails,
riding, fishing and even dry skiing,
but it is here. In summer, special
events include children's picnics
and kite flying displays. Enjoy.

🕐 All year: daily 7am–sunset
£ Adm free
✳ Visitor centre, Ranger supervision
🅰 Signs from M2 jnct 3/4 and A278
♿ ⬛ ☕ ℗

Chart Gunpowder Mills

Westbrook Walk, Faversham, Kent
☎ 0795 534542

The only gunpowder mill left in
Britain. Reputed to have made
explosives for both Nelson and
Wellington. Well restored and
displayed.

🕐 Apr–Sep, Sat/Sun/BH 2–5
£ Adm free
🅰 M2 jnct 6
🚉 Faversham 15 min
🅿

Chartwell

Westerham, Kent TN16 1PS
☎ 0732 866368

Winston Churchill lived here for
more than 40 years. It almost smells
of his famous cigar smoke. Special
exhibitions of wartime, his uniforms
and gifts received. Studio with his
paintings. Admission by timed
ticket.

🕐 Apr–Oct, Tue–Thu 12–5.30,
   Sat/Sun/BHM 11–5.30; Nov/phone
£ Hse/Gdn: Ad £4.50, Chd £2.25.
   Gdn only £2/£1
🅰 B2026
♿ ♨ 🍴 🛍 🅿 NT

Chatley Heath Semaphore Tower

Old Lane, Cobham, Surrey
☎ 0932 862762

Until the telephone, this semaphore
system, used by Nelson's navy to
pass messages from ports like
Plymouth to London, was the
world's fastest means of long-
distance communication. See how it
was done.

🕐 Late Mar–beg Oct, Sat/Sun/BH
   (+Wed/Surrey sch hol) 12–5
£ Ad £1.60, Chd (8–16)/SC £1
🅰 M25/A3
♨ 🅿

Chessington World of Adventures

Leatherhead Rd, Chessington KT9 2NE
☎ 0372 727227

Toytown Truckers joins rides like
the Runaway Mine train, Dragon
World, old favourite the Fifth
Dimension and, of course, the
Vampire Ride. The zoo, safari
skyway and teeming market square
let you draw breath.

🕐 Easter–end Oct, daily 10–5.30
   (9pm Jul/Aug); last adm 3
£ Ad £13,
   Chd £10.75,
   SC £5.75
🅰 M25 jnct 9, A243
🚉 Chessington S, 10 min
♿ ♨ ☕ 🍴 🛍 🅿

Chichester Harbour Water Tours

West Itchenor, Chichester, W Sussex
☎ 0243 786418

Cruise gently for 1½ hours around this area of outstanding natural beauty and the busy bustle of boating at Chichester.

🕐 Summer: daily from 10.30;
   last trip 7pm
£ Ad £3.50, Chd £1.50
🅰 A286
☕ 🅿

Day at the Wells

Corn Exchange, The Pantiles,
Tunbridge Wells TN2 5QJ
☎ 0892 546545

Welcome to 1740, the world of Beau Nash, travelling by stagecoach and taking the health-giving waters. A walk through history with life-like models and costumed figures, ending in a glamorous crinolined ball. Special commentary for children.

🕐 Daily: Apr–Oct 10–5; Nov–Mar 10–4
£ Ad £3.75, Chd (5–15)/SC £2.95, f/t
🅰 Town centre
🚉 Tunbridge Wells 10 min
♿ 🛍 🅿

Dickens Centre

Eastgate House, High St,
Rochester ME1 1EW
☎ 0634 844176

They are all here. Tiny Tim, Mr Pickwick, Oliver Twist, not to mention the author himself, in this walk-through assembly of fact and fiction in Charles Dickens' England.

🕐 All year, daily 10–5.30
£ Ad £2.60, Chd/SC £1.60, f/t
🅰 Town centre
🚉 Rochester 5 min
🛍

Dover Castle & Hellfire Corner

Dover, Kent
☎ 0304 201628

The castle claims almost 2,000 years as a fortress sitting on the famous White Cliffs. Hellfire Corner is a World War II maze of secret tunnels, started in the Napoleonic wars, from which the relief of Dunkirk was planned. Atmospheric reconstruction.

🕐 Daily: Apr–Sep 10–6; Oct–Mar 10–4;
   last adm 45 min before
£ Ad £5.25, Chd (5–15) £2.60,
   SC £3.95, f/t
🅰 Above town
🚉 Dover Priory (bus link)
♿(res) 🍴 🍽 🍴 🛍 🅿 EH

Drusillas Park

Nr Alfriston, E Sussex BN26 5QS
☎ 0323 870234

Meerkats, monkeys, penguins,
parrots and much more, including a
farmyard, a miniature railway and
adventure playground. Close
contact with many of the animals.

🕐 Daily: summer 10–5; winter 10.30–4
£ Ad £4.95, Chd (3–12) £4.35,
  SC/♿ £3.35
🅰 A27, E of Lewes
♿ ⛏ 🍴 🛍 🅿

Filching Manor Motor Museum

Jevington Rd, Wannock,
Polegate, E Sussex BN26 5QA
☎ 0323 487838

Four-wheel fanatics will love the
100 or so motors gathered here. You
can understand why Paul
McCartney owned the 1927
Hispano-Suiza. Malcolm Campbell's
1937 *Bluebird*, and a collection of
armour.

🕐 10–30–4.30:
  Apr/May Thu–Sun,
  Jun–Oct daily; Nov/Dec
  Sat/Sun
£ Ad £3, Chd/SC £2, f/t
🅰 A27, A22
♿ ⛏ ☕ 🛍 🅿

Eurotunnel Exhibition Centre

St Martin's Plain, Cheriton High St,
Folkestone CT19 4QD
☎ 0303 270111

Does everything but actually take
you to France. Huge model
railway system, realistic simulation
of actual journey, walk-round full-
size shuttle wagon. See how it was
all built.

🕐 Daily: summer 10–6; winter 10–5
£ Ad £3.60, Chd/SC £2.20, f/t
🅰 M20 jnct 12, A16
🚉 Folkstone 3 miles
♿ ⛏ ☕ 🛍 🅿

Fort Fun

Royal Parade, Eastbourne BN22 7LU
☎ 0323 642833

Older children can hurtle round on
a runaway train, sledge on grass, or
brave a roller coaster. The younger
head for the gentler pursuits of
Rocky's Adventureland.

🕐 Ft Fun: Easter–Oct Sat/Sun 10–6
  (daily/sch hol).
  Rocky's: all year, daily 10–6
£ Ft Fun: Ad £1.70, Chd £3.95, SC 50p, f/t;
  Rocky's: Chd £2.50, (Ad free)
🅰 Town centre
🚉 Eastbourne 25 min
♿ ⛏ ☕ 🅿

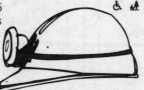

Gatwick Airport Spectator Area

South Terminal Bldg,
Gatwick Airport RH6 0NP
☎ 0293 503843

Plane spotting.
Some spotters
take radios to
listen to
pilot/control
tower chat.

🕐 Daily: late
Mar–Sep 8–7;
Oct–late Mar 9–4
💷 Ad 60p, Chd/SC 30p
🅰 M23 jnct 9
🚻 Gatwick
♿ ☕ 🍴 🛍 🅿

Gatwick Zoo

Russ Hill, Charlwood, Surrey RH6 0EG
☎ 0293 862312

A selection of exotic birds. And, in
large enclosures and an island,
monkeys, wallabies and meerkat,
and a walk-through tropical area
with free-flying butterflies.

🕐 Easter–Oct, daily
10.30–6; Nov–Mar,
Sat/Sun/sch hol
10.30–dusk
💷 Ad £3.50,
Chd (3–14)
£2.50,
SC £3
🅰 M23 jnct 9/10
♿ 🎢 ☕ 🛍 🅿

Grand Shaft

Snargate St, Dover, Kent
0304 201200

A real oddity. This challenging
triple staircase, built in 1809, goes
straight down (or up) for 43m
from the barracks on the cliff tops
to the town.

🕐 Late May–beg Sep, Wed–Sun 2–5
💷 Ad £1, Chd/SC 50p
🅰 Above town
🚻 Dover Priory 15 min

Hastings Sea Life Centre

Rock–A–Nore Rd, Hastings TN34 3DW
☎ 0424 718776

Get into deep waters here and see
British lobsters, sharks and octopus.
Special sea-lab feature for children
with a 3D film and underwater
tunnel.

🕐 All year, daily 10–6 (Jul–Sep 10–8)
💷 Ad £4.25, Chd (4–14) £2.95, SC £3.45
🅰 Old Town area
🚻 Hastings & St Leonards
1½ miles
♿ ☕ 🛍 🅿

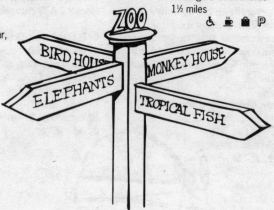

Hever Castle & Gardens

Nr Edenbridge, Kent TN8 7NG
☎ 0732 865224

Childhood home of Anne Boleyn
and where she was courted by
Henry VIII. Lots of royal
connections and an exhibition of
miniature houses too good to be
called dolls' houses. A maze, and
open-air theatre in summer.

🕐 Daily, mid Mar–beg Nov. Gdn 11–6,
   Castle 12–6 (5 winter)
💷 Ad £5.20, Chd (5–16) £2.60, SC £4.70.
   Gdn only: £3.80/£2.20/£3.30; f/t
🅰 B2026, SE of Edenbridge
⌗ Hever 15 min
♿ ☕ 🍴 🛍 ℗

Historic Dockyard

Chatham, Kent ME4 4TE
☎ 0634 812551

The Royal Navy built ships here
from 1586 to 1962. Now the 80-acre
site is turned over to historic
remembrance and re-creation. The
last ship, the submarine *Ocelot*, is
being restored. The ropeworks
show you how ropes were made,
and you can get a flavour of it
all from keel to
crow's-nest.

🕐 Easter–Oct,
   daily 10–5;
   Feb/Mar/Nov,
   Wed/Sat/Sun
   10–4; last adm 4/3
💷 Ad £5.50, Chd £2.75,
   SC £4.80, f/t
🅰 M20 jnct 6, M2 jnct 3
⌗ Chatham 15 min
♿ ☕ 🍴 🛍 ℗

Hollanden Farm Park

Great Hollanden Farm, Mill Lane,
Hildenborough, Sevenoaks TN15 0SG
☎ 0732 832276

Some pretty unusual sheep, goats
and pigs as well as horses and waterfowl, and a newly created Iron Age
village. Strawberry farm with trailer
rides and adventure playground.

🕐 Easter–Sep, daily 10.30–5
💷 Ad £3.40, Chd £2.20, SC £2.75
✳ PYO fruit
🅰 A21, B245
♿ ⛺ ☕ 🛍 ℗

Howletts Wild Animal Park

Bekesbourne, Canterbury, Kent
☎ 0227 721286

Has the largest breeding group of
gorillas outside America and one of
the largest collections of tigers in the
world. African elephants, chimps
and cheetahs as well.

🕐 Daily: summer 10–7 (last adm 5);
   winter 10–1hr before dusk
💷 Ad £6.50, Chd (4–15)/SC £4.50
🅰 A2, S of Canterbury
⌗ Bekesbourne
   15 min
♿ ⛺ ☕
🛍 ℗

193

Kent & East Sussex Railway

Town Station, Tenterden TN30 6HE
☎ 0580 765155/762943 t/table

No fewer than 16 steam trains travel
the 7 miles from Tenterden to
Northiam, tackling some steep hills
en route. Play area and railway
shop.

🕐 Jul–Aug daily; other times/phone
💷 Rtn: Ad £5.80, Chd (2–15) £1,
   SC £4.50
✳ Special events
🅰 A28 (for both stns)
🚏 Ashford/Hastings (bus link)
♿ ⛺ ☕ 🍽 🅿

Leeds Castle

Nr Maidstone, Kent ME17 1PL
☎ 0622 765400

Arguably the prettiest royal palace,
it packs in not just a showpiece
castle but parks with a maze,
grottoes, aviaries, concerts and
events.

🕐 Daily: Mar–Oct 10–5; Nov–Feb 10–3
💷 Ad £7, Chd £4.80, SC £6.
   Park only: £5.50/£3.30/£4.50; f/t
🅰 M20 jnct 8
🚏 Bearsted (not w/ends)
♿ ⛺ ☕ 🍽 🛍 🅿

Long Man

Wilmington, E Sussex

The tallest of all chalk figures, the
Wilmington man is 73m long, cut
deeply into Windover Hill with a
staff in each hand. His origin is a
complete mystery: some people
place him as far back as the Iron
Age.

🕐 All year, all day
💷 Adm free
🅰 A27, W of Polegate

Museum of Kent Life

Lock Lane, Sandling, Maidstone ME14 3AU
☎ 0622 763936

All about hops etc, but the bit
everyone heads for is *The Darling
Buds Of May* show. You can look
around Ma Larkin's kitchen or have
your photo taken beside Pop's old
blue truck.

🕐 Apr–Oct, daily 10–5.30
💷 Ad £3, Chd/SC £1.50, f/t
🅰 M20 jnct 6, A229
🚏 Maidstone E or W, 1½ miles
♿ ⛺ ☕ 🛍 🅿

Museum of Shops

20 Cornfield Tce, Eastbourne BN21 4NS
☎ 0323 737143

A whole street of shops from
various areas and eras in Britain;
50,000 exhibits packed into 3 floors.
How we lived then.

🕐 Apr–Oct, daily, 10–5.30; Nov–Mar
  (not Jan) 10–5
£ Ad £2, Chd (5–15) £1, SC £1.50
🅰 Nr War Memorial roundabout
⊞ Eastbourne 10 min
▮

Old Lighthouse

Dungeness, Kent
☎ 0679 21300

Exactly the kind of lighthouse you
draw when you are very young -
tall, round and narrow. You can
climb the 167 steps to the top to see
the 3-ton lens and the lantern, and
find out how it worked. This was
the fourth lighthouse to be built
here since the 17th century. The
erection of the nearby nuclear
power station, between the Old
Lighthouse and the sea, prompted
the building of a fifth. Visits
weather permitting.

🕐 Daily: Apr–Oct 10.30–5.30;
  Nov–Mar Sat/Sun 12–3
£ Ad £1, Chd/SC 50p
✳ Romney, Hythe & Dymchurch Rlwy [qv]
🅰 Off B2075 at Lydd
♿ Ⓟ

Old Town Gaol

Town Hall, Biggin St, Dover, Kent
☎ 0304 201200

The cellars of the ancient town hall
are turned into a full-scale Victorian
prison with lots of audio-visual
tricks to give authenticity. Attend a
trial, visit the cells, see them sewing
mailbags. Be good.

🕐 Jun–late Sep, Mon–Sat 10–4.30,
  Sun 2–4.30; Sep–May/phone
£ Ad £3.20, Chd(5+)/SC £1.90
🅰 Town centre
⊞ Dover Priory 5 min

Paddle Steamer
Kingswear Castle

The Historic Dockyard, Chatham ME4 4TQ
☎ 0634 827648

A rare chance to board a working
paddle steamer. The *Kingswear
Castle*, built 1924, churns her way
down the Medway with style. A 2½-
hour afternoon cruise, plus a range
of special theme sailings.

🕐 May–Sep/Dec; phone for details
£ From: Ad £3.95, Chd £2.95,
  SC £3.50, f/t
🅰 M2 jnct 3, A2
⊞ Chatham 10 min
▮ Ⓟ

Palace Pier

Madeira Drive, Brighton, E Sussex
☎ 0273 609361

Traditional seaside fun. Funfair, penny arcades (electronic now), candyfloss... Or you can just look out to sea.

🕐 Daily: summer 9–2am; winter 11–11
£ Adm free
🅰 On sea front
🚉 Brighton 10 min
♿ ☕

Penshurst Place & Gardens

Penshurst, Tonbridge TN11 8DG
☎ 0892 870307

Splendid medieval manor. Apart from the portraits, tapestries and fine furniture, there is a toy museum, a neat Tudor garden, nature and farm trails, and an adventure playground.

🕐 Late Mar–beg Oct, daily
   (Hse 12–5.30, Gdn 11–6); rest
   Mar/Oct, Sat/Sun; last adm 5
£ Ad £4.95, Chd £2.75, SC £4.50.
   Gdn only: £3.50/£2.25/£3
✳ Special events
🅰 A21, B2176
⛽ 🍴 🛍 Ⓟ

Planet Earth at Garden Paradise

Avis Road, Newhaven BN9 0DH
☎ 0273 512123

Earthquakes, volcanoes (simulated in noise and heat), dinosaurs (motorised and life-size); plus the World Of Plants, re-creating deserts and tropical rainforest. Miniature passenger railway and play area.

🕐 Daily: Mar–Oct 10–5.30; Nov–Feb
   10–4.30
£ Ad £2.99, Chd (5–14) £2.50, f/t
🅰 A26, A259
🚉 Newhaven 10 min
♿ ⛽ ☕ 🛍 Ⓟ

Port Lympne Wild Animal Park

Lympne, Hythe, Kent CT21 4PD
☎ 0303 264646

All safari-style with rhinos, antelopes and elephants living in parkland. There is a 'gorillararium', and trailer trips through the animal paddocks.

🕐 Daily: summer 10–7 (last adm 5);
   winter 10–1hr before dusk
£ Ad £6.50, Chd (4–15)/SC £4.50
✳ Pre–book trailer rides
🅰 M20 jnct 11, A20
🚉 Ashford (bus link)
♿ ⛽ ☕ 🛍 Ⓟ

River Wey & Godalming Navigations

Dapdune Wharf, Wharf Rd,
Guildford GU1 4RR
☎ 0483 61389

This is as far south as you can go on Britain's inland waterways. There is the towpath to walk or 19½ miles to glide along in tranquil delight, slipping past locks and weirs first dug out around 1670. Dapdune Wharf has a horse-drawn barge display.

🕑 All year, dawn–dusk
💷 Adm free
✳ Horse–drawn boat trips (0483 414938)
🚗 M25, A3
♿ Ⓟ

Romney, Hythe & Dymchurch Railway

New Romney Station,
New Romney TN28 8PL
☎ 0679 62353/63256

Real steam railway, but everything scaled down to one-third normal size. The tiny trains haul up to 200 passengers at 25mph across 15 miles of Romney Marsh. You can inspect the engine shed and see the toy museum at the station. Link with Old Lighthouse at Dungeness [qv].

🕑 Mar–Oct; phone for details
💷 Full rtn: Ad £7.30, Chd (3–15) £3.65, SC £4.86, f/t
✳ Santa train/Dec
🚗 A259 (all stns)
🚌 Ashford/Hastings (bus link)
♿ 🍴 ☕ 🛍 Ⓟ

Roman Painted House

New St, Dover, Kent CT17 9AJ
☎ 0304 203279

The rooms they have excavated were buried by Roman soldiers 1,800 years ago as they built new defences. Originally a Roman hotel, and you won't see better Roman paintings this side of the Alps. Artefacts etc.

🕑 Apr/Jun/Sep/Oct, Tue–Sun/BH 10–5 (May 10–6); Jul/Aug, daily 10–6
💷 Ad £1.50, Chd/SC 50p
🚗 Town centre
🚌 Dover Priory 5 min
♿ 🛍 Ⓟ

Rowlands Confectionery

17 Old High St, Folkestone CT20 1RL
☎ 0303 254723

If you ever wondered how they got the place name into sticks of rock, this confectioner's demonstration explains all.

🕑 Daily: summer 10–6; winter 10–5
💷 Adm free
🚗 Nr town centre
🚌 Folkestone 30 min

Royal Pavilion

Old Steine, Brighton BN1 1UE
☎ 0273 603005

This farmhouse conversion,
instigated by the future George IV
in 1786, cost so much money the
royal family had to beg parliament
for cash. Fantastically lavish; among
the bits to make you gasp are the
music room, kitchen and silver gilt
collection.

🕐 Daily: Jun–Sep 10–6; Oct–May 10–5
💷 Ad £3.75, Chd £2.10, SC £2.75, f/t;
    ♿free
🅰 Town centre
🚉 Brighton 10 min
♿ ☕ 🛍

Smugglers Adventure

St Clement's Caves,
West Hill, Hastings TN34 3HY
☎ 0424 422964

The history of smuggling is
celebrated in a whole acre of caves
cut in the hillside, peopled with life-
size figures and sound and light
effects. Museum and audio-visual
show.

🕐 Daily: Apr–Sep 10–5.30; Oct–Mar
    11–4.30
💷 Ad £3.60, Chd £2.30, SC £2.95, f/t
✳ West Hill Cliff Rlwy, or walk
🅰 Above Old Town
🚉 Hastings & St Leonards 1½ miles
🛍

🔻 Shipwreck Heritage Centre

Rock–A–Nore Rd, Hastings TN34 3DW
☎ 0424 437452

The big sound and light show takes
you through a medieval shipwreck
in a simulated dock. Then they
show you pieces salvaged from
wrecks over 3,000 years. Other
highlights: radar scan of Channel
shipping and live NASA satellite
weather reports.

🕐 Daily: Easter/Jun/Sep, 10.30–5;
    Jul/Aug 10.30–6,
    Apr/May, 12–5
💷 Ad £2, Chd £1.25,
    SC £1.50, f/t
✳ Deaf loop
🅰 Old Town area
🚉 Hastings &
    St Leonards 1½ miles
♿ 🛍 🅿

South Foreland Lighthouse

St Margaret's–at–Cliffe, Dover
☎ 0892 890651

Built in 1843, the lighthouse was
used by Marconi for the first radio
communications as an aid to
navigation. A couple of miles walk
to reach it.

🕐 Apr–Oct, Sat/Sun/BHM 2–5.30
    💷 Ad £1, Chd 50p
    🅰 B2058
    🅿 NT

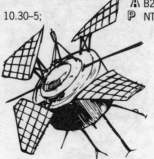

South of England Rare Breeds Centre

Highlands Farm, Woodchurch,
Ashford, Kent TN26 3RJ
☎ 0233 861493

Working 90-acre farm with 55 rare breeds. Milking and shearing displays, children's corner where animals can be handled, horse-drawn rides and nature trails.

🕐 Daily: Apr–Sep 10.30–5.30;
   Oct–Mar 10.30–4.30
💲 Ad £3, Chd 85p, SC £2.50; rides 80p
✳ Holiday events
🅰 A2070, B2067
♿ ⚲ 🍽 🛍 🅿

Stoneywish Country Park

Spatham Lane, Ditchling,
E Sussex BN6 8SU
☎ 0273 843498

Roam free to watch wildfowl on the lakes or examine the collection of old photos and farm machinery. Good pets' corner and large play area.

🕐 Mar–Oct, daily 10–7; Nov–Feb,
   Sat/Sun 10–5
💲 Ad £2, Chd £1, SC £1.75
🅰 B2116
♿ ⚲ 🍵 🛍 🅿

Sussex Falconry Centre

Locksacre Aquatic Nursery, Wophams Lane, Birdham, Chichester PO20 7BS
☎ 0243 512472

Many of the birds here have been rescued, including owls, falcons and hawks. Flying displays in good weather during summer.

🕐 Mar–Oct, Tues–Sun 9.30–5
💲 Ad £1.95, Chd/SC £1.25
🅰 A286, S of
   Chichester
♿ 🍵 🛍 🅿

Tangmere Military Aviation Museum

Tangmere Airfield, Tangmere,
Chichester PO20 6ES
☎ 0243 775223

One of the Battle of Britain airfields, with memorabilia from those days. You can also see Meteor and Hunter jets, and have a go on a real flight simulator.

🕐 Daily: Mar–Oct 10–5.30;
   Nov–Feb 10–4.30
💲 Ad £2.50, Chd £1
🅰 A27, E of Chichester
♿ ⚲ 🍵 🛍 🅿

Thorpe Park

Staines Road, Chertsey, Surrey KT16 8PN
☎ 0932 562633

Exciting rides include the Calgary
Stampede, the pirate rides on
Treasure Island, a white water trip
and a jolly Teacup ride. Waterbuses
and landtrains get you around.
Special rides for younger ones plus
a cinema and roller skating.

🕐 Daily: late Mar–late Oct, 10–5
  (Jul/Aug 10–6)
£ Ad £11.25, Chd (under 14) £10.25, f/t
🅰 M25 jnct 11/13
♿ ⛺ ☕ 🍴 🛍 🅿

Washbrooks Farm Centre

Brighton Rd, Hurstpierpoint, W Sussex
☎ 0273 832201

Contact with farm animals and their
young, including rare breeds.
Tractor and trailer rides and an
adventure playground.

🕐 All year, daily 9.30–5
£ Ad £1.75,
  Chd/SC £1.50,
  f/t
🅰 A23
♿ ⛺ ☕
🛍 🅿

Weald & Downland Open Air Museum

Singleton, nr Chichester, W Sussex
☎ 0243 811348

Over 35 restored and re-created old
buildings, including a medieval
farmhouse, a later, working,
watermill and a village school. Set
in a country park with woodland
walks and nature trail.

🕐 Mar–Oct, daily
  11–6 (last adm 5);
  Nov–Feb/phone
£ Ad £4.20, Chd £2.10,
  SC £3.70, f/t
🅰 A286, N of Chichester
⛺ ☕ 🛍 🅿

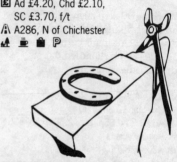

Whitbread Hop Farm

Beltring, Paddock Wood, Kent TN12 6PY
☎ 0622 872068

The oast house setting is
impressive, with a good
exhibition of workshops,
carts and farming equipment,
and all about hops. Shire horses
and, less predictably, birds of
prey on view.

🕐 Daily: summer 10–6; winter 10–4
  (last adm 5/3)
£ Ad £4.95, Chd (5–15) £3,
  SC/♿ £3.50
✻ Hot air ballooning etc
🅰 B2015
♿ ⛺ ☕ 🍴 🛍 🅿

White Cliffs Experience

Market Square, Dover CT16 1PB
☎ 0304 210101

Multi-media history show you can join in. You can 'talk' to Romans, step aboard an early ferry, feel what it was like after a World War II air raid. And so on.

🕐 Late Mar–Oct, daily 10–6.30
(last adm 5); Nov–Mar/phone
💷 Ad £4.99,
Chd (4–14) £3.50,
SC £3.99, f/t
🅰 Town centre
🚉 Dover Priory
5 min
♿ ♨ ☕ 🅿

Wildfowl & Wetlands Centre

Mill Rd, Arundel, W Sussex BN18 9PB
☎ 0903 883355

Famous reserve. You can watch the swans, ducks and geese from concealed hides, from the viewing gallery at the visitor centre or at the length of your arm, for many of the birds will take food from your hand.

🕐 Daily: summer
9.30–5.30;
winter 9.30–4.30 (last
adm 4.30/3.30)
💷 Ad £3.95, Chd(4+) £2,
SC £2.95, f/t
🅰 A27
🚉 Arundel 20 min
♿ ♨ 🍴 🛍 🅿

Avon
Cornwall
Devon
Somerset
Isles of Scilly

American Museum

Claverton Manor, Bath BA2 7BD
☎ 0225 460503

A taste of the real America. You can
see a Conestoga, the wagon that
conquered the West, a Cheyenne
tepee, the captain's cabin from a
New England whaler. No Big Macs,
no bubble gum, not a Coke in sight.

🕐 End Mar–beg Nov, Tue–Sun 2–5,
  BH Sun/Mon 11–5
💷 Ad £5, Chd £2.50, SC £4.50.
  Grnds: £2/£1
🅰 A36, 3¼ miles SE of Bath
☕ ☖ 🏠 Ⓟ

Arlington Court

Arlington, Barnstaple, Devon EX31 4LP
☎ 0271 850296

The house is stuffed with collections
of things like exotic shells, model
ships and costumes. A carriage
collection is in the stables, and there
are carriage rides. In the lovely park
Jacob sheep and Shetland ponies
safely graze.

🕐 Hse/Gdn/Park: end Mar–Oct,
  Sun–Fri 11–5.30. Footpaths:
  Nov–Mar, dawn–dusk
💷 Ad/Chd £4.60. Gdn only: £2.40
🅰 A39, 7 miles NE of Barnstaple
♿ ⛲ ☕ 🍴 🏠 Ⓟ NT

Automobilia

The Old Mill, St Stephen,
St Austell PL26 7RX
☎ 0726 823092

A 50-car museum where enthusiasts
can buy (and sell) bits for their
own classic cars. Others can just
look and enjoy.

🕐 Jun–Sep, daily
   10–6; Apr/May/Oct, Sun–Fri 10–4
💷 Ad £3, Chd(6+) £1.50, SC £2.50, f/t
🅰 A3058, W of St Austell
♿ ☕ 🛍 🅿

Babbacombe Model Village

Hampton Ave, Babbacombe,
Torquay TQ1 3LA
☎ 0803 328669

One of the great English model
villages. It covers 4 acres and is laid
out with a whole midget town,
countryside, lakes, waterfalls,
roads, railways, the lot.

🕐 Daily: Easter–Oct 9am–10pm; winter 10–4
💷 Ad £3.50, Chd (3–13) £2.25,
   SC £2.95, f/t
🅰 2 miles E of Torquay
♿ 🅿

Bath Ghost Walk

Garrick's Head, Bath BA1 5LY
☎ 0225 463618

The 2-hour walk starts from the
Nash Bar and takes in the spookier
aspects of the city. Not the sort of
thing Jane Austen would have
written about.

🕐 Starts 8pm. May–Oct, Mon–Fri;
   Nov–Apr, Fri
💷 Ad £3, Chd/SC £1.50
🅰 Next to Theatre Royal
▦ Bath 10 min

Becky Falls

Manaton, Bovey Tracey, Devon
☎ 064722 259

Fifty beautiful acres of woodland
valley, with waterfalls, streams,
glades and much undisturbed
wildlife. The idea is to guide people
round, but leave them alone to
enjoy the brush with nature.

🕐 Easter–Nov, daily
   10–6/dusk
💷 £3.50 per car
🅰 B3344
♿ ☕ 🍽
🛍 🅿

Bickleigh Castle

Bickleigh, Tiverton, Devon EX16 8RP
☎ 0884 855363

This part 900-year-old house
contains the country's most
complete collection of World War II
spy and escaping gadgets, ranging
from home-made 'German'
work papers to magnetic
compass buttons and silk
handkerchiefs which are
actually maps. There are
also displays on the *Mary
Rose* and *Titanic* (family
connections), and a spooky
tower.

🕐 Easter/Apr–May,
   Wed/Sun/BH 2–5.30;
   Jun–beg Oct, Sun–Fri
£ Ad £3.20, Chd (5–15) £1.60
🏁 A396, S of Tiverton
♨ ☕ 🛍 🅿

Bristol Zoo Gardens

Guthrie Rd, Clifton, Bristol BS8 3HA
☎ 0272 738951

Home for some 300 species. Young
humans can try Zoo Olympics to
see if they can jump as far as a
kangaroo or swing like a gibbon in
the adventure
playground.

🕐 Daily: summer
   9–6; winter 9–5
£ Ad £5.50,
   Chd £2.50, SC £4
🏁 M5 jnct 17/18;
   signs from city
♿ ⛲ 🍴 🛍 🅿

Bristol Industrial Museum

Princes Wharf, Wapping Rd,
Bristol BS1 4RN
☎ 0272 251470

Bristol's industrial heritage on land,
sea and air. Vintage road transport
from bikes to buses is displayed
along with a helicopter, a mock-up
of Concorde and the maritime
history of the city. A model railway
covers the tracks.

🕐 All year, Tue–Sun 10–5
£ Ad £1, Chd free,
   SC 50p
🏁 City docks
🚃 Bristol Temple
   Meads 20 min
♿ 🛍 🅿

Canonteign Falls & Country Park

Christow, Exeter, Devon EX6 7NT
☎ 0647 52434

Perched on the edge of Dartmoor,
an abundant supply of water and
some clever engineering creates
parkland with bouncing, bubbling
cascades, rushing waterfalls and 5
ornamental lakes. Plus miniature
ponies, a farm history collection,
waterfowl and cream teas.

🕐 Mar–mid Nov, daily
   10–5.30
£ Ad £3, Chd £2,
   SC £2.50
🏁 A38, B3193
♿ ☕ 🅿

Cheddar Showcaves

Cheddar Gorge, Somerset BS27 3QF
☎ 0934 742343

Deep and spectacular caves with
silent pools, and one with a
waterfall. There is a display of an
ancient burial chamber and a cave
dwelling, then comes Crystal Quest,
half tour half 'dungeons and
dragons' light show. Busy outside
too, with glassblowers, sweet-
makers and a cheese shop.

You can climb to the clifftop and
visit the **Black Rock Nature
Reserve**. There, you can take a 1½-
mile circular walk through
woodland and downland which
contains around 200 species of
wildflowers and trees, including the
Cheddar Pink, found only here.

🕒 Daily: Easter–Sep 10–5.30;
  Oct–Mar 10.30–4.30
£ Ad £5, Chd £3, f/t, ♿free
🅰 A371
♿(res) ☕ 🎒 🅿

Children's Adventure Land

Verbeer Manor, Willand,
Cullompton, Devon EX15 2PE
☎ 0884 33312

In 75 acres, canoes on the lake,
nature walks, pitch and putt, giant
slides, go-karts, Dinosaurland, an
aerial walkway and a pirate ship.
Crazy golf, an assault course, pets'
corner and soft play area are
squeezed in too.

🕒 All year, daily 10–dusk
£ Ad/Chd(3+) £3.50, SC £2.50
🅰 M5 jnct 27/28
♿ ☕ 🎡 🎒 🅿

Chewton Cheese Dairy

Priory Farm, Chewton Mendip,
Bath BA3 4NT
☎ 0761 241666

Learn all about Cheddar cheese-
making, live and on video.
Afterwards, nip out to see the rare
breeds and the owls, then back for a
cheese sandwich.

🕒 All year, daily; cheese–making not
  Thu/Sun
£ Ad £2, Chd (4–14) £1, SC £1.50
🅰 A39
♿(res) 🐑 🎡 🎒 🅿

Chysauster Ancient Village

New Mill, Penzance, Cornwall TR20 8XA
☎ 0736 61889

Enter the Iron Age. Nine oval-
shaped houses front the first
identifiable village street in
England, with doors all carefully set
to avoid the winds on the hillside.
Well preserved.

🕒 Easter–Oct, daily 10–6;
  Nov–Mar, Tue–Sun
£ Ad £1.35, Chd 65p, SC £1
🅰 B3311, N of Penzance
🚌 Penzance (bus link)
🎒 🅿

Clifton Suspension Bridge

Tollhouse, Bridge Rd, Clifton, Bristol
☎ 0272 732122

Brunel's spectacular masterpiece.
Built between 1836 and 1864, the
bridge is a dizzy 75m above the
Avon. In high winds it can move as
much as 30cm, but it never closes.

🕐 All year, daily
💷 On foot free; car 15p
🅰 M5 jnct 18/19; signs from city

Cornish Seal Sanctuary

Gweek, Helston, Cornwall TR12 6UG
☎ 0326 221361

You can visit the seals
in hospital and see
how they are treated
for pollution
damage and
injury. A series
of pools is
home to
more seals,
sea lions
and
penguins.
The sanctuary also has a nature trail
by a stream, and play areas.

🕐 Daily: summer 9–6;
winter 10–5
💷 Ad £4.50,
Chd £2.95,
SC £3.50
🅰 A394
♿ 🎪 ☕ 🎁 🅿

Cotehele

St Dominick, Saltash, Cornwall PL12 6TA
☎ 0579 50434

A 15th-century house with the
original furniture and no electric
light, perched on a cliff garden
which winds its way down to its
own quay and sailing barge on the
beautiful, rugged Cornish coastline.
Working mill with cider press.
Limited to 600 visitors a day.

🕐 Apr–Oct, Sat–Thu. Hse: 12–5.30/dusk
Mill: 11–5.30/dusk
Gdn: daily 11–5.30/dusk
💷 All-in: £5. Gdn/Mill £2.50
🅰 8 miles SW of Tavistock
🚂 Calstock 2 miles
☕ 🎪 🎁 🅿 NT

Cricket St Thomas Wildlife & Leisure Park

Chard, Somerset TA20 4DD
☎ 0460 30755/0891 884501

Now has Crinkly Bottom Village
complete with Mr Blobby's house to
add to the elephants, jaguars and
sea lions. You can travel on the
scenic railway, visit the children's
park with its rare breeds, or walk
beside the lake to see deer,
wallabies, camels and
flamingoes.

🕐 All year, daily
10–6/dusk
💷 Ad £6.80, Chd (4–14) £5,
SC £6, ♿ free
🅰 A30 Chard/Crewkerne
♿ 🎪 ☕ 🎪 🎁 🅿

Dairyland Farm World

Summercourt, Newquay, Cornwall
TR8 5AA
☎ 0872 510246

There is a giant milking
parlour with a viewing
gallery, a country life
museum, soft play area and
approachable pets in a playground.
Or nature trails, pony rides, hay
rides and an assault course.

🕐 Late Mar–Oct, 10.30–5.30; last adm 4
£ Ad £4.50, Chd £3.30, SC £4.20, f/t
⚠ A3058, 4 miles SE of Newquay
⚐ ☕ 🛍 🅿

Dobwalls Family Adventure Park

Nr Liskeard, Cornwall PL14 6HD
☎ 0579 20325/20578 info

Miniature
steam and
diesel locos pull passengers
through scenery with a frontier
flavour. Part of a themed complex
which also offers a huge Adventureland with high cable walkways, and
a Babes In The Wood section for
younger children. Crazy golf, radio-
controlled trucks and boats,
hillbilly shooting gallery, and more.

🕐 Easter–Sep, daily 10–6; Oct,
  Sat/Sun+h/term 10–5; last adm 1½hr
  before
£ Ad £6.50, Chd/SC £4.50 (£4.50/£3.50
  after 2.30), f/t
⚠ A38
♿ ⚐ ☕ 🛍 🅿

Exmoor Bird Gardens

South Stowford, Bratton Fleming,
Barnstaple EX31 4SG
☎ 05983 352

The gardens, a natural calling point
for native waterfowl, are enhanced
by a collection of tropical birds,
many of which wander free
through the 12-acre landscaped
grounds. A Tarzanland assault
course distracts the young.

🕐 Daily: April–Oct 10–6; Nov–Mar 10–4
£ Ad £3, Chd £2, SC £2.50, f/t
⚠ A399
♿ ⚐ ☕
🛍 🅿

Exmoor Brass Rubbing Centre

Watersmeet Rd, Lynmouth,
N Devon EX35 6EP
☎ 0598 52529

The centre offers beginners a whole
range of brasses to copy, and gives
advice and help with techniques.
Could become the habit of a
lifetime.

🕒 Easter–Sep, Mon–Fri 11–4.30
(sch hols, daily 10–5)
£ Adm free. Rubbing: from £1.35
⚠ Town centre
♿ 🛍 ℗

Exploratory, The

Bristol Old Station, Temple Meads,
Bristol BS1 6QU
☎ 0272 252008/225944 info

Understanding why the world's
biggest guitar doesn't play high
notes, and why mirrors confuse
your brain, can be a lot of fun. Well,
it is here, in this interest-packed
hands-on science exhibition.

🕒 All year, daily 10–5
£ Ad £4, Chd(5+) £2.50
⚠ Next to Temple Meads stn
🚉 Bristol Temple Meads
♿ 🖥 🛍 ℗

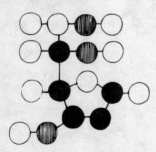

Flambards Victorian Village Theme Park

Culdrose Manor, Helston,
Cornwall TR13 0GA
☎ 0326 574549

A life-size Victorian village stocked
with shops and period dress, and a
Blitzed street brought back from the
past. Plus science exhibits,
sideshows, historic planes, 3D
cinema shows and fast-driving
simulators.

🕒 Apr–Oct, daily 10–5.30
(7.30pm Mon–Thu sch hols)
£ Ad £7.95 (over 54, £3.95),
Chd (4–13) £6.95, f/t
⚠ A394/A3083
♿ 🥤 🖥 🛍 ℗

Fleet Air Arm Museum

Yeovilton, Ilchester, Somerset BA22 8HT
☎ 0935 840565

Starts with a VC won by shooting
down a Zeppelin airship, then takes
you, via torpedo-dropping and
kamikaze pilots, right up to a
Falklands veteran helicopter with
bullet holes in it. Then you can look
over the second Concorde ever
built, sit in real aircraft cockpits, try
the Super X flight simulator, and
board an aircraft carrier.

🕒 Daily: Apr–Oct 10–5.30;
Nov–Mar 10–4.30
£ Ad £5.50, Chd £3, SC £4.50, f/t
⚠ A303, B3151
♿ 🥤 🍴 🛍 ℗

Glendurgan Garden

Mawnan Smith, Falmouth,
Cornwall TR11 5JZ
☎ 0326 250906

A stunning sub-tropical garden, but
the real excitements are
the Giant's Stride (a
sophisticated rope
swing across a
gap) and the
famous laurel
maze, laid out
in 1833 and
now reopened
after 3 years'
restoration work.

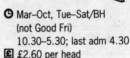

🕐 Mar–Oct, Tue–Sat/BH
 (not Good Fri)
 10.30–5.30; last adm 4.30
💷 £2.60 per head
🅰 4 miles SW of Falmouth
🛆 🅿 NT

Goonhilly Satellite Earth Station

Goonhilly Downs, Helston,
Cornwall TR12 6LQ
☎ 0326 221333

Goonhilly has been in the
forefront of things ever since the
first Russian satellites were
tracked. Nowadays the
giant satellite dishes are
catching, untangling and
bouncing on the products
of very advanced
technology. How it is all
done is explained partly by
exhibits (visitors can
operate a TV dish), partly
by audio-visual displays.

🕐 Apr–Oct h/term, daily 10–6
💷 Ad £3, Chd/SC £1.50
✳ Bus tour of complex
🅰 B3293 from Helston
🛆(res) 🍽 🛆 🅿

Gnome Reserve

West Putford, Bradworthy,
N Devon EX22 7XE
☎ 0409 241435

Over 1,000 garden gnomes and
pixies, plus more than 250 species of
plants in the wildflower and herb
garden. Visitors can see pottery
pixies being baked. Plenty of gnome
video opportunities.

🕐 Mid Mar–Oct, daily 10–6
💷 Ad £1.50, Chd £1, SC £1.25
🅰 A388, 10 miles S of Bideford
🛆 🅿

House of Marbles & Teign Valley Glass

The Old Pottery, Pottery Rd, Bovey Tracey,
Devon TQ13 9DS
☎ 0626 835358

Glass-blowing and the intricate
decorative work is what you see
and admire, but the marbles are
more fun for the young. They have
the largest range of glass ones in the
world.

🕐 All year, Mon–Fri 9–5
 (+Sun/BH 10–3, Easter–Sep)
💷 Adm free
🅰 A382
🛆 🍽 🍴 🛆 🅿

International Helicopter Museum

Weston Airport, Locking Moor Rd,
Weston–super–Mare BS22 8PP
☎ 0934 635227

Irresistible to lovers of whirly-birds.
The museum has more than 50
helicopters and autogiros. You'll
love the simulator: everybody
'crashes' first time.

🕐 Daily: Apr–Oct 10–6; Nov–Mar 10–4
£ Ad £3, Chd £2, SC £2.50, f/t
🅰 M5 jnct 21
♿ ☕ 🛍 🅿

Kents Cavern Showcaves

Ilsham Rd, Wellswood, Torquay TQ1 2JF
☎ 0803 215136

Spectacular
natural limestone
cave system
with evidence of
very early
human
occupation, then of Iron and Bronze
Age inhabitants. Guides deliver a
polished 45-minute tour.

🕐 All year, daily
10–5 (9pm peak
season)
£ Ad £3.25,
Chd (5–15) £2, f/t
🅰 B3199, N of town
centre
☕ 🛍 🅿

Lands End

Sennen, Penzance, Cornwall
TR19 7AA
☎ 0736 871501

A multi-media, multi-sensory
experience. Set out as a kind of
labyrinth of legends, it mixes King
Arthur, Celtic mythology, a kind of
Tolkien quest and lots of lights,
battles in darkness, and that kind
of thing.

🕐 All year, daily 10–dusk
£ Ad £5.50 (£3.50 winter), Chd/♿ free
🅰 End of A30
♿ ☕ 🍴 🛍 🅿

Lydford Gorge

The Stables, Lydford Gorge,
Okehampton, Devon EX20 4BH
☎ 082 282 441/320

Three-mile walk round a scarily
steep wooded ravine, past 27m-high
White Lady waterfall. The Devil's
Cauldron, a sheer-sided pothole
scoured by the River Lyd and tackled
on narrow paths, is the fun bit.

🕐 End Mar–Oct, daily 10–5.30;
Nov–Mar, 10.30–3 (to waterfall only)
£ £2.80 per head
✳ Children's guide
🅰 A386, S of Okehampton

🌳 ☕ 🅿 NT

Lynmouth Cliff Railway & Valley of Rocks
Lynmouth, Devon
☎ 0598 52225 (TIC)

The 274m cliff railway was built in 1890 and lifts gently up a 30° gradient to the top, giving a spectacular view. Take the cliff path to the Valley of the Rocks, where wind has carved limestone pillars into fantastic shapes with names like Ragged Jack, The Devil's Cheesewring and Castle Rock, which sits over a 244m drop to the Bristol Channel.

🕐 Feb–Nov, 8–7
£ Ad 35p, Chd 20p
🅰 From sea front
♿ 🅿

Maritime Museum
The Haven, Exeter EX2 8DP
☎ 0392 58075

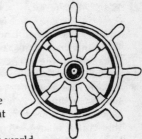

A fleet of floating wonders. There is a dugout, a coracle, a gondola, the smallest boat to circumnavigate the world - a total of more than 100 craft, many of which you can board.

🕐 Daily: Apr–Sep 10–5; Oct–Mar 10–4; last adm 4/3
£ Ad £3.75, Chd £2.25, SC £2.95, f/t
✳ Free ferry trips across canal
🅰 Signs from city centre
🚉 Exeter St Thomas 5 min
♿(res) 🍴 🎁 🅿

Miniature Pony Centre
Moretonhampstead, Devon TQ13 8RG
☎ 0647 432400

It started with miniature ponies and just grew - pintos, palominos, Arabs, shires and Lipizzaners, and still has the amazing miniatures.

🕐 Easter–Oct, Sat–Thu 10.30–5 (Jul/Aug 10–5)
£ Ad £3.95, Chd (3–16) £2.95, SC £3.25, f/t
🅰 B3212, 3 miles W of M'stead
♿ 🧒 🍴 🎁 🅿

🌼 Morewellham Quay Open Air Museum

Morewellham, Tavistock, Devon PL19 8JL
☎ 0822 832766

Until 1900 Morewellham was the most important copper port in Britain. Now the quayside has been turned into a living museum. Wharfs have been restored, period boats sit awaiting cargo, the blacksmith primes his bellows and the staff are all dressed in Victorian costumes. There is also a Victorian farmyard.

🕐 All year, daily 10–5
💷 Ad £6.75, Chd (3–16) £4.60, SC £6, f/t
🅰 A390
♿ ☕ 🍽 🏠 🅿

Mr Bowler's Business

Bath Industrial Heritage Centre,
Julian Rd, Bath BA1 2RH
☎ 0225 318348

J.B.Bowler, plumber, gas-fitter, bell-hanger and entrepreneur, ran the kind of business premises where nothing was thrown away. The factory lay virtually untouched for many years. Now restored, it is a delight. Try the Cherry Ciderette from his Soda Fountain.

🕐 Easter–Oct, daily 10–5;
Nov–Mar, Sat/Sun
💷 Ad £3, Chd/SC £2, f/t
🅰 Nr The Circus
🚻 Bath 25 min
☕ 🏠

Museum of Costume

Assembly Rooms, Bennett St,
Bath BA1 2QH
☎ 0225 461111

This outstanding collection takes you through 400 years of fashion. Displays change, but there are usually around 200 dressed figures in period settings, plus 1,000 accessories and jewellery items from liberty bodices to cuff links.

🕐 All year, Mon–Sat 10–5, Sun 11–5
💷 Ad £3.20, Chd (8–18) £2. Cmbd tkt with Roman Baths [qv]: £6.60/£3.50; f/t
🅰 Nr The Circus
🚻 Bath 20 min
♿ 🏠

Norwood Farm

Bath Rd, Norton St Philip, Bath BA3 6LP
☎ 0373 834356

Thirty different rare breeds of livestock on show, including young animals that can be fed and handled. Organic produce for sale.

🕐 Easter–Sep, daily 11–6
💷 Ad £3, Chd(3+) £1.75, SC £2.50
🅰 B3110, 6 miles S of Bath
♿ 🛝 ☕ 🏠 🅿

Papers Past

Longstone Heritage Centre,
St Mary's, Isles of Scilly
☎ 0720 22924

The Centre's main display is of
shipwrecks, but Papers Past shows
how those wrecks and other events
in history have been reported by the
Press. You can buy newspapers of
the day you were born.

🕐 Apr–Oct, daily 10.30–4.30
💷 Ad £2.50, Chd £1.25, SC £2.25
🅰 Telegraph Rd
♿ ⛲ 🍴 🛍

Paradise Park

Glanmor House, Hayle, Cornwall TR19 6AQ
☎ 0736 753365

A huge collection of rare and
endangered birds on show. The
park runs an owl conservation
project and has flying displays by
eagles (Easter-Oct), as well as being
home to the World Parrot Trust.

🕐 All year, daily 10–5
💷 Ad £4.95, Chd £2.95, SC £3.95
🅰 A30 at Hayle
🚉 Hayle 15 min
♿ ⛲ ☕
🛍 🅿

Pennywell: Devon Farm & Falconry Centre

Buckfastleigh, Devon TQ11 0LT
☎ 0364 642023

Among the attractions (apart from
the toddlers' farm, pets' corner and
falconry demos) are strange delights
such as ferret racing and worm
charming. Events all day.

🕐 Easter–Oct, daily 10–6; Nov–Mar/phone
💷 Ad £3.95, Chd £2.85, SC £3.65, f/t
🅰 A38
♿ ⛲ ☕ 🛍 🅿

Plymouth Dome

The Hoe, Plymouth PL1 2NZ
☎ 0752 600608

There are not many museums
where you can say the views are a
knockout, but it is true in this
imaginative, modern, glass-topped
place where computers, radar and
TV screens take you from Sir
Francis Drake and the Armada up
to life as it is lived today - and
beyond.

Nearby is **Smeaton's Tower**, an
18th-century lighthouse that was
moved from Eddystone Rocks to
Plymouth Hoe in 1884 (☎ 0752
600608).

🕐 All year, daily 9–5.30 (7.30pm summer)
💷 Ad £3.40, Chd £2.25, SC £2.70, f/t
🅰 On The Hoe
🚉 Plymouth 20 min
♿ ☕ 🛍

Poldark Mine Heritage Complex
Wendron, Helston, Cornwall TR13 0ER
☎ 0326 573173

The Romans worked the tin mine nearly 2,000 years ago. Now arranged as 3 separate routes of tunnels and underground chambers, some 61m down, ranging from an easy tour for the less agile to paths for the fit and fearless. Above ground is a well-staged history of Cornish tin. Less seriously, the Cobra Slide and a shooting gallery.

🕓 Easter–Oct, daily 10–6; last adm 4
£ Ad £5.25, Chd(5+) £2.80, £4.25
🄰 B3297, N of Helston
⚑ ☕ 🍴 🛍 🅿

Quince Honey Farm
North Rd, South Molton, Devon EX36 3AZ
☎ 0769 572401

You can see bees, closely and in safety, in observation hives, in specially designed opening hives and even in a post-box.

🕓 Easter–Sep, daily 9–6; Oct 9–5
£ Ad £2.90, Chd £1.45, SC £2.35
🄰 In town
⚑ ☕ 🛍 🅿

Postal Museum
8 Broad St, Bath BA1 5LJ
☎ 0225 460333

On 2 May 1840, the world's first postage stamp was sent from this building. The history is recorded here, and a full-scale Victorian post office shows how things have changed (no queue). Activity room for children.

🕓 All year, Mon–Sat 11–4, Sun 2–4
£ Ad £2, Chd(7+) 80p, SC £1.40, f/t
🄰 City centre
🚉 Bath 15 min
♿(res) ☕ 🛍

Radford Farm & Shire Horse Stables
Radford, Timsbury, Bath BA3 1QF
☎ 0761 470106

The centre of attention is the big shire horses, but what requires more concentration is milking the goats. Then there are nature trails, craft areas and a pets' corner.

🕓 Apr–Oct, daily 10.30–5
£ Ad £3, Chd £2, SC £2.50
🄰 A39, B3115
⚑ ☕ 🛍 🅿

River Dart Country Park

Holne Park, Ashburton,
Newton Abbot TQ13 7NP
☎ 0364 652511

This is action country. The trees are full of rope bridges and Tarzan swings. There is an Anaconda Run which is a kind of adventure tunnel, safe swimming, and riding on those warm, rough Dartmoor ponies.

🕐 Easter–Sep, daily 10–5
💷 Ad £3.75, Chd/SC £2.75, f/t
🅰 A38
🏕 � 🍴 🎒 🅿

Roman Baths Museum

Pump Room, Abbey Churchyard, Bath
☎ 0225 461111

It was a Celtic sacred spring before the Romans turned it into Britain's first health hydro. The water still bubbles up at 46.5°C, and the Great Bath, centrepiece of the complex, is remarkably intact. The museum has coins, jewellery and other artefacts.

The waters can be tasted in the 18th-century **Pump Room** above, the social centre of Georgian Bath. Most, though, prefer to settle for a cup of tea in the elegant surroundings.

🕐 Apr–Sep, daily 9–6;
  Oct–Mar, Mon–Sat 9.30–5,
  Sun 10.30–5
💷 Ad £5, Chd £3. Cmbd tkt
  with Museum of Costume [qv]:
  £6.60/£3.50; f/t
✳ Floodlit Aug, 8pm–10pm
🅰 Next to Abbey
🚏 Bath 10 min
♿ � 🍴 🎒

St Agnes Leisure Park

Penwinnick Rd, St Agnes,
Cornwall TR5 0PA
☎ 0872 552793

Solid attractions like scaled-down replicas of Cornish buildings, a model of Gulliver pegged out by Lilliputians, a film set-style haunted house and dinosaur models. Rides and amusements.

🕐 Easter–Oct, daily 10–4 (last adm);
  summer hols 10–9
💷 Ad £4.10, Chd £1.75, SC £3.60, f/t
🅰 B3277, S of St Agnes
♿ � 🎒 🅿

St Michael's Mount

Marazion, Penzance, Cornwall TR17 0HT
☎ 0736 710507/710265 (tide/ferry)

Spectacular castle and tiny village on a rocky outcrop 91m above the sea. The rising tide cutting visitors off from the mainland is part of the romance of this 14th-century castle, with its cramped passageways, grand banqueting hall and fearsome armoury.

🕐 Apr–Oct, Mon–Fri 10.30–5.30.
  Winter/phone
💷 Ad/Chd £3.20, f/t
🅰 A394
🚏 Penzance 3 miles
� 🍴 🎒 🅿 NT

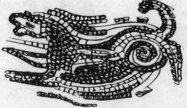

215

Seaton Electric Tramway

Riverside Depot, Harbour Rd, Seaton,
Devon EX12 2NQ
☎ 0297 21702/20375

Britain's only narrow-gauge
tramway system. A real trip back in
time in these open-top gliders, as
they swoop along the scenic 3 miles
beside the River Axe from Seaton to
Colyton.

🕐 Apr–Sep, daily 10–5; Oct, Mon–Fri
💷 Ad £3.70, Chd £2.20, SC £3.20, f/t
🅰 A3052
♿ ⏛ 🎁 🅿

⚘ Secret World

New Road Farm, E Huntspill,
Highbridge, Somerset TA9 3PZ
☎ 0278 783250

There is an observation sett where
you can spy on badgers, a nocturnal
house where animals move in the
dark but are still seen by visitors,
and a spot where foxes sunbathe.
Also on view, 60 or so farm and
wildlife creatures, nature trail, play
areas and visitor centre.

🕐 Mar–Oct, daily 10–6; Nov–Feb,
Sat/Sun 10–5
💷 Ad £3.75, Chd £2.50, SC £3.25
🅰 M5 jnct 22/23
♿ ⏛ 🎁 🅿

Shire Horse Adventure Park

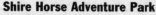

Tredinnick, Wadebridge,
Cornwall PL27 7RA
☎ 0841 540276

The shire horses are the stars, and
have their own show along with
miniature Shetland ponies. In Old
Macdonald's Barn, children have
hands-on experience of rabbits,
lambs, goats and pot-bellied pigs.
There is a nature trail, farm
museum and agility course, and a
soft-play 'house' on 4 floors.

🕐 Apr–Oct, daily 10–5 (not Sat in Oct)
💷 Ad £4.50, Chd (3–14) £2.95, SC £4
🅰 A39, 8 miles N of Newquay
♿ ⏛ 🍴 🎁 🅿

South Devon Railway

The Station, Buckfastleigh,
Devon TQ11 0DZ
☎ 0364 642338

The romance of steam joins the
delights of Devon scenery, with a
maze and riverside picnic area.
There is even a First Class Pullman
car for this 14-mile round trip. Then
you can look in the engine sheds.
See the **Buckfast Butterfly Farm
& Otter
Sanctuary** nearby
(☎ 0364 642916).

🕐 Phone for
timetable
💷 Vary

🅰 A38
♿ ⚘ ⏛ 🍴 🎁 🅿

SS Great Britain
Great Western Dock,
Gas Ferry Rd, Bristol BS1 6TY
☎ 0272 260680

The world's first propeller-driven ocean vessel, the creation of that great engineer, Isambard Kingdom Brunel. Abandoned in the Falklands and brought home to Bristol, restoration is well under way - as you can see.

🕐 Daily: summer 10–6; winter 10–5
🎫 Ad £2.90, Chd(5+) £1.90, SC £1.90
🅰 City docks
🚉 Bristol Temple Meads (bus link)
♿ 🚻 🏠 🅿

Tamar Otter Park & Wild Wood
North Petherwin, Launceston,
Cornwall PL15 8LW
☎ 0566 785646

One of the few places where you can see otters in natural conditions. Feeding time is at noon and 3.30 daily. In the 20 acres of Wild Wood, the red deer roam free.

🕐 Apr–Oct, daily 10.30–6
🎫 Ad £3.80, Chd (5–16) £2.30, SC £3.30
🅰 B3254, NW of Launceston
♿ 🅰 🚻 🏠 🅿

Theatre Royal Tour
Sawclose, Bath BA1 1XX
☎ 0225 448815

The 45-minute tour of this much admired Georgian theatre takes you behind the scenes and sketches the colourful history. Look out for the ghost of the Grey Lady. You don't have to book.

🕐 All year, Wed/Sat 11am
🎫 Ad £2, Chd £1
🅰 City centre
🚉 Bath 10 min

Tropical Bird Gardens
Rode, Bath BA3 6QW
☎ 0373 830326

More than 1,000 exotic birds in 17 acres of landscaped gardens and woods. Flamingoes and penguins by the lakes, brilliantly coloured parrots and macaws in the trees. The Woodland Steam Railway runs in summer.

🕐 Daily: summer
   10–6; winter
   10–dusk;
   last adm 1hr
   before
🎫 Ad £3.90,
   Chd (3–15) £2,
   SC £3.40
🅰 Btwn A36 & A361
♿ 🚻 🏠 🅿

🦔 Twiggy Winkies Farm & Hedgehog Hospital

Moorview Farm, Denbury Rd,
East Ogwell, Newton Abbot TQ12 6BZ
☎ 0626 62319

Feed a lamb, groom a pony, ride a donkey, collect eggs, cuddle a rabbit, and more. You can also learn how sick and injured hedgehogs are cared for. Cuddling is difficult.

🕐 Easter–Oct, daily 10–5
💷 Ad £3.50, Chd (2–14) £2.25, SC £3
🅰 A381, SW of Newton Abbot
♿ (res) ☕ 🎁 🅿

Underground Passages

Boots the Chemist Corner, High St, Exeter
☎ 0392 265887

People with claustrophobia should not go on the tour. If you do, it is a revelation of how ingenious the 13th-century monks and city fathers were. The narrow passages are part of a complex series of tunnels which supplied water to the entire city. A museum explains all.

🕐 Easter–Oct, Mon–Sat 10–4.45
(last tour); winter/phone
💷 Ad £2.10, Chd £1.10, f/t
🅰 City centre
🚋 Exeter Central 5 min

Wheal Martyn China Clay Heritage Centre

Carthew, St Austell, Cornwall PL26 8XG
☎ 0726 850362

The great slashes of white against the heathland mark where china clay is dug out. At the centre are 2 china clay works beside a giant waterwheel, and a site trail and video tell the history of the industry. There are also 26 acres with adventure and nature trails and working steam engines.

🕐 Apr–Oct, daily 10–6 (last adm 5)
💷 Ad £3.90, Chd £1.95, SC £3.10, f/t
🅰 B3274, 2 miles N of St Austell
🚋 St Austell (bus link)
🚻 ☕ 🎁 🅿

Wheelwright & Gypsy Museum

Loxton, Axbridge, Somerset BS26 2HX
☎ 0934 750841

The wheels being made would fit caravans once used by Romany gypsies, and those caravans, brightly painted, are here along with old-fashioned fairground exhibits like swing boats, hooplas, coconut shies and the rest.

🕐 Jul–Aug, daily 10–7; Apr–Jun/Sep–Oct,
Wed–Sun 10–7; winter/phone
💷 Ad £2.50, Chd £1, SC £1.75, f/t
🅰 A38, 15 miles S of Bristol
♿ 🚻 ☕ 🎁 🅿

218

Willows & Wetlands Centre

Meare Green Court,
Stoke St Gregory, Taunton TA3 6HY
☎ 0823 490249

The same family have been making baskets here for 150 years. Now they reveal the whole process, from willow tree to wastepaper basket. Genuine rural skills. Also environmental display.

🕒 All year, Mon–Sat 9–5.
Tours: Mon–Fri 10–12/2–4
💷 Ad £1.95, Chd £1, SC £1.50
🛣 A361, A378
♿ 🏠 🅿

♥ Wookey Hole Caves

Wookey Hole, Wells, Somerset BA5 1BB
☎ 0749 672243

Two thousand years ago, primitive man used the mysterious network of caves and underground rivers to bury their dead. Today it is brought spectacularly to life with huge, strategically lit stalagmites and stalactites. Outside is an Edwardian fairground, an old-fashioned penny arcade and the last mill in Britain making hand-made paper.

🕒 Daily: summer 9.30–5.30;
winter 10.30–4.30
💷 Ad £5.60, Chd (4–16) £3.60,
SC £4.90, f/t
🛣 2 miles W of Wells
🔥 🍴 🏠 🅿

World in Miniature

Bodmin Rd, Goonhavern, Truro TR4 9QE
☎ 0872 572828

Detailed models of the world's famous buildings, a full-size replica of Tombstone, wildest town in the West, a wrap-round cinema, and entertaining activities. A world of fun.

🕒 Apr–Oct, daily 10–4 (last adm);
Jul/Aug 10–5
💷 Ad £4, Chd £1.75, SC £3.50, f/t
🛣 B3285, E of Goonhavern
♿ 🍵 🏠 🅿

World of Model Railways

Meadow St, Mevagissey,
St Austell, Cornwall PL26 6UL
☎ 0726 842457

Miniature creations of whole chunks of landscape, including an English suburb, an Alpine ski resort and Cornwall's china clay mining. Some 2,000 models, with 50 trains running on time through it all.

🕒 Easter/May–Oct, daily 11–5
💷 Ad £2.25, Chd/SC £1.75, ♿free
🛣 Nr town centre
♿ 🏠

Yarner Wood National Reserve

Nr Bovey Tracey, Devon
☎ 0626 832330 (Warden)

A mixture of mainly oak woodland
and wild Dartmoor heathland,
rising to 300m above sea level at its
western end. There is a 1½-mile
nature trail and a twice-as-long
Woodland Walk. Good spot for a
picnic. Becky Falls [qv] is a couple
of miles up the road.

🕐 All year, all day
£ Adm free
/!\ Btwn Manaton and Bovey Tracey
℗

Yelverton Paperweight Centre

4 Buckland Tce, Leg o' Mutton,
Yelverton, Devon PL20 6AD
☎ 0822 854250

Hundreds and hundreds of glass
paperweights wink, twinkle, glare
and flash at you. The other half of
the Centre sells modern and artist-
made paperweights. Very tempting.

🕐 All year. Days/times vary, phone
£ Adm free
/!\ A386, B3212
♿ 🚻 🛍 ℗

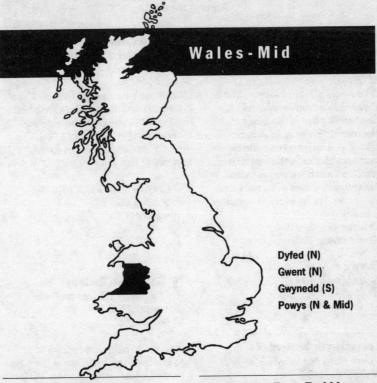

Dyfed (N)
Gwent (N)
Gwynedd (S)
Powys (N & Mid)

Aberaeron Sea Aquarium & Animal Kingdom

2 Quay Parade, Aberaeron,
Dyfed SA46 0BT
☎ 0545 570142

The big aquarium tanks have special displays, including one on how animals camouflage themselves. You can see how scorpions tend their young, pet a rabbit or two, and see things in microscopic detail.

🕐 Easter–Oct, daily 11–5
   (summer 10.30–8.30)
£ Ad £2.50, Chd £1.25, SC £2
🅰 Harbour
♿ (res) 🛍

Abergwynant Farm Trekking Centre

Dolgellau, Gwynedd LL40 1YF
☎ 0341 422377

The centre has 50 horses and points out that riding experience is not essential. Minimum age for riders on 2-hour trips is 8 years. Very scenic, good hacking country. Hard hats provided - you have to look after the other end yourself.

🕐 All year, daily. Phone re times
£ £7.50 (1hr); £10.50 (2hr)
🅰 Off A493
🅿

Aberystwyth Cliff Railway
Cliff Railway House,
Cliff Tce, Aberystwyth SY23 2DN
☎ 0970 617642

Created as a 'conveyance of Gentlefolk', this is the longest electric cliff railway in Britain, taking you 131m to find the biggest camera obscura in the world, from which you can see 26 peaks and 1,000 square miles of country and shoreline. Trains every 10 minutes.

🕒 Easter–Oct, daily 10–6
(end Jul/Aug 10–9)
💷 Rtn: Ad £1.85, Chd £1, SC £1.60, f/t
🅰 N end of prom
🚉 Aberystwyth 10 min
☕

Aberystwyth Yesterday
6 Laura Place, Aberystwyth SY23 2AU
☎ 0970 617119

Quirky, personal collection of items from old adverts and kitchen equipment to historical documents, creating a picture of a century of life in the 'capital' of Mid Wales.

🕒 Apr–Nov, daily 10–5; Dec–Mar, Mon–Sat 10–5
💷 Adm free
🅰 Above Aberystwyth rlwy stn
🚉 Aberystwyth

Aeron Express Aerial Ferry
The Quay, Aberaeron, Gwent
☎ 0970 617642

Originally devised in 1885 by Capt John Evans, the 4-seater carriage is hung on cables over the harbour, and ferrymen work pulleys to whisk passengers across to the opposite quay.

🕒 Easter/Spr BH–Sep, daily 10–6
💷 50p single, £1 rtn
🅰 Harbour
🅿

Bala Lake Railway
The Station, Llanuwchllyn, Bala,
Gwynedd LL23 7DD
☎ 067 84 666

Add the exciting cindery scent of steam trains to a trip along the edge of the largest natural lake in Wales. Its 4½ miles contain a legendary hidden palace and the gwyniad, a trout-like fish very rarely caught.

🕒 Easter–Oct; phone re times
💷 Rtn: Ad £4.80, Chd £2.80, f/t
✳ Bonfire Night Special, Santa train
🅰 A494, B4403
☕ 🅿

Borth Animalarium

Borth, Dyfed SY24 5NA
☎ 0970 871224

Small, friendly animals, with the
emphasis on observation. You can
marvel at mice as well as wallabies,
lemurs and bright, tropical birds.

🕐 Daily: Easter–Sep 10–6; Oct 11–4
💷 Ad £2, Chd £1, SC/♿ £1.25
🅰 On sea front
⧚ Borth 15 min
♿ ☕ 🎁 🅿

Bwlch Nant-yr-Arian Visitor Centre

Rheidol Forest, Ponterwyd, Powys
☎ 0974 261404

Victorian writer and poet George
Borrow had this place in mind
when he wrote *Wild Wales*. Walks
from the Visitor Centre include
trails along old trenches used to
carry water to lead mines, and a 5-
mile marked track punctuated by
wood sculptures.

🕐 Easter–Sep, daily 10–5;
Jul/Aug 10–6
💷 Adm free
🅰 A44, W of Ponterwyd
♿ ⛺ ☕ 🅿

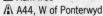

Cantref Trekking & Riding Centre

Upper Cantref, Brecon, Powys LD3 8LR
☎ 0874 86223

Cantref offer lessons for complete
beginners, and experienced guides
accompany riders. They insist upon
(and provide) hard hats.

🕐 All year, daily 10.30 & 2
💷 £6.50 (1hr), £9.50 (2hr),
£16.50 (day ride)
✳ Farmhouse B&B
🅰 A40, B4558
🅿

Cardigan Island Coastal Farm Park

Clyn–Yr–Ynys, Gwbert–on–Sea,
Cardigan SA43 1PR
☎ 0239 612196

The Dyfed Wildlife Trust looks
after this nature reserve on the
largest island off the Dyfed coast.
Rare bottle-nosed dolphins are
visitors, there is a colony of Atlantic
grey seals and a flock of wild Soay
sheep, plus rare British breeds and a
llama. The new waterfowl centre
has an international roll call of duck
and geese.

🕐 All year, dawn–dusk
💷 £1 at turnstile
🅰 A487, B4548
☕ 🅿

🏵 Centre for Alternative Technology

Machynlleth, Powys, SY20 9AZ
☎ 0654 702782

Seven acres showing how the world can live without destroying natural resources and the environment. Wind, power, solar energy, organic growing and free animals...there is even a water-powered cliff railway near the adventure playground.

🕐 Daily: summer 10–5; winter 11–4. Phone first
💷 (Inc rail up) Ad £4.50, Chd £2.50, SC £3.50, f/t
🅰 A487, 2 miles N of Machynlleth
♿ 🍴 🅿

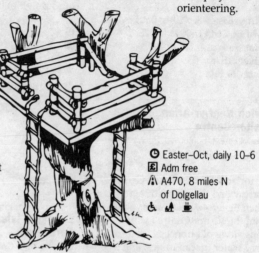

Coed y Brenin Forest Park

Ganllwyd, Dolgellau, Gwynedd LL40 2HY
☎ 0341 40666

Wander among a sea of fir trees, or tear around the mountain bike centre before picnicking by the water. Children's play area, orienteering.

🕐 Easter–Oct, daily 10–6
💷 Adm free
🅰 A470, 8 miles N of Dolgellau
♿ 🏕 ☕

Ceredigion Museum

Coliseum, Terrace Rd, Aberystwyth SY23 2AQ
☎ 0970 634212

Cinema turned museum with locally important memories, including a completely re-created traditional cottage and some model boats.

🕐 All year, Mon–Sat 10–5 (+Sun/sch hols)
💷 Adm free
🅰 Via TIC/town centre
🚉 Aberystwyth 5 min
♿

Derwen Welsh Cob Centre

Pennant, Llanon, Dyfed FY23 5JN
☎ 0545 570250

The Welsh cob is perhaps the most versatile breed of horse in the world. Tough workhorse, easy to ride, elegant and with a light carriage, the breed has been exported all over the globe. Here, visitors can see the pick of the breed - in harness, at play or peacefully raising foals.

🕐 All year, daily 11–5
💷 Ad £2.50, Chd 50p
🅰 B4577, N of Aberaeron
♿ 🛍 🅿

Felin Crewi Watermill

Felin Crewi, Penegoes,
Machynlleth, Powys SY20 8NH
☎ 0654 703113

From raw grain
to buttered
toast...you can
see the whole
process at this
working water-
powered flour mill.
Riverside walk with
nature trail.

🕒 Easter–Sep, daily 10–5
💶 Ad £1.60, Chd 80p, SC £1.30, f/t
🅰 A489, 2 miles E of Machynlleth
♿ ☕ 🏠 🅿

Gigrin Farm Nature Trail

South St, Rhayader, Powys LD6 5BL
☎ 0597 810243

A working farm with
access to specially
designed nature,
farm and
woodland walks.
Lots of wildlife to
spot.

🕒 Easter–Nov,
daily 10–8
💶 Ad £1.50, Chd 50p
🅰 A470
⛺ 🅿

Felinwynt Butterfly Centre

Rhos Maen, Felinwynt, Cardigan SA43 1RT
☎ 0239 810882

Even the tearoom here is tropical.
Multi-coloured foreign butterflies
and exotic plants,
and an exhibition
about rainforests.

🕒 Last Sun May–last
Sun Sep, daily
10.30–5
💶 Ad £1.75,
Chd 75p,
SC £1.50
🅰 A487, N of Cardigan
♿ ☕ 🏠 🅿

Harlech Castle

Castle Square, Harlech,
Gwynedd LL46 2YH
☎ 0766 780552

This is what
medieval
castles are all
about. A World
Heritage Site,
Harlech Castle
perches high on
a crag and is
defended by
circles within circles. Soaked in
history, it was built by James of St
George, one of the top castle
builders of all time. It also has great
views of rugged Snowdonia.

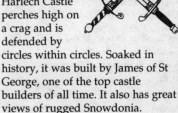

🕒 Late Mar–late Oct, daily
9.30–6.30; late Oct–late Mar
9.30–4 (Sun 11–4)
💶 Ad £2.90, Chd/SC £1.80, f/t
🅰 A496
🚋 Harlech 5 min
🅿 🎧

Lake Vyrnwy Reserve

Bryn Awel, Llanwddyn, Powys SY10 0LZ
☎ 0691 73278

One of the gem reserves run by the RSPB. Woodland, forest, lakes, sparrow-hawks, buzzards and peregrine. You should also look for badgers, red squirrels and rare butterflies. Visitor centre.

🕐 Apr–Xmas
   daily 10.30–5.30; end
   Dec–Mar, Sat/Sun only
£ Adm free
⚠ B4393
♿ ☕ Ⓟ

Llanarth Pottery

Llanarth, Dyfed SA47 0PU
☎ 0545 580584

Introduce yourself to the magic of mud. Here you can see clay turned into stoneware, shaped, coloured and baked by craftsmen - and you can take some home.

🕐 Workshop: all year, Mon–Fri 9–5
£ Adm free
⚠ A487, 3½ miles S of Aberaeron
♿ 💼 Ⓟ

Llanfair Slate Caverns

Llanfair, Harlech, Gwynedd LL46 2SA
☎ 0766 780247

Put on a hard hat and wrap up warm to see the great caves hollowed out by slate miners 61m underground. The work was all done by candlelight, and when your guide switches off the lights it is immense, dark and spooky.

🕐 Easter–end Oct, daily 10–5
£ Ad £2.30, Chd £1.30,
   SC £1.40, f/t
✳ Children's farmyard
⚠ A496, 1 mile S of Harlech
🚉 Pensarn 15 min
☕ Ⓟ

▼ Llywernog Silver-Lead Mines

Ponterwyd, Aberystwyth SY23 3AB
☎ 0970 85620

The huge, working waterwheel is an exciting introduction to mining adventure. You can tour underground with cap lamps, see where ore was processed and try your hand at panning for the silver it contained.

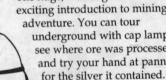

🕐 Easter–Oct, daily 10–6
£ (Inc tour) Ad £3.95, Chd £2.25,
   SC £3.50, f/t
⚠ A44, 1 mile W of Ponterwyd
♿ ☕ Ⓟ

Maes Artro Tourist Village

Llanbedr, Barmouth, Gwynedd LL45 2PZ
☎ 0341 23467

A street of old-time shops, an
adventure playground with totem
poles, giant outdoor draught games,
an aquarium, plus an original
Spitfire with recorded dogfight
sounds (you can retreat to a real air
raid shelter). RAF rescue helicopter,
military tanks and rural heritage
exhibition.

🕒 Easter–Sep, daily 10–5.30
£ Ad £2.75, Chd/SC £2
✳ Free return visits during same week
🅰 A496
⊞ Llanbedr Halt 5 min
♿ ☕ 🎁 🅿

Model Aircraft Exhibition

Brooklands, Cellan, Lampeter SA48 8HX
☎ 0570 422604

For aeromodellers and aviation
buffs, 500 model planes, each a
different type or mark, and most of
which have flown with the RAF or
Fleet Air Arm. Children must be
over 10.

🕒 Jul–Sep, Wed only.
   Tours: 10.30/1.45/3.15
£ Ad 60p, Chd 20p (donation)
🅰 B4343, N of
   Lampeter
🅿

Mr Puzzle's Jigsaw World & Teddy Bear Wonderland

10 Broad St, Hay-on-Wye, Herefordshire
☎ 0497 821440

Browsers are welcome in this town
of bookshops (one stocks 250,000
secondhand volumes) and this
specialist shop with 1,000 teddy
bears and 2,500 jigsaw
puzzles offers a lot
of browsing.

🕒 All year, Mon–Sat
   9–6, Sun 10–6
£ Adm free
🅰 Opp town clock
🅿

Museum of Welsh Woollen Industry

Drefach–Felindre, Llandysul,
Dyfed SA44 5UP
☎ 0559 370929

Wool, weaving and cloth were a
major industry and this is bang in
the centre of where it all happened.
There is a working mill and you can
see how it was done.

🕒 Apr–Sep, Mon–Sat 10–5;
   Oct–Mar, Mon–Fri 10–5
£ Ad £1, Chd 50p,
   SC 75p, f/t
🅰 A484, near
   Pentrecagal
☕ 🅿

Offa's Dyke

Offa's Dyke Assoc, Knighton,
Powys LD7 1EW
☎ 0547 528753

King Offa of Mercia dug this big
ditch and threw the spoil up as an
8m-high bulwark to defend his
kingdom. Modern walkers are
grateful to him. Offa's Dyke Path
runs 80 miles from Chepstow to
Prestatyn. It can be ambled on over
short stretches, while fit, pioneering
spirits do it all.

🕒 All year, dawn–dusk
£ Adm free
🅰 Consult TIC
♨ Ⓟ

Powis Castle

Welshpool, Powys SY21 8RF
☎ 0938 554336

The famous gardens surrounding
this lavish castle often feature on
TV gardening programmes. The
amazing gilded state bedchamber
dates from 1688.

🕒 Apr–Jun/Sep–Oct Wed–Sun;
    Jul/Aug Tue–Sun. Castle/Mus:
    12.30–4. Gdn: 11–5.30
£ All-in: Ad £5.80, Chd £2.90.
    Gdn only: £3.80/£1.90
✳ Braille guide
🅰 A483
♿ ♨ 🏠 Ⓟ N

Severn Valley Quad Trekking

Broniarth, Newtown, Powys SY16 3AN
☎ 0686 625560

The 4-wheel all-terrain machines are
a kind of cross between Land
Rovers and ride-on lawnmowers,
and can go up hills, down dales and
along the beds of mountain streams
on this 300-acre territory. Helmets,
waterproofs and guides provided.

🕒 All year: daily 10–6
£ Big Trek (over 12s): £10
    Mini Trek (6–12): £5
🅰 Off A483, N of Newtown
♨ Ⓟ

Shell Island

Llanbedr, Gwynedd LL45 2PJ
☎ 034 123 217/453

Shell Island is a much-loved
camping resort and beach area, with
as many as 200 different kinds of
shells to gather. Also noted for its
wildflowers and good rock pools for
children to explore.

🕒 All year, daily
£ £3 per car
🅰 A496, signs from Llanbedr Bridge
♿ ⛽ ♨ 🍽 🏠 Ⓟ

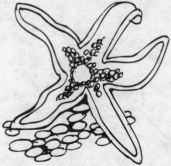

Talyllyn Railway
Wharf Station, Tywyn, Gwynedd LL36 9EY
☎ 0654 710472

It has been running since 1865 from a little town on a 3-mile beach, up into the mountainside. The beach is brilliant, the mountain has great walks, and the station has a museum packed with engines and railway relics.

🕐 Apr–Oct, daily; phone re times
🎫 Ad £6.80, Chd £3.40,
   SC £5.80, f/t
🅰 A493, B4405
♿ ☕ 🅿

Vale of Rheidol Railway
Park Ave, Aberystwyth SY23 1PG
☎ 0970 625819

Twelve miles to Devil's Bridge on narrow gauge steam tracks, with spectacular, wooded views on one of the Great Little Trains of Wales. The return trip lasts 3 hours, single journey 1 hour.

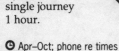

🕐 Apr–Oct; phone re times
🎫 Vary
🅰 Next to rlwy stn
🚉 Aberystwyth
☕ 🅿

Welsh Royal Crystal
5 Brynberth Industrial Estate, Rhayader,
Powys LD6 5EN
☎ 0597 811005

High class glass. See crystal blown and handcut by craftsmen on a conducted tour covering the whole process from molten blob to finished piece.

🕐 All year, daily 9.30–4.30.
   Tours Mon–Fri
🎫 Ad £2, Chd/SC £1, f/t
🅰 Signs from A44 and town clock
♿ ☕ 🛍 🅿

Welshpool & Llanfair Light Railway
The Station, Llanfair Caereinion,
Powys SY21 0SF
☎ 0938 810441

Started in 1903 to take local people to market, saved by steam enthusiasts and now a tourist favourite. The railway runs 8 miles through choice scenery to Welshpool where you can visit Powis Castle [qv].

🕐 Jul–Sep, daily; other times/phone
🎫 Rtn: Ad £6, Chd(5+) £3, SC £5.20, f/t
🅰 A458 (for either stn)
🚉 Welshpool (mainline) 1 mile
♿ ☕ 🅿

W H Smith Museum

24 High St, Newtown, Powys SY16 2NP
☎ 0686 626280

In 1792, W.H.Smith Esq began
selling newspapers in London's
New Fetter Lane. The story from
that modest start to the familiar
retail chain of today is told in this
small museum, which has
models of early station
bookstalls and a 'Read all
about it!' newsboy
among other
memorabilia. The shop
below is as it was in
1927 - except for the
merchandise.

🕐 All year, Mon–Sat 9–5.30
   (not some BH)
💷 Adm free
🛣 Town centre
🚉 Newtown 10 min
🛍

Ynys-Hir Bird Reserve

Eglwysfach, Machynlleth, Powys SY20 8TA
☎ 0654 781265

The biggest complex of bird hides
and marked walks in Wales. The
reserve covers woodland, wetland,
peat bog and open hillside. All 3
species of woodpecker and 64 other
species breed here
regularly. Visitor
centre.

🕐 All year: daily
   9–9/dusk
💷 £3 (RSPB
   members free)
🛣 A487, 6 miles
   S of Machynlleth
♿ (res) ☕ 🛍 🅿

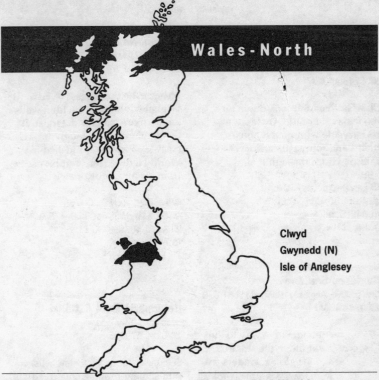

Clwyd
Gwynedd (N)
Isle of Anglesey

Alice In Wonderland Visitor Centre

3/4 Trinity Square, Llandudno LL30 2PY
☎ 0492 860082

Alice Liddell, the little girl to whom Lewis Carroll first told the stories of *Wonderland* and *Through the Looking Glass*, used to go to Llandudno on holiday. That connection led, in 1933, to a statue of the White Rabbit. The Centre has walk-through settings with tapes of the tales.

🕒 Easter–Nov, daily 10–5;
   Nov–Mar, Mon–Sat 10–5
£ Ad £2.50, Chd £1.95, SC £2.20
🛣 Town centre
🚉 Llandudno 2 min
♿ Ⓟ

Anglesey Bird World

Dwyran, Anglesey, Gwynedd LL61 6RP
☎ 0248 440627

You can start at Swan Lake, but the main attraction is 1,000 birds in the tropical house. A mini zoo and railway, goats, sheep and donkeys, a bouncy castle and more.

🕒 Easter–Sep, daily 10–6
£ Ad £2.85, Chd/SC £1.85, f/t
🛣 A4080
♿ ☕ Ⓟ

Anglesey Model Village

Parc Newborough, Anglesey,
Gwynedd LL61 6RS
☎ 0248 440477

Play Gulliver and look down on a
model layout of the Anglesey
countryside with model houses,
towns and tourist attractions. Model
railway chugs through it all.

🕒 Easter–Oct, daily 10–5
£ Ad £1.50, Chd/SC £1
🅰 A4080, nr Newborough
♿ ☕ Ⓟ

Anglesey Sea Zoo

Brynsiencyn, Anglesey, Gwynedd LL61 6TQ
☎ 0248 430411

Imaginative way to look
at life in the sea around
Anglesey. Undersea
'wreck' area, walk
through a tide
tank and a big
fish 'forest'.
You can touch
some of the sea
creatures.

🕒 Daily: Mar–Oct
10–5, Nov–Feb
11–3
£ Ad £3.95,
Chd £2.95, SC £3.50, f/t
🅰 A4080
♿ ☕ Ⓟ

Beaumaris Castle

Beaumaris, Gwynedd LL58 8AP
☎ 0248 810361

Meant to be the biggest of Edward
I's castles, with walls within walls
within more walls and a moat. It
would have been a tough nut to
crack if he had ever finished it.
World Heritage Site, but best seen
from the air, unfortunately.

🕒 Apr–Sep, daily 9.30–6.30;
   Oct–Mar, Mon–Sat 9.30–4, Sun 11–4
£ Ad £1.50, Chd/SC £1
🅰 A545
Ⓟ EH

Beaumaris Gaol & Court

Beaumaris, Gwynedd
☎ 0286 679098

See dark, damp Victorian cells,
punishment rooms and a treadmill,
before standing in the dock where
people were once sent to the
gallows. Not many people stay long
in the condemned cell.

🕒 Late May–Sep, Mon–Fri 11–5.30,
   Sat/Sun 2–5; Easter/May, Sat/Sun only
£ Ad £2.80, Chd/SC £2.10, f/t.
   Gaol only: £2.30/£1.55
🅰 Town centre

Butlin's Starcoast World
Pwllheli, N Wales LL53 6HX
☎ 0758 701441

Butlins in full swing. White-knuckle boomerang roller coaster, space-age flight simulator, giant cable car and more. Try the hurtling thrill of the (sub-tropical) watersplash, the fun fair, or gentler pleasures like the boating lake and miniature railway.

🕐 Mid Feb–Oct 10–10; last adm 4
£ Ad £5.50, Chd(3+) £5, SC £3
⚠ A497, E of Pwllheli
🚏 Butlin's stop
♿ ⚕ 🍴 🛍 Ⓟ

Betws-y-Coed Motor Museum
Betws–y–Coed, Gwynedd LL24 0AH
☎ 0690 710760

Vintage Aston Martins, Maseratis, Rolls-Royces, as well as beautifully polished MGs and Morrises. A child's racing car, motorbikes, and a jet engine used in a world speed record. *Brrm brrm.*

🕐 Mar–Nov, daily 10–6
£ Ad £1, Chd 60p, SC 65p
⚠ Town centre, nr rlwy stn
🚏 Betws–y–Coed
♿ Ⓟ

Bryntirion Open Farm
Dwyran, Anglesey, Gwynedd
☎ 0248 430232

On the edge of miles of sand dunes in a National Nature Reserve. You can get close to the farm animals, then look at rare breeds or roam lake and woodland walks.

🕐 Late May–Sep, Sun–Fri 10.30–5.30
£ Ad £2.25, Chd £1.80
⚠ A4080
♿ 🦽 ⚕ 🛍 Ⓟ

Butterfly Palace
Menai Bridge, Ynys Mon, Gwynedd LL59 5RP
☎ 0248 712474

Hundreds of exotic butterflies lilting past, and a very creepy crawly insectarium and reptiles who watch *you*. The pets' corner has animals you won't mind petting.

🕐 Daily: Mar–Oct 10–5; Nov–Dec 11–3
£ Ad £3.25, Chd £1.95, SC £2.75, f/t
⚠ From Menai/Britannia bridges
♿ 🦽 ⚕ 🛍 Ⓟ

Caernarfon Air World

Caernarfon Airport,
Dinas Dinlle, Gwynedd LL54 5TP
☎ 0286 830800

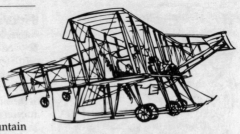

It all started with a beach airstrip which became a World War II airfield and then, with helicopters, a mountain rescue centre. Now you can sit in aircraft cockpits and play with controls, view a Dambusters exhibit and goggle at a huge model aircraft display. Caernarfon Pleasure Flights, also at the airport, runs pleasure trips over Snowdon.

🕐 Daily: Mar–Sep 9–5, Oct–Nov 9–4.30
£ Ad £3.50, Chd £2.50, f/t
🅰 A487, A499
♿ ☕ 🍴 🅿

Caernarfon Castle

Castle Ditch, Caernarfon LL55 2AY
☎ 0286 677617

Showpiece castle where Prince Charles was invested as Prince of Wales in 1969. Castle's story is told in audio-visual display in Eagle Tower, overlooking Menai Strait. Regimental museum of Royal Welch Fusiliers includes huge Russian cannon. Only one Welshman has ever been Prince of Wales: Llewellyn the Last.

🕐 Late Mar–late Oct, daily 9.30–6.30; late Oct–late Mar, 9.30–4 (Sun 11–4)
£ Ad £3.50, Chd/SC £2.50, f/t
🅰 Town centre
🛍 🅿 EH

Conwy Butterfly Jungle

Bonlondeb Park, Conwy, Gwynedd
LL32 8DU
☎ 0492 593149

The Welsh love butterflies. You will see metal ones decorating houses throughout the principality. This collection of tropical butterflies amid exotic flowers has egg-to-adult flier displays.

🕐 Daily: Apr–Sep 10–5.30, Oct 10–4
£ Ad £2.50, Chd/SC £1.75, f/t
🅰 Next to town centre quay
🚉 Conwy 3 min
♿ 🛍 🅿

Conwy Valley Railway Museum

The Old Goods Yard, Betws–y–Coed, Gwynedd
☎ 0690 710568

Steam fans will go loco. This site contains everything from full-size steam engines to elaborate working model railway systems. You can go on train *and* tram rides, then eat in the dining car.

🕐 Easter–Nov, daily 10.30–5.30
£ Ad £1 Chd/SC 50p; train ride 75p
🅰 Next to rlwy stn
🚉 Betws–y–Coed
♿ ☕ 🅿

Dolwyddelan Chocolate House

Old School, Church St, Dolwyddelan,
Gwynedd LL25 0SG
☎ 06906 579

From this ancient village set in
forest comes a Welsh dragon - made
in red chocolate. You can watch all
the stages of creating chocs from a
special gallery. Mouth watering.

🕐 Easter–Oct, daily 10–4.30
   (Sat/Mon no chocolate–making)
£ Adm free
🅰 A470
⊞ Dolwyddelan 3 min
♿ 🍴 🎁 🅿

Ffestiniog Power Station

Tan–y–Grisiau, Blaenau Ffestiniog,
Gwynedd LL41 3TP
☎ 0766 830310

They run the millions of gallons of
water down pipes and through
turbines to create electricity. Then
they use some of that to pump the
water back up, and then...
Fascinating introduction to hydro
electricity.

🕐 May–Oct, Sun–Fri 10–4.30
£ Ad £2.50, Chd/SC £1.35
🅰 A496
🍴 🅿

Erddig

Nr Wrexham, Clwyd LL13 0YT
☎ 0978 355314

This stately country house has 2
halves, Upstairs and Below Stairs,
so you can see how the other half
lived. Perfectly
preserved
kitchens, laundry
and staff quarters,
while overhead a
state bedroom,
fine pictures
and good
living. Good
gardens,
video
presentations.

🕐 Apr–Aug Sat–Wed: Gdn 11–6,
   Hse 12–5
£ Upstairs: Ad £5, Chd £2.50.
   Below Stairs: £3.20/£1.60
🅰 A483
⊞ Wrexham General 1½ miles
♿ 🍴 🍽 🎁 🅿 NT

Ffestiniog Railway

Harbour Station, Porthmadog,
Gwynedd LL49 9NF
☎ 0766 512340

Not so much a railway, more an
enchanting trip through
the Snowdonia
national park. There
are 6 halts between
Porthmadog and
Blaenau Ffestiniog,
13½ miles of
narrow gauge
mainline in
miniature, spiralling
up past woods
and waterfalls.
Historic (and modern)
rolling stock.

🕐 Mar–Nov, daily; phone re times
£ Vary; 1 chd (5–15) free with each adult
✳ Jazz trains etc/summer
🅰 A487, A497
⊞ Porthmadog/B Ffestiniog
♿ 🍴 🍽 🅿

Gloddfa Ganol Slate Mine
Blaenau Ffestiniog, Gwynedd
☎ 0766 830664

The world's biggest slate mine.
Watch open-cast blasting from the
Mining Museum after the
underground tour, and see
craftsmen work the slate. Land
Rover guided tours extra. Train ride
and play areas.

🕐 Easter–Oct, Mon–Fri 10–5.30
💷 Ad £3.75, Chd £2
🚗 A470, N of town
♿ 🍴 🎒 🅿

Great Orme Mines
Great Orme, Llandudno LL30 2XG
☎ 0492 870447

Complex set in Great Orme Country
Park. Travel in cable-drawn 1902
tramcars to the summit for the
views. The free shuttle bus is to
Bronze Age copper mines where the
digging is now done by
archaeologists. There is an audio-
visual display, and then you have
the park with rare wildlife and an
adventure playground.

🕐 Mar–Nov, daily 10–5
💷 Ad £3.80, Chd £2.40, f/t
✳ Mineral specimens for sale
🚗 Tram/shuttle bus from Great
   Orme Summit
♿

Greenwood Centre
Port Dinorwic, Gwynedd LL56 4QN
☎ 0248 671493

Entertaining look at trees, covering
Welsh oaks and druids, rainforests
and the biggest trees on earth. How
to build an oak-framed house, and
find out which grows faster, a
tropical or British tree. Topped off
with a forest walk.

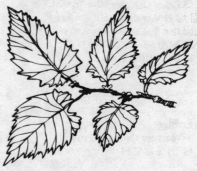

🕐 Mar–Oct, daily 10–5.30
💷 Ad £2.75, Chd £1.85, SC £2.25
🚗 A487, N of Caernarfon
♿ 🎒 🅿

Harlequin Puppet Theatre
Cayley Promenade, Rhos on Sea,
Colwyn Bay
☎ 0492 548166

Britain's first permanent puppet
theatre delights not only children
but puts on special shows for the
adults, too. A class act.

🕐 Summer, daily 3 & 8; other sch hols
   3pm; term time/phone
💷 Ad £3.35, Chd £2.50, SC £2.85
🚗 Signs from prom
♿ 🅿

Inigo Jones Slateworks

Y–Groeslon, Caernarfon, Gwynedd
☎ 0286 830242

Craftsman-carved memorials,
plaques, ornaments. Young visitors
can have a go at engraving and
watch polishing techniques.
Calligraphy exhibition.

🕐 Easter–Sep, Mon–Fri 9–5,
   Sat–Sun 10–4; Sep–Mar Mon–Fri 9–5
💷 Ad £2, Chd/SC £1.50
🛣 A487, 6 miles S of Caernarfon
 ♿ ☕ 🅿

Llanberis Lake Railway

Llanberis, Caernarfon LL55 4TY
☎ 0286 870549

Set in Padarn Country Park which
has woodland walks to see old
mines (and the mine hospital). One
of the Great Little Trains of Wales
puffs gently round the lake, which
is a busy water sports centre.

🕐 Daily: Mar 11.30–3, Apr–May 11–4,
   Jun–Sep 11–4.30
💷 Rtn: Ad £3.60, Chd £2, f/t
✳ Picnic stop at Cei Llydan
🛣 A4086
 ♿ 🚻 ☕ 🅿

Llanfairpwll

Llanfairpwll Stn, Llanfairpwll,
Gwynedd LL61 5UJ
☎ 0248 717171

All the action is because Llanfair etc
has the longest place name in
Britain, or perhaps the world.
Tourist complex around the station,
selling the world's longest platform
ticket. The name was actually
invented by a Victorian
businessman to promote tourism.

🕐 Easter/May–Oct, Mon–Sat 9–5.30,
   Sun 10.30–5; Nov–Apr, Mon–Sat 9–5,
   Sun 12–5
💷 Adm free
🛣 A5
🚉 Llanfairpwll
 ♿ ☕ 🅿

Llangollen Canal

Ribbon Plate, The Old Wharf,
Trevor, Llangollen LL20 7TP
☎ 0978 823 215

Start at the wharf for trips along
Telford's astonishing 'canal in the
sky', the Pontcysyllte Aqueduct,
37m above the Dee Valley. There is
a choice of trips, including horse-
drawn boats, and a range of prices.
The nearby Canal Exhibition Centre
has all the facts.

🕐 Mar–Oct, daily 10–7.30
💷 40 min trip: Ad £1, Chd 50p;
   other trips/phone
🛣 A539, 4 miles E of Llangollen
 ♿ 🍴 🅿

Llechwedd Slate Caverns

Blaenau Ffestiniog, Gwynedd LL41 3NB
☎ 0766 830306

Victorian slate mining lives again
with this meticulous re-creation.
Two underground, floodlit, tours
include trip on miners' tramway
and an underground lake. On the
surface, a 19th-century village
complete with shops, pub and
lock-up.

🕐 Daily: Mar–Sep 10–5.15 (last tour);
   Oct–Feb 10–4.15
💷 Tour: Ad £4.75, Chd £3.25, SC £4.25
🅰 A470
♿ ☕ 🅿

Loggerheads Country Park

Loggerheads, Mold, Clwyd CH7 1SW
☎ 0352 85586

Nature trails in the countryside of
old lead mines. The pit wheel still
stands, and the watermill, with
visitor centre, has been
painstakingly restored. Special
events for children.

🕐 All year, daily
💷 Adm free
🅰 A494, 4 miles from Mold
♿ 🍴 🅿

Museum of Childhood

1 Castle St, Beaumaris,
Anglesey LL58 8AP
☎ 0248 712498

Nine rooms of nostalgia packed
with teddy bears, toy trains, dolls'
house...2,000 items spanning 150
years, all about being young.

🕐 Mid Mar–Oct, Mon–Sat 10.30–5.30,
   Sun 12–5 (last adm 4.30/4)
💷 Ad £2.50, Chd £1.25, SC £1.50
🅰 Opposite castle
🛍 🅿

Penrhos Coastal Park

Ynys Mon, Anglesey LL65 2JD
☎ 0407 760949

This 200-acre estate lies in an Area
of Outstanding Natural Beauty, and
has coastal walks with panoramic
views. The woods are home to
badgers, the sand and sea hosts to
oyster-catchers, cormorants and
great-crested grebe.

🕐 All year, daily.
   Info centre: May–Sep 11–3
💷 Adm free
✳ Cycling restricted
🅰 A5 nr Holyhead
♿ ☕ 🅿

Penrhyn Castle

Bangor, Gwynedd LL57 4HN
☎ 0248 353084/371337 info

Looks real, but the castle is a Victorian creation, packed with goodies like full-size train engines, adventure playground and, because the people who built it became rich selling slate, solid slate beds and tables.

In **Bangor**, there is a garden next to the cathedral made only from plants mentioned in the Bible - including nettles!

🕐 End Mar–end Oct, Wed–Mon.
Castle: 12–5 (Jul/Aug 11–5). Grnds: 11–6
💷 Ad £4.40, Chd £2.20, f/t
🛣 A5/A55
♿ ⚶ ☕ 🎒 Ⓟ NT

Piggery Pottery

Y Glyn, Llanberis, Gwynedd LL55 4EL
☎ 0286 872529

You don't just watch skilled people produce immaculate pots, you can take a lump of clay and have a go yourself, and then paint the result.

🕐 All year, daily 9.30–6
(w/ends Nov–Mar 11–4)
💷 Adm free
🛣 A4086
♿ ☕ Ⓟ

Porthmadog Pottery

Snowdon Mill, Snowdon St,
Porthmadog LL49 9DF
☎ 0766 512137

Take home a pot you made by yourself, or just enjoy the squish of moulding clay. You can paint your own pot or watch experts show how it should be done.

🕐 Apr–Oct, Mon–Fri 9.30–5.30
(+ w/ends Jul/Aug). Other times/phone
💷 Ad 50p, Chd free. Charge for DIY potting
🛣 Signs from town centre
🚉 Porthmadog 15 min
♿ 🎒 Ⓟ

Portmeirion Village

Portmeirion, Gwynedd, LL48 6ET
☎ 0766 770228

An entire fantasy village, each house different, as if an Italian architect had bumped into Walt Disney and together they had reconstructed interesting buildings they had found all over Britain. Fountains, waterfalls, statues. Setting for the cult TV series *The Prisoner*.

🕐 All year, daily 9.30–5.30
💷 Ad £3, Chd (5–15) £1.30, SC £2.40
🛣 A496, A487
☕ 🍽 🎒 Ⓟ

Power of Wales

Amgueddfa'r Gogledd,
Llanberis, Gwynedd LL55 4UR
☎ 0286 870636

Audio-visual linking of the mining
of coal, slate and gold, and how it
all ties in with the 10 miles of
tunnels creating the Dinorwig
storage power station.
Imaginatively presented by Merlin
the wizard from the King Arthur
legends.

🕐 Phone for details
💷 Ad £5, Chd £2.50, SC £3.75
🅰 A4086 Llanberis by–pass at
    Padarn Lake
♿ 🅿

Queen of the Sea Cruises

Ger–y–Parc, 20 Ffordd Eryri, Caernarfon
☎ 0286 672772

A 40-minute cruise to see the
dramatic seashore and cliffs
splitting Anglesey from the rest of
Wales, and the bridge which spans
the gap.

🕐 Easter–Oct, daily 11–6
💷 Ad £2.75, Chd £1.50, SC £2.30
🅰 Harbour/Slate Quay
☕ 🅿

Rhyl Sea Life Centre

East Parade, Rhyl, Clwyd LL18 3AF
☎ 0745 344660

Recently opened aquarium you can
walk through past sharks, stingray,
octopus, down to oysters and
shrimps.

🕐 Daily: Jun–Oct 9.30–7, Nov–May 9–5
💷 Ad £4.25, Chd £2.95, SC £3.45
🅰 On sea front
🚉 Rhyl 10 min
♿ ☕ 🅿

Rhyl Skytower

West Promenade, Rhyl, Clwyd
☎ 0745 355068 (TIC)

Swirl gracefully, turning as you rise
the 73m to the tower's top from
where you have an eagle's-eye view
of the North Wales coast.

🕐 Easter/Apr–May, Sat/Sun 10–6;
    Jun–mid Sep, daily 10–6 (8pm Jul/Aug)
💷 Ad £1.10, Chd/SC 80p
🅰 On prom
🚉 Rhyl 10 min
♿ 🅿

Rhyl Sun Centre

Promenade, Rhyl, Clwyd LL18 3AQ
☎ 0745 344433

Indoor water fun. Watch from an
overhead railway as others swim
through waves; battle through a
tropical rainstorm or test your
courage on the huge Dragon Flume.
Natural wet weather entertainment.

🕐 Late Mar–late Sep, daily 10–8.30;
   Oct/phone
💷 Ad/Chd(3+) £3.75
🅰 On sea front
♿ ☕ 🍴 🅿

South Stacks Cliff Reserve

Swn-y-Mor, South Stack,
Holyhead LL65 1TH
☎ 0407 764973

Puffins, razorbills and guillemots
nest here in thousands, and the
visitor centre overlooks auk nesting
site. Closed circuit TV watches
nearby nests. Marked walks along
tops of sheer cliffs.

🕐 Apr–Sep, daily 11–5
💷 Adm free
🅰 Signs from Holyhead/Trearddur
☕ 🅿

Snowdon Mountain Railway

Llanberis, Caernarfon LL55 4TY
☎ 0286 870223

A 2½-hour up and downer. The
steam loco climbs 4 ⅝ miles up
Snowdon, pushing a passenger
coach. It takes about an hour and
there is not an inch of level track all
the way. Very busy attraction; fine
days in mid summer are packed, so
arrive early. On a clear day you can
see Ireland's Wicklow Mountains
and peaks in the Lake District.
Other days Snowdon's head is in
cloud and you can see nothing: they
might even cancel the train.

🕐 Mid Mar–Nov, 9–5; phone re timetable
💷 Pk season rtn: Ad £13, Chd £9.30
✳ Advance bookings
🅰 A4086
♿ ☕ 🅿

Sygun Copper Mine

Beddgelert, Gwynedd LL55 4NE
☎ 076686 595/564 info

Caverns in a canyon where copper
was mined until 1903. Tunnels lead
through stalagmites and stalactites
with traces of copper, gold and lead;
40-minute tour with audio-visuals,
lighting effects and lots of steps.

🕐 Apr–Sep, Mon–Fri 10–5, Sat 10–4,
   Sun 11–5; Oct–Mar/phone
💷 Ad £3.75, Chd £2.50, SC £3.25
🅰 A498, A4085
☕ 🅿

Victorian School of Three Rs

Parade St, Llangollen, Clwyd
☎ 0978 860794

Re-creation of Victorian schoolroom
where you can see what it was like
to go to school in the 19th-century.
Those not paying attention will
have to stand in the corner.

🕑 Easter–Oct, daily 11–4.30
💷 Ad £1, Chd 65p, SC 85p
🅰 Signs from Market St car park
♿ 🅿

Welsh Mountain Zoo

Colwyn Bay, Clwyd
☎ 0492 532938

The animals are in natural
surroundings. Flying sea eagles and
chimpanzees in groups are the great
attractions.

🕑 Daily: Apr–Sep 9.30–5;
   Oct–Mar 9.30–4
💷 Ad £4.95, Chd £2.95, SC £3.95, f/t
🅰 A55
🚌 Colwyn Bay (free minibus)
♿ ☕ 🅿

Wylfa Nuclear Power Station

Cemaes Bay, Anglesey,
Gwynedd LL67 0DH
☎ 0407 733431

This 2-reactor station produces
enough electricity to power 2
Liverpool-sized cities. Visitor centre
with detailed exhibition of how
domestic nuclear power is created.

🕑 All year, daily 9.30–4.30 (tours/phone)
💷 Adm free
🅰 Nr Cemaes/A5025
♿ ☕ 🅿

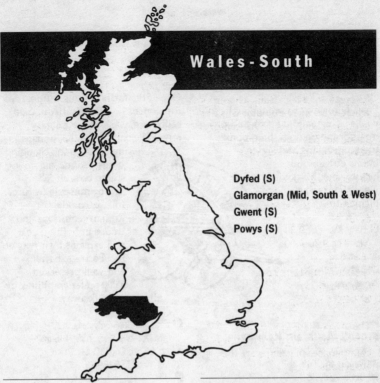

Wales - South

Dyfed (S)
Glamorgan (Mid, South & West)
Gwent (S)
Powys (S)

Barry Island Pleasure Park
Barry, S Glamorgan CF6 8ZD
☎ 0446 741250/732844

A short walk from the sands of
Whitemore Bay is the bright,
swirling, whirling fun of more than
50 rides, including the white-
knuckle log flume. Also Bugs Attic
multi-media show for children.
Smartyboots should know Barry is
not an island, but a peninsula.

🕐 Easter–Sep, daily 11–10
💷 Per ride/groups of rides
✳ Fri 'Family Night'; Tue/Thu special offers
🅰 M4 jnct 33
🚏 Barry Island (opp)
🚇 🅿

 ## Big Pit Mining Museum
Blaenafon, Gwent NP4 9XP
☎ 0495 790311

Wales' oldest colliery. After a 90m
descent in the pit lift cage, visitors
don real miners' safety helmets and
lamps and ex-miners give them a
tour of coal faces and pit pony
stables. On the surface are an engine
house, pithead baths and exhibition.

Pontypool & Blaenafon Railway
runs steam trains to Big Pit (☎ 0495
792263, evenings).

🕐 Mar–Nov, daily; other times/phone.
   1st tour 10am/last 3.30
💷 Ad £4.95, Chd (5–16) £3.50, SC £4.50, f/t
✳ No under 5s down pit
🅰 A4042, A4043
♿ 🎪 🚇 🅿

Brecon Beacons Mountain Centre

Libanus, S of Brecon, Powys LD3 7DW
☎ 0874 623366

From here you can see the highest peaks in the national park and pick up information on sailing, pony trekking, caving and sights in this outstanding beauty spot. Marked woodland walks, picnic sites.

🕑 Daily: Mar–Oct 9.30–5;
   Nov–Feb 9.30–4.30
£ Adm free
🅰 A470
♿ ♨ ☕ Ⓟ

Brecon Mountain Railway

Pant Station, Merthyr Tydfil,
M Glamorgan CF48 2UP
☎ 0685 722988

One of the Great Little Trains of Wales covers this 2-mile steam-driven narrow gauge trip from outside Merthyr Tydfil to a lake at the foot of the Brecon Beacons.

🕑 Apr–Oct, daily;
   phone re times
£ Ad £3.90,
   Chd £1
🅰 A465, 3
   miles N of Merthyr
♿ ☕ Ⓟ

Caerleon Roman Fortress Baths

High St, Caerleon, Gwent NP6 1AE
☎ 0633 422518

One of the farthest flung outposts of the Roman Empire, Caerleon, then called Isca, was a major military town. The baths were the Romans' leisure centre: pool, changing rooms and mosaic floors still to be seen. The nearby museum features full-size models of Roman centurions and troops in fighting gear, and explains their way of life. Fortress, barracks and well-preserved 5,000-seater amphitheatre all a short walk away.

🕑 Late Mar–late Oct, daily 9.30–6.30;
   late Oct–late Mar, 9.30–4 (Sun 2–4)
£ Ad £1.50, Chd/SC £1, f/t
🅰 M4 jnct 25, B4596
Ⓟ EH

Caerphilly Castle

Caerphilly, M Glamorgan CF8 1JL
☎ 0222 883143

Massive, moated, 30-acre castle was state of the art in 13th-century defensive systems, has a tower which leans more than the one at Pisa, and an armour and shield bedecked Great Hall. Built by Norman conqueror Gilbert the Red.

🕑 Late Mar–late Oct, daily 9.30–6.30;
   late Oct–late Mar, 9.30–4 (Sun 2–4)
£ Ad £2, Chd/SC £1.50
🅰 A468
▦ Caerphilly 10 min
Ⓟ EH

Cardiff Castle

Castle St, Cardiff CF1 2RB
☎ 0222 822083

Started life as a Roman fort, became a medieval fortress and then a millionaire's showplace home. Look for marble mantelpieces inset with precious lapis lazuli, and silver, copper and brass world map set in the floor. Also museums of 1st Queen's Dragoon Guards and Welch Regiment, with models, uniforms, medals and taped battle sounds.

🕐 Daily: Mar/Apr/Oct 10–5;
   May–Sept 10–6; Nov–Feb 10–4.30
£ (Inc museums) Ad £3.30 Chd/SC £1.70
/i\ City centre
▦ Cardiff Central 5 min
& ♿

Carreg Cennan Castle

Tir-y–Castell Farm, Trapp,
Llandeilo, Dyfed SA19 6UA
☎ 0558 822291

A steep climb to this dramatic ruin which perches on top of a sheer limestone cliff like something out of Tolkien's *Lord of the Rings*. Walled passage to cave under castle, and you have to go through hill farm where you can examine rare farm breeds.

🕐 Daily: late Mar–late Oct 9.30–7.30;
   late Oct–late Mar, 9.30–4
£ Ad £2, Chd/SC £1.50
/i\ A483, 4 miles SE of Llandeilo
♨ P EH

Chepstow Castle

Bridge St, Chepstow, Gwent NP6 5EZ
☎ 0291 624065

Norman castle, centre of Civil War battles, set in medieval town. Has exhibition of life-size Roundheads and Cavaliers, and weapons. You can see where Henry Marten, who signed King Charles' death warrant, was later locked up for 20 years.

🕐 Late Mar–late Oct, daily 9.30–6.30;
   late Oct–late Mar, 9.30–4 (Sun 11–4)
£ Ad £2.90, Chd/SC £1.65, f/t
/i\ M4 jnct 22, A466
▦ Chepstow 5 min
P EH

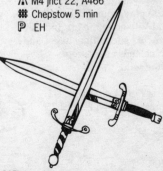

Coney Beach Pleasure Park

Esplanade, Porthcawl,
M Glamorgan CF36 5BY
☎ 0656 788911

Up-to-date version of an old-fashioned promenade fun fair, with shooting galleries, bingo, helterskelter and carousel. Roll up, roll up.

🕐 Easter–Sep, daily 11–7 (10pm Jul/Aug)
💷 Adm free
☕ 🅿

Cosmeston Lakes Country Park & Medieval Village

Lavernock Rd, Penarth,
S Glamorgan CF62 5TR
☎ 0222 701678

Roam in 200 acres of meadows, lakeside and woods. Rich in bird life, riding available, and an adventure playground. Visit the Medieval Village in the grounds, a reconstructed site with cottages and barns, plus hens and sheep wandering wild.

🕐 Daily: summer 11–5; winter 11–3
💷 Park: free. Village: Ad £1, Chd 75p
🅰 B4267
♿ ⛲ ☕ 🅿

Cwmcarn Forest Drive

Cross Keys, Gwent, NP2 7FA
☎ 0495 272001

This 7-mile drive gives panoramic views across 8 counties from marked mountain and woodland walks. Adventure play areas and visitor centre.

🕐 Apr–Oct, daily 11–7
💷 £2 per car
🅰 M4 jnct 28, A467
♿ ⛲ ☕ 🅿

Dan-yr-Ogof Showcaves

Abercraf, Upper Swansea Valley,
W Glamorgan SA9 1EJ
☎ 0639 730284/730693

Nine miles of caves, and more still unexplored, make this the biggest showcave site in Western Europe. Main visitor area is a half-mile maze of stalactites and stalagmites. Cathedral Cave has 13m 'Dome of St Pauls', Bone Cave displays cave archaeology. Outside is an 'Iron Age' farm, dinosaur park and shire horse centre.

🕐 Late Mar–late Oct, daily 10–5
💷 Ad £5.50, Chd £3.50
🅰 A4067 btwn
   Swansea/Brecon
☕ 🅿

🌺 Dolaucothi Roman Gold Mines

Pumsaint, Llanwrda, Dyfed SA19 8RR
☎ 0558 650359

The Romans were serious
gold miners here by
AD75, and built refining
aqueducts for open cast
and deep mines to
supply the imperial
mint. Guided
underground tours, gold
panning, video display
and visitor centre.
No samples.

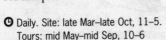

🕐 Daily. Site: late Mar–late Oct, 11–5.
  Tours: mid May–mid Sep, 10–6
💷 Tour/Site: Ad £4.80, Chd £2.40.
  Site: £3/£1.50
✳ No under 5s underground
🅰 A482, btwn Lampeter/Llanwrda
♿ ☕ 🛍 🅿 NT

Felin Geri Centre

Cwm–cou, Newcastle Emlyn, Dyfed
☎ 0239 710810

How-they-lived-then comes alive
with a 16th-century working
watermill, falconry displays,
sawmill and fishing museum. Also
adventure fort.

🕐 Easter–Oct, daily 10.30–5.30
💷 Ad £2, Chd £1, SC £1.50
🅰 B4333, NW of Newcastle Emlyn
⛺ ☕ 🛍 🅿

Folly Farm

Begelly, Kilgetty, Dyfed SA68 0XA
☎ 0834 812731

Working dairy farm gives visitors a
go at hand-milking cows.
Sheep dog demos.
Indoor and outdoor
play areas, nature trail,
rides on farm trailer.
After that there are
good beaches around
Saundersfoot, including
one at Wiseman's Bridge
where Winston
Churchill watched D-
Day rehearsals.

🕐 Easter–Sep, daily 10–5.30; Oct 11–5
💷 Ad £3, Chd (3–15) £2, SC £2.50
✳ Rally kart tracks extra
🅰 A478 btwn Tenby/Narberth
♿ ☕ 🍴 🅿

Gower Farm Museum

Llanddewi, W Glamorgan
☎ 0792 391247

How it was to farm in Wales 100
years ago, with live animals and
displays of old buildings and
techniques. Meet today's animals on
the farm trail. Near
smuggling coast with
spectacular cliff walks
and good beaches.

🕐 Jun–Sep, daily
  10–5; Apr–May,
  Sat–Sun only
💷 Ad £1.25,
  Chd/SC 75p
🅰 A4118
♿ ☕ 🅿

Groggshop

Broadway, Pontypridd,
M Glamorgan CF37 1BH
☎ 0443 405001

Pontypridd produced Tom Jones
and Evan and James James who
wrote the Welsh national anthem,
but this attraction is mainly for
rugby fans to see unique sculptures
(groggs) of famous rugby players,
plus other celebrities. Retail shop -
fun if you are in the area.

🕐 All year. Mon–Fri 9–5,
　　Sat 10–5, Sun 2–4
£ Adm free
/i\ Town centre
⏣ Pontypridd 15 min

Gunsmoke & Seven Sisters Sawmills

Seven Sisters, Neath,
W Glamorgan SA10 9EI
☎ 0639 700288

The attraction is not the working
sawmill or woodworking
demonstrations but the Wild
West re-creation of
Gunsmoke Cowboy
Town, where folk
dress up and have
daily shoot-outs.
Also an adventure
playground.

🕐 Apr–Sep, daily 11–6
£ Ad £1.90, Chd/SC
　　£1.70
/i\ A4109, 7 miles NE
　　of Neath
☕ P

Gwili Railway

Bronwydd Arms Station,
Carmarthen SA33 6HT
☎ 0267 230666

Steam trains run 1½ miles along
GWR branch line to secluded
woodland riverside. Elaborate
working signal box to see. You can
have a snack in 1968 BR buffet car.

🕐 Late July/Aug 11–4.30;
　　phone re timetable
£ Ad £2.50 Chd/SC £1.25
/i\ A484, 3 miles from town centre
♿ ☕ P

Kidwelly Castle

Castle Rd, Kidwelly, Dyfed SA17 5BQ
☎ 0554 890104

Spectacular 12th-century castle
　　stronghold overlooking River
　　　Gwendraeth. With round
　　　towers and keeps, it is the
　　　castle of children's imaginings.
　　　Much used by film makers in
　　　knightly epics. Guided tours.

🕐 Late Mar–late Oct, daily
　　9.30–6.30;
　　late Oct–late Mar 9.30–4
　　(Sun 11–4)
　£ Ad £2, Chd/SC £1.50
　/i\ A484
⏣ Kidwelly 10 min
☕ 🍽 🛍 P EH

Llancaiach Fawr Living History Museum
Nelson, Treharris, M Glamorgan CF46 6ER
☎ 0443 412248

Restored haunted manor house once visited by Charles I. Guides are servants in 17th-century dress. Visitors can dress up, lounge in furniture and try the stocks. Has ghost tours in winter.

🕘 All year, Mon–Fri 10–5, Sat–Sun 10–6;
last adm 3.30/4.30
💷 Ad £3.30, Chd £1.90, SC £2
🅰 B4254 Nelson/Gelligaer
♿ 🍴 🛍 🅿

Manorbier Castle
Manorbier, Tenby, Dyfed
☎ 0834 871394/871317

Overlooking the sea, with a beach below the ramparts, this 13th-century castle has waxwork displays of Tudor children, a dungeon and drawbridge. If it seems familiar it is because the BBC filmed *The Lion, the Witch and the Wardrobe* in and around Manorbier.

🕘 Easter–Sep, daily 10.30–5.30
💷 Ad £1.50, Chd/SC 60p
🅰 A4139, B4585
🚉 Manorbier 15 min
🛍 🅿

Llangloffan Farmhouse Cheese Centre
Castle Morris, Dyfed
☎ 03485 241

Follow cheese-making from milking time to Welsh rarebit. The farmhouse has Jersey cows and other animals you can get close to. Play area.

Nearest town is Fishguard, site of last invasion of British mainland. French forces led by an Irish-American were routed largely by the ladies of the town in 1797.

🕘 Cheese–making:
May–Sep,
Mon–Sat 10–12.30;
Apr/Oct,
Mon/Wed/Thur/Sat
💷 Ad £1.75, Chd £1.25
♿ ☕ 🛍 🅿

Margam Country Park
Port Talbot, W Glamorgan, SA13 2TJ
☎ 0639 871131/881635

Parkland covering 800 acres. See Iron Age pigs, fallow deer, and the under 8s beating a path through one of the world's largest hedge mazes. Also visit the midget houses of Fairytale Land Village. Pony trekking and adventure playground, plus fine orangery for adults.

🕘 Apr–Sep,
daily 10–7;
Oct–Mar,
Wed–Sun 10–5;
last adm 5/3
💷 Ad £3.10,
Chd/SC £2.05,
f/t
🅰 M4 jnct 38
♿ ☕ 🛍 🅿

Maritime & Industrial Museum

Museum Square, Maritime Quarter,
Swansea SA1 1SN
☎ 0792 650351/470371

Warehouse/dockside display of
marine and Swansea history with
working woollen mill. Mumbles
railway, first in world to carry
passengers, ran along dockside.
Crazy lighthouse, fun statues
including one of Captain Cat from
Dylan Thomas' *Under Milk Wood*.

🕐 All year, Tue–Sun/BH 10.30–5.30
🅳 Adm free
🅰 By Marina
♨ Swansea High St 15 min
♿ ☕ 🛍 🅿

Model House Craft & Design Centre

Bull Ring, Llantrisant,
W Glamorgan CF7 8EB
☎ 0443 237758

Visitors are not encouraged at the
Royal Mint, located at the local
business park, but in this ex-
workhouse you can see a unique
exhibition of historic minting
machinery and coins. High
class craftsmanship displays
in adjoining modern visitor
centre.

🕐 May–22 Dec, Tue–Sun 10–5;
    2 Jan–Apr Wed–Sun 12–5
🅳 Adm free
🅰 Old Town
♿ 🛍 🅿

Monmouth Castle & Museum

Priory St, Monmouth, Gwent NP5 3XA
☎ 0600 713519 (Museum)

The castle is a ruin, but is
where Henry V was
born. The museum
has some of the very
best bits of the life
of another hero,
Horatio Nelson,
including the
fighting sword he
carried at Trafalgar.

🕐 All year, Mon–Sat
    10–1 & 2–5, Sun 2–5
🅳 Castle: free.
    Mus: Ad £1, SC 50p,
    Chd free
🅰 Town centre
♿ 🛍 🅿

Museum of the Home

7 Westgate Hill, Pembroke SA71 4LB
☎ 0646 681200

Amazing collection of household
objects of the last 300 years.
Everything from
kettles to boot
polish and
scrubbing
boards like great
granny used to
use. Especially good
on games, toys, reading
and illumination.

🕐 May–Sep, Mon–Thu 11–5
🅳 Ad £1.20, Chd/SC 90p
    (no under 5s)
🅰 Opp castle
♨ Pembroke 15 min
🛍 🅿

National Coracle Centre & Flour Mill

Cenarth Falls, Newcastle Emlyn, Dyfed SA38 9JL
☎ 0239 710980

See folk make and sail one-man basket boats of designs dating back to Roman times. Nine varieties of Welsh coracles plus international versions. Display on poaching techniques, all housed in working water-powered 17th-century flour mill.

🕐 Easter–late Oct, Sun–Fri 10.30–5.30
💷 Ad £1.50, Chd 50p
🛣 A484, W of Newcastle Emlyn
♿

Oakwood Park

Canaston Bridge, Dyfed SA67 8DE
☎ 0834 891376/891373

One ticket lets you ride roller coasters, drive go-karts, visit a Western gold-rush town, all set in 80 landscaped acres - and you ride into town on a miniature train.

🕐 Late Mar–Sep,
daily 10–6;
Oct/phone
💷 Ad/Chd(10+) £7.45;
Chd (3–9) £6.45;
SC £5.45
🛣 A4075, 2½ miles
SW of Narberth
♿ ☕ 🍴 🅿

Oceanarium & Marine Life Centre

42 New St, St David's, Dyfed SA62 6SS
☎ 0437 720453/721665

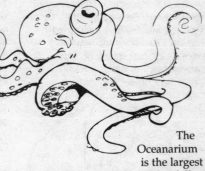

The Oceanarium is the largest sea aquarium in Wales with a full range of sharks, rays, giant clams, octopuses and the rest. The Marine Life Centre is based on the local seaside with rock pool life, sea caves and a tank showing how ships are wrecked.

St David's is Britain's smallest city and pilgrims have visited the cathedral for 1,000 years. A medieval pope declared two pilgrimages to St David's were equal to one to Rome. Three equalled a visit to Jerusalem.

🕐 Daily: summer
9–6; winter 10–4
💷 Ad/SC £2.25,
Chd £1.50
🛣 Town centre
♿ ☕ 🎁 🅿

Parc le Breos Burial Chamber
Parkmill, W Glamorgan

Ancient site of Stone Age settlers
with 6,000-year-old burial chamber
foundations. Further up the little
valley, Cathole Cave contained
bones of woolly rhinoceros and
mammoth. Not dramatic, but
interesting.

🕐 All year
💷 Adm free
🅰 A4118

Pembrey Country Park
Pembrey, Dyfed
☎ 0554 833913

A 7-mile stretch of sands butts on to
this 520-acre park for the active and
energetic. Everything from
birdwatching to a dry ski slope,
taking in pony treks, forest walks,
play areas and a narrow gauge
railway.

🕐 All year, dawn–dusk
💷 £2.50 per car; activity prices
🅰 A484, 5 miles W of Llanelli
♿ ☕ 🅿

Pembroke Castle
Pembroke, Dyfed SA71 4LA
☎ 0646 684585/681510

Great castle, one of the finest of the
many in Wales, perched on a bluff
above Pembroke River. Huge inside
with 23m-high round tower
with views for miles.

🕐 Daily: Apr–Oct 9.30–6; Nov–Mar 10–4
💷 Ad £2, Chd(5+)/SC £1.20, f/t
🅰 End of Main St
🚃 Pembroke 15 min
♿ ☕ 🎁 🅿

Pembrokeshire Motor Museum
Keeston Hill, Haverfordwest,
Dyfed SA62 6EJ
☎ 0437 710950

Collection of cars and motorcycles
from the earliest to modern classics,
Brighton Run veterans and grand
prix contenders. Also the largest
model car collection in
the UK. For
the non-
motoring
minded, the
visitor centre
includes
pottery and
crafts.

🕐 Easter–Oct,
   daily 10–6
💷 Ad £2.50, Chd £1, SC £2, f/t
🅰 A487, 4 miles NW of
   Haverfordwest
♿ 🍴 ☕ 🅿

Penscynor Wildlife Park

Cilfrew, Neath, W Glamorgan SA10 8LF
☎ 0639 642189

Penguins, flamingoes and a tropical
house with free-flying exotic birds.
You can also see monkeys,
aquarium fish and sea lions, and be
chairlifted to the alpine slide, drive
bumpa boats and radio-controlled
cars. Adventure playground.

🕐 Daily: Easter–Sep 10–6;
　Oct–Mar 10–dusk
🅔 Ad £4, Chd(3+)/SC £3, f/t
🅰 Off A465 at Aberdulais r/about
♿(res) ☕ Ⓟ

Sirhowy Valley Country Park

Cross Keys, Gwent
☎ 0495 270991

This lovely 1,000-acre park offers
riverside and woodland walks,
heritage sites, picnic areas and a
visitor centre.

🕐 Daily; car park closes 5.30 (Apr–Sep),
　4.30 (Oct–Mar)
🅔 Adm free
🅰 A4048
♿ ⛺ Ⓟ

Plantasia

Parc Tawe, North Dock,
Swansea SA1 2AL
☎ 0792 474555

Massive
computer-
controlled
glasshouse
with 3 climate zones:
desert, humid and
tropical, with plants to suit. There
are 5,000 of them in 850 varieties,
complete with matching lizards,
insects, snakes and spiders. Aviary
with exotic birds.

🕐 All year, Tue–Sun
　10.30–5.30
🅔 Ad £1, Chd/SC 75p
🅰 Eastern approach
　(Fabian Way), signs
🚉 Swansea 10 min
♿ 🛍 Ⓟ

🕯 Techniquest

72 Bute St, Pierhead, Cardiff CF1 6AA
☎ 0222 460211

Exciting, active, hands-on popular
science. Walk through 'solid' objects
and 'fly' in a mirror. Holograms,
computer chips and magnets
produce magical and instructive
effects.

🕐 All year, Tue–Fri+sch hols 9.30–4.30,
　Sat/Sun/BH 10.30–5
🅔 Ad £3, Chd/SC £1.60, f/t
🅰 End of Bute St
🚉 Bute Road 5 min
♿ ☕ 🛍 Ⓟ

Teifi Valley Narrow Gauge Railway

Station Yard, Henllan, Llandysul,
Dyfed SA44 5TD
☎ 0559 371077

Steam and diesel engines puff and chuff 1½ miles through woods to viewable engine shed. Playgrounds, barbecue areas, nature trail. Train ticket lasts all day.

🕐 Easter–Oct, daily 10.30–5
£ Ad £3, Chd(3+) £1.50, SC £2.75
🅰 A484, 3 miles E of Newcastle Emlyn
♿ ☕ 🅿

Tredegar House

Newport, Gwent NP1 9YW
☎ 0633 815880

Beautiful 17th-century stately home in 90 acres. Carriage rides and guided tours of house (including servants' quarters) and garden, but you make your own way to boating lake, craft centre and adventure play farm.

🕐 Easter–Sep,
   Wed–Sun/BH
   11.30–4;
   Oct Sat/Sun only
£ Ad £3.50,
   Chd/SC £2.70
🅰 2 miles W of town
   centre
♿ ☕ 🅿

Wales Aircraft Museum

Cardiff–Wales Airport, Rhoose, Cardiff
☎ 0446 711141

Step aboard a Viscount airliner, examine a Vulcan or Canberra bomber. More than 30 propellor and early jet planes. Model aircraft for sale.

🕐 May–Sep, daily 10–6
£ Ad £1.50, Chd £1
🅰 A4226, B4265
☕ 🎁 🅿

Welsh Folk Museum

St Fagans, Cardiff, S Glamorgan CF5 6XB
☎ 0222 569441

Re-erected brick by brick, or stone by stone, a Celtic village, Victorian shops, farmhouses, the smallest post office in Wales and an old school are among historical buildings set in 100 acres around manor house. Demonstrations of lost and traditional crafts.

🕐 Apr–Oct, daily 10–5; Nov–Mar,
   Mon–Sat 10–5
£ Ad £4, Chd £2, SC £3
🅰 M4 jnct 33, A4232
♿ ☕ 🍴 🅿

Welsh Hawking Centre

Weycock Rd, Barry CF6 9AA
☎ 0446 734687

Over 200 birds of prey including
eagle owls, merlins, peregrine
falcons, snowy owls. Birds can be
seen hatching and rearing young in
spring and early summer.
Childrens' animal park with petting
area for rabbits, sheep, donkeys, etc.
Daily flying displays, adventure
playground.

🕐 All year, daily 10.30–5
£ Ad £3, Chd £2
/!\ A4226, N of Barry
♿ ☕ 🏠 🅿

Welsh Miners' Museum

Afan Argoed Forest Park, Cynonville,
Port Talbot SA13 3HG
☎ 0639 850564

This display of the home life and
working times of South Wales
colliers captures the lifestyle of the
mining valleys. Within spitting
distance of Pontrhydyfen where
Richard Burton was born.

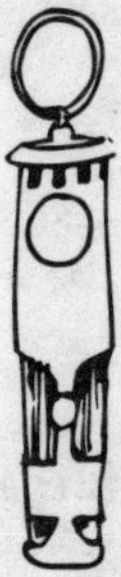

🕐 Daily: Apr–Oct 10.30–6;
　　Nov–Mar 10.30–4.30
£ Ad 50p, Chd/SC 25p
✳ Bike hire
/!\ M4 jnct 40; A4107,
　　6 miles NE of Port Talbot
♿ ☕ 🏠 🅿

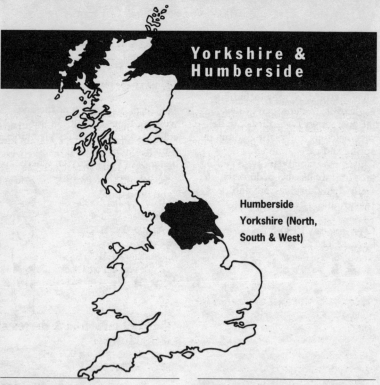

Humberside
Yorkshire (North,
South & West)

Abbey House Museum

Kirkstall Rd, Leeds LS5 3EH
☎ 0532 755821

Three streets have been re-created,
complete with full-size shops from a
forgotten age. You can walk into
Castelow's the chemists, Sagar's the
ironmongers... Or visit the toy
gallery, with delights from a
Victorian dolls' house to Ninja
turtles.

🕐 All Year, Mon–Fri 9.30–5,
   Sat 10–5, Sun 1–5
£ Ad £2, Chd(5+) 50p, SC £1
⚠ A65, 2 miles W of Leeds
⧓ Leeds 2 miles
🅿

Abbeydale Industrial Hamlet

Abbeydale Rd South, Sheffield S7 2QW
☎ 0742 367731

It really *is* a small village, reflecting
the industry of Sheffield. The razor-
sharp scythes that reaped the
world's harvests for centuries were
made at Abbeydale. You can see a
water-driven grinding shop, a
furnace and people working in the
restored Victorian workshops.

🕐 All year, Tue–Sat 10–5, Sun 11–5
£ Ad £2.50, Chd/SC £1.25
✳ Working Days (phone)
⚠ A621, 6 miles SW of Sheffield
♿ ☕ 🅿

ARC, The
St Saviourgate, York YO1 2NN
☎ 0904 654324

Archaeology comes to life in this restored ancient church. Visitors can use computers to trace hidden walls, stitch a Roman sandal, pick a Viking padlock or meet real archaeologists. Serious fun.

🕐 All year, Mon–Fri 10–5, Sat/Sun 1–5
💷 Ad £3.20, Chd/SC £2.10
🄰 City centre
🚻 York 10 min
♿(res) EH

Beck Isle Museum of Rural Life
Bridge St, Pickering, N Yorks YO18 8DU
☎ 0751 73653

A collection of the curious, marvellous, mysterious and commonplace, drawn from the last 200 years, displayed in 27 different settings ranging from pubs to plough barns. An Edwardian nursery and print shop too.

🕐 Mar–Oct, daily 10–5
💷 Ad £1.75, Chd 75p, SC £1.50
🄰 Town centre
🚻 North York Moors line
🅿

Big Sheep & Little Cow
The Old Watermill, Aiskew,
Bedale, N Yorks DL8 1AW
☎ 0677 422125

The Dexter cows here are almost smaller than the sheep, but both are milked. Visitors can feed lambs and stroke calves; then there is a cheese-tasting and a chance to sample sheep's milk ice cream. Pony rides and farm quiz.

🕐 Easter–Sep, daily 10.30–6
   (other times by appt)
💷 Ad £2.50, Chd/SC £2
🄰 Off A684 at Aiskew
♿(res)

Bradford Industrial & Horses at Work Museum
Moorside Rd, Bradford BD2 3HP
☎ 0274 631756

All of Bradford's industrial life is here, especially Samson and his friends - heavy horses still pulling the carts and drays that once thronged the city's streets. The rest, set in a 19th-century spinning mill, includes trains, trams and a neat contrast between the mill owner's house and his workers' cottages.

🕐 All year, Tue–Sun/BHM 10–5
💷 Adm free
🄰 A658, N of Bradford
♿ ☕ 🅿

Brimham Rocks
Nr Ripon, N Yorks

Spectacular rock formations. These sandstone stacks are probably the nearest we have in Britain to the rugged Indian country seen in Westerns. Great for walking - but if you see smoke signals, worry.

🕐 All year, daily. Centre/shop:
  May–Oct daily
£ Adm free; pkg £1.30
🅰 B6265, SW of Ripon
♿ ☕ 🎁 🅿

Calder Valley Cruising
The Marina, New Rd, Hebden Bridge, W Yorks HX7 8AD
☎ 0422 845557

The narrowboat *Sarah Siddons* takes you on a relaxing trip through Pennine scenery along the Rochdale Canal. Horse drawn and motor cruises.

🕐 Jun–Sep, daily 10–5; other
  times/phone
£ From: Ad £2, Chd £1, f/t
🅰 A646
🚃 Hebden Bridge 10 min
♿(prior notice) ☕ 🅿

Calderdale Industrial Museum
Square Rd, Halifax HX1 1RE
☎ 0422 358087

Could you believe a museum that smells of toffee? That hisses like a steam engine? This one does. Synchronised staging and sense effects bring back to life once-thriving local industries from mining to carpet weaving.

🕐 All year, Tue–Sat/BHM 10–5, Sun 2–5
£ Ad £1.50, Chd/SC 75p
🅰 Town centre
🚃 Halifax 5 min
♿ ☕ 🅿

Cannon Hall Open Farm
Cawthorne, Barnsley S75 4AT
☎ 0226 790427

Lambs to cuddle in Spring. Sweaters from the angora rabbits for sale. Viewing gallery to see pigs, British and Vietnamese; and yes, those are wallabies and a llama.

🕐 Mid Feb–Oct, Tue–Sat 11–4.30,
  Sun/BH 11–5
£ Ad £1.50, Chd (3–15)/SC £1
🅰 A635, 5 miles W of Barnsley
♿ ☕ 🎁 🅿

Caphouse - Yorkshire Mining Museum

Caphouse Colliery, New Rd, Overton,
Wakefield WF4 4RH
☎ 0924 848806

This is a *real* coal mine. Wear
sensible shoes, wrap up warm, then
ride the cage 137m into the earth.
See how you would like to dig a
76cm coal seam. Up above, the
adventure playground might seem
tame, so see the pit ponies or walk
the nature trail. Allow 4 hours.

🕐 All year, daily 10–5
£ Ad £5.50, Chd £4, SC £4.55, f/t
✳ No under 5s underground
/ĭ\ A642
♿ 🛝 ☕ 🍽 ℗

Castle Howard

York YO6 7DA
☎ 0653 648333

The largest and most opulent stately
home in Yorkshire. Starred in TV's
Brideshead Revisited, has Van Dyck
and Gainsborough on the walls, and
there is room for a good adventure
playground, a lake with boat trips,
nature walks and 1,000 acres to
stroll in.

🕐 Mid Mar–Oct, daily. Grounds 10am,
   Castle 11am; last adm 4.30
£ Ad £6, Chd £3, SC £5, f/t
/ĭ\ A64
♿ ☕ 🍽 ℗

Colour Museum

Perkin House, 82 Grattan Rd,
Bradford BD1 2JB
☎ 0274 390955

This place could make your life
brighter. Visitors can operate
experiments with light, colour
dyeing and printing. One of the
delights is making your own
rainbows.

🕐 All year, Tue–Fri 2–5,
   Sat/sch hols 10–4
£ Ad £1.10, Chd/SC 65p, f/t
/ĭ\ Town centre
🚉 Bradford InterCh/Foster's Sq 10 min
♿

Cruckley Animal Farm

Foston–on–the–Wolds, Driffield,
N Humb YO25 8BS
☎ 0262 488337

Fifty varieties of farm animals,
including rare breeds, on this 60-
acre working farm. Tours include
milking, chick-hatching and
meeting Sylvester the pot-bellied
pig, who starred in TV's Children
in Need appeal.

🕐 Late Apr–Sep, daily 10.30–6
£ Ad £2.15, Chd(3+)/SC £1.35
/ĭ\ B1249 from Driffield
♿ 🛝 ☕ 🛍 ℗

Dewsbury Museum

Crow Nest Park, Heckmondwike Rd,
Dewsbury, W Yorks WF13 2SA
☎ 0924 468171

A world of contrasts in two
galleries. The Children At Work
gallery has a reconstructed coal
mine, just one place where
children worked. The
Children at Play
concentrates on dolls and
toys, and has a re-
created 1940s classroom.

🕐 Daily: Nov–Feb 12–5;
    Mar–Oct, Mon–Fri 10–5,
    Sat/Sun 12–5
£ Adm free (charge to groups)
Ⓐ 1 mile from town centre
▓ Dewsbury 15 min
♿(res) 🅿

Eden Farm Insight

Old Malton, N Yorks YO17 0RT
☎ 0653 692093

See how wheat becomes bread,
barley becomes beer and sugar beet
sugar; then find out how a combine
harvester works. All this on an
active farm with a pets'
paddock, planned walks
and old-time farming
displays.

🕐 Spring–Oct,
    Sun–Fri 10.30–4.30
    (last adm)
£ Ad £2.50, Chd £1.50,
    SC £2, f/t
Ⓐ A169, nr Eden Camp
♿ 🧒 ☕ 🎁 🅿

Eden Camp

POW Camp No 83, Malton, N Yorks
☎ 0653 697777

This is war! The camp once held
German POWs and now re-creates
an award-winning picture of life
during World War II. The Blitz,
rationing, bomber raids and more
are reproduced with sight, sound,
smell and even smoke. Children
won't want to miss the puppet
show, and there are two adventure
playgrounds. In one, older children
'escape' via a tunnel. Allow 3 hours.

🕐 Mid Feb–23 Dec, daily 10–5;
    last adm 4
£ Ad £3, Chd/SC £2
Ⓐ A64, N of Malton
♿ ☕ 🍴 🅿

Elsham Hall Country & Wildlife Centre

Brigg, Humberside DN20 0QZ
☎ 0652 688698

If you have 400 acres
you can pack a lot in,
and here they have
falconry, working
craftsmen, a jetty
where you can
feed the carp, a
butterfly house,
animal farm,
theatre and more.
If you feel like a
walk, you can see at
least 80 different kinds of British
forest tree.

🕐 Easter–mid Sep, daily 11–5
£ Ad £3.95, Chd £2.50, SC £3
Ⓐ M180 jnct 5
♿ ☕ 🍴 🎁 🅿

Embsay Railway

Embsay Station, Embsay,
Skipton BD23 9QX
☎ 0756 794727/795189 info

They have 14 or so steam
trains here, some of which
dress up as Thomas the
Tank Engine for special
events. The 2½-mile trip to
Holywell takes 40 minutes,
and they do it up to 6 times a
day. It's a toot!

🕐 All year. Phone re times
💷 Ad £2.80, Chd £1.40, SC £2
✳ Special events
🅰 A59
⧟ Skipton 2 miles
♿ ♨ ☕ 🅿

Eureka! The Museum for Children

Discovery Rd, Halifax HX1 2NE
☎ 0422 330069/0426 983191 info

So absorbing that sometimes they
let people stay only 3 hours. Find
out how much your bones weigh,
what makes your heart beat, feed
Giant Mouth machine and find out
what happens to the food you eat.
And that's just for starters.

🕐 All year, daily 10–5 (7pm Wed;
   Mon until 2pm term time)
💷 Ad/Chd(13+) £4.50,
   Chd (3–12) £3.50, f/t
🅰 Next Halifax rlwy stn
⧟ Halifax
♿ ☕ 🎒 🅿

Falconry UK

The Walled Garden, Sion Hill Hall,
Kirby Wiske, Thirsk YO7 4EU
☎ 0845 587522

Many of the hawks, owls
and falcons you see are
under threat in the
wild, especially the
American Bald
Eagle. Flying
displays 3 times
a day, weather
permitting.

🕐 Easter–Oct, Tue–Sun/BHM 10.30–5.30
💷 Ad £3, Chd/SC £2.50
🅰 A167, S of Northallerton
♿ ☕ 🅿

Flamingo Land Fun Park

Kirby Misperton, Malton,
N Yorks YO17 0UX
☎ 0653 668585

White Knuckle Valley, where The
Bullet, Thunder Mountain and The
Twist wait to scare the pants off
you, runs right down the middle of
this theme park. Elsewhere, milder
events like laser shows and circuses
beckon. The bird walk, one of the
biggest privately owned zoos in
Europe, and live stage shows will
help you relax.

🕐 Easter–Oct, daily 10–6 (off pk 5pm)
💷 Ad/Chd(4+) £8, f/t
🅰 A64/A170, 8 miles E of Malton
♿ ☕ 🍴 🎒 🅿

Fosse Hill Jet Ski Centre

Catwick Lane, Brandesburton,
Driffield, N Humb YO25 8SB
☎ 0964 542608

For the very active family. The
centre specialises in jet skiing on the
lake, but you can also have a go on
go-karts or
try bungy
jumping.

🕐 All year, daily
   10–dusk
£ Per activity
🄰 A165, 7 miles NE
   of Beverley
♿ (prior notice) 🖭 Ⓟ

Harewood House

Harewood, Leeds LS17 9LQ
☎ 0532 886331

They don't build houses like this
any more. Set in 1,000 acres
landscaped by Capability Brown,
worked on by Robert Adam,
furniture by Chippendale. The
paintings would make Italians drool
with envy. You feel the adventure
playground should have been
designed by the SAS. Four-acre bird
garden.

🕐 Mid Mar–Oct, daily 10–4.30 (last adm).
   Hse from 11am
£ Ad £5.75, Chd £3, SC £5, f/t.
   Bird gdn/grnds: Ad £4.50,
   Chd £2.50, f/t
🄰 A61
♿ 🖭 🍴 📷 Ⓟ

Haworth Museum of Childhood

117 Main St, Haworth, Keighley,
W Yorks BD22 8DP
☎ 0535 643593

Overshadowed by the Bronte
parsonage up the road, this little
museum is well worth a visit for its
fine collection
of toys, dolls and
games from Victorian
days to the present. Look out
for the Meccano and working
Hornby Dublo trains.

🕐 Easter–Oct, daily 10.30–5.30;
   Nov–Mar Sat/Sun/sch hols 10.30–5
£ Ad £1, Chd/SC 50p
🄰 Haworth town centre
🚂 Keighley & Worth Valley line
♿ Ⓟ

Holmfirth Postcard Museum

Huddersfield Rd, Holmfirth,
Huddersfield HD7 1JH
☎ 0484 682231

Local company Bamforths have
been producing cheeky postcards
for 100 years. This collection is not
only historic, it's funny too. You can
also see the comedy films they
made 1908-14, with local people as
the stars.

The town also stages a **Last of
the Summer Wine Exhibition**
because the TV series has been
made here since 1972. Lots of
pictures and memorabilia. (Daily
10–5.30 - ☎ 0484 681362)

🕐 All year, Mon–Sat 10–4, Sun 12–4
£ Ad £1, Chd 50p
🄰 Town centre
♿ Ⓟ

Jorvik Viking Centre
Coppergate, York YO1 1NT
☎ 0904 643211

Step aboard a time craft and travel back 1,000 years. This dark ride through the excavated Viking city of York (Jorvik) takes you in movement, sight, sound and smells past busy market stalls, smoke-fired houses and a bustling quayside, to the archaeological dig and 10th-century houses standing where they were found. A gallery has many of the uncovered treasures.

🕐 Daily, Apr–Oct 9–7; Nov–Mar 9–5.30
£ Ad £3.95, Chd(5+) £2
🅰 City centre
🚉 York 15 min
♿ ℗ EH

Keighley & Worth Valley Railway
Keighley Station, Keighley BD22 8NJ
☎ 0535 645214/647777 info

Five miles of steam railway, with 6 stations and some fine scenery. One station starred in *The Railway Children*, another is a stopping place for Bronte pilgrims, while a third is Britain's smallest station. Gas-lit in winter.

🕐 Phone re times
£ Full rtn: Ad £4.50, Chd/SC £2.25, f/t
✳ Rover tkt; special events
🚉 Keighley stn is on A650
♿ 🛁 🚻 ℗

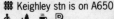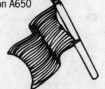

Kilnsey Park & Trout Farm
Kilnsey, Skipton, N Yorks BD23 5PS
☎ 0756 752150

Children can have a go at fishing with the tackle provided or they can just feed the trout being farmed. Pony trekking and an adventure playground provide a youthful challenge.

🕐 All year, daily 9–5.30 (dusk in winter)
£ Adm free. Animals/fish areas:
  Ad £1.50, Chd £1
🅰 B6160, N of Threshfield
♿ 🛁 🚻
🍽 🛍 ℗

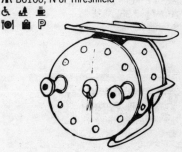

Kinderland
Burniston Rd, Scarborough YO12 6PE
☎ 0723 354555

Aimed at 14s and under, with solid equipment, a gentle water chute, crazy golf and an indoor play area. Nothing too elaborate, nothing too scary, but a huge amount to do and no one over-excited.

🕐 Easter–Sep. Phone re times
£ From: Ad/Chd £3.25, SC £2.25
🅰 Signs from town centre
🚉 Scarborough 1½ miles
♿ 🛁 🚻 🛍 ℗

Kirklees Light Railway

Railway Station, Clayton West,
Huddersfield HD8 9PE
☎ 0484 865727

Miniature railway gives you a
stylish and scenic ride on its narrow
15in gauge down an old Lancs &
Yorks Rlwy branch line. Plus
children's playground with
miniature fairground rides and
working model vehicles.

🕐 All year; phone for details
💷 Ad £3, Chd £2
🅰 M1 jnct 38, A636
♿(prior notice)
☕ 🛍 🅿

🎪 Lightwater Valley Theme Park

North Stainley, Ripon HG4 3HT
☎ 0765 635321/635368 info

This is the world of The Ultimate, at
1½ miles long, the biggest roller
coaster in the world. Then there is
the Soopa Loopa which loops the
loop twice, then does a triple
horizontal spiral. If that is not
enough, The Rat rollercoasts
through a sewer system 12m
underground at breakneck speed.
Wow!

🕐 Easter–Oct; phone for details
💷 Height 1.33m+ £8.50,
    under 1.33m £6.95 (under 5s free)
✳ Live shows; Grandparents (Fri) £2.95
🅰 A6108
♿ 🍴 ☕ 🍽 🅿

Middleton Railway

The Station, Moor Rd, Hunslet,
Leeds LS10 2JQ
☎ 0532 710320

When you have travelled on the
Middleton, you have travelled on
the oldest commercial railway in
the world.

🕐 Phone for details
💷 Ad £1.60, Chd 80p, f/t
🅰 M1 jnct 45
🅿

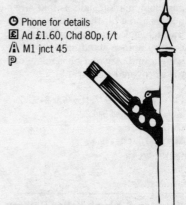

Mother Shipton's Cave & Petrifying Well

Prophecy House, Knaresborough HG5 8DD
☎ 0423 864600

Mother Shipton, England's most
famed prophetess, recorded by
Samuel Pepys as foretelling the Fire
of London, was born in the cave 500
years ago. Next to it is the
petrifying well which turns objects
hung under its cascade into stone;
easily explained in science, but
visitors still marvel.

🕐 Easter–Halloween, 9.30–5.45;
    Nov–Mar 10–4.45
💷 Ad £3.95, Chd £2.95, SC £3.65, f/t
✳ Nature walk, adv playgnd
🅰 A59
🚉 Knaresborough 15 min
♿(res) 🍴 🍽 🅿

Museum of Automata
9 Tower St, York YO1 1SA
☎ 0904 655550

It all goes with clockwork. Pigs climb ladders, cows jump over moons, birds sing in cages, and you can make the modern ones work on your own in a kind of end-of-the-pier show. A moving experience.

🕐 All year, daily 9.30–5.30 (Jan 10–4)
💷 Ad £3.20, Chd £1.95, SC £2.80, f/t
🅰 City centre
🚇 York 15 min
♿ 📷

Museum of Badges & Battledress
The Old Chapel,
The Green, Crakehall,
Bedale, N Yorks DL8 1HP
☎ 0677 424444

This private collection fills 2 floors with more than 50 mannequins dressed to kill. Army, Navy, Air Force, Home Guard, Land Army, Red Cross - if they have badges, they're here.

🕐 Easter–Sep,
Tue–Fri/BH 11–5,
Sat/Sun 1–5
💷 Ad £1, Chd 50p,
SC 80p, f/t
🅰 A684, 3 miles W of Leeming Bar
🅿

National Fishing Heritage Centre
Alexandra Dock, Grimsby DN31 1UF
☎ 0472 344867

Grimsby was the biggest fishing port in the world just 100 years ago. Museum displays show why and an environmental 'trip' on a steam trawler gives you more than a feel of what it was like to be a fisherman. The only thing missing is a bucket of icy salt water over you.

🕐 All year, daily 10–6
💷 Ad £3.10, Chd £2.30, SC £2.50, f/t.
Cmbd tkt for trawler:
£3.90/£2.90/£3.15, f/t
🅰 Signs in city centre
🚇 Grimsby 5 min
♿ ☕ 🅿

National Museum of Photography, Film & TV
Pictureville, Bradford BD1 1NQ
☎ 0274 727488/726083

The biggest cinema screen in Britain is here. Five storeys high, with a projector the size of a Ford Escort. The only remaining public 3-projector Cinerama screen in the world. See yourself as newscaster on the Nine O'Clock News or flying on a magic carpet on TV.

🕐 All year, Tue–Sun
10.30–6
💷 Adm free; cmbd tkt
IMAX/Cinerama £6
🅰 City centre
🚇 Bradford Interchange 5 min
♿ ☕ 📷 🅿

National Railway Museum

Leeman Rd, York YO2 4XJ
☎ 0904 621261

Everything from a replica of
Stephenson's *Rocket* to Channel
Tunnel trains. There are 3 halls, and
favourite items are royal trains from
Queen Victoria onwards; *Mallard*,
the world's fastest steam loco; and
Magician's Road, a hands-on gallery
for children.

🕐 All year, Mon–Sat 10–6, Sun 11–6;
   last adm 5
£ Ad £4.20, Chd £2.10, SC £2.80, f/t
🅰 Behind York rlwy stn
🚉 York 3 min
♿ ⛲ 🍴 🛍 🅿

Nunnington Hall

Helmsley, N Yorks YO6 5UY
☎ 0439 748283

Two magic things to look for in this
old manor house. First, the
collection of 22 miniature rooms, all
one-eighth full size and furnished.
Second, the display of work by the
British Toymakers' Guild, which is
almost too good to play with.

🕐 Apr–Oct, Tue–Thu/Sat/Sun 2–6
   (Jul/Aug, Sat/Sun/BHM 12–6);
   last adm 5
£ Hse/Gdn: Ad £3.50, Chd £1.50.
   Gdn: Ad £2, Chd free
🅰 B1257, SE of Helmsley
♿(res) ☕ 🛍 🅿 NT

North Yorkshire Moors Railway

Pickering Station, Pickering YO18 7AJ
☎ 0751 472508/473535 info

Steam railway built by George
Stephenson. The route travels 18
miles through the wild beauty of
the North York Moors National
Park. Stop off at Newtondale Halt
(where no cars can go) or
Goathland, known as Aidensfield to
fans of TV's *Heartbeat*.

🕐 Apr–Oct, daily. Phone re times/winter
£ Pk/Off–pk rtn: Ad £8.50/£7.90,
   Chd £4.30/£4, SC £6.40/£5.90; f/t
✳ Santa special
🅰 Town centre
♿ ☕ 🛍 🅿

Original Ghost Walk of York

Kings Arms, Ouse Bridge, York
☎ 0904 646463

In a city old enough to have a
thousand ghosts, a skilled story-
teller walks you through the areas
and retells the legends.

🕐 All year, nightly 8pm
£ Ad £2.50, Chd £2
🅰 City centre
🚉 York 10 min
🅿

Pennine Boat Trips

Waterside Court, Coach St,
Skipton BD23 1LH
☎ 0756 790829

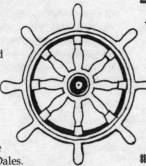

The way to relax and explore the 200-year-old Leeds & Liverpool Canal. The 75-minute trip glides smoothly through the Yorkshire Dales.

🕐 Daily: Apr/Oct 1.30;
   May/Jun/Sep
   1.30/3; Jul/Aug 11.30/1.30/3/4.30
💷 Ad £2.50, Chd £1.50, SC £2.20
🛈 Signs from High St
🚉 Skipton 5 min
♿ ☕ 🅿

Penny Arcadia

Ritz Cinema, Market Pl, Pocklington,
York YO4 2AR
☎ 0759 303420

Pinball machines, toy cranes that grab sweets, Test Your Strength, Speak Your Weight, and What the Butler Saw slot machines were popular for years. You can see why.

🕐 Daily: Easter/Jun–Aug 10–5;
   May/Sep 12.30–5
💷 Ad £3, Chd/SC £2
🛈 A1079
♿ 🅿

Pickering Trout Lake & Fun Fishing

Newbridge, Newton Rd,
Pickering YO18 8JJ
☎ 0751 474219

You can see how a trout farm operates and feed the fish, and have a go at fishing for them too. Don't be too good - you have to buy all you catch.

🕐 Mar–Oct, daily 10–dusk;
   Nov–Feb, Sat/Sun
💷 £4 per head; hire of bait/fly rod £1
🛈 Next to rlwy stn
🚉 Pickering (N York Moors Rlwy)
♿ ☕ 🅿

Ripon Prison & Police Museum

St Marygate, Ripon, N Yorks
☎ 0765 690799

A policeman's lot may not be a happy one, but when you walk into the cells here, you will see that it was tougher for Victorian villains. The other half of the museum traces

local police history and their successes in filling the cells above.

🕐 Jul/Aug, Mon–Sat 11–5, Sun 1–5;
   Apr–Jun/Sep/Oct, daily 1–5
💷 Ad £1, Chd 50p, SC 60p
🛈 Nr cathedral
🅿

Royal Pump Room Museum

Crescent Rd, Harrogate HG1 2RY
☎ 0423 503340

Here is the original sulphur well
which started the health craze of
'taking the waters'. Samples are
given to visitors to taste. Beware: it
is the strongest sulphur well in
Britain.

🕐 All year, Mon–Sat 10–5,
    Sun 2–5 (Oct–Apr to 4)
💷 Ad £1, Chd/SC 60p
🏠 Town centre
🚉 Harrogate 15 min
♿

Ryedale Folk Museum

Hutton–le–Hole, York YO6 6UA
☎ 0751 417367

More than 2,000 years of local life in
a dozen reconstructed buildings.
You can examine an Elizabethan
manor, the oldest daylight
photographic studio in the country,
and a furnished gypsy caravan.

🕐 End Mar–Oct, daily 10–5.30;
    last adm 4.30
💷 Ad £2.50, Chd £1.25, SC £2, f/t
🏠 A170
♿ 🛍

Sea Life Centre

Scalby Mills,
Scarborough YO12 6RP
☎ 0723 376125

Are you watching the sharks or are
they watching you? Visitors walk
see-through tunnels in vast tanks
holding all sorts of sea creatures, so
views are really close-up. Quiz trails
and feeding displays.

🕐 All year, daily 10–6 (10–5 winter)
💷 Ad £4.35, Chd (4–14) £3.25, SC £3.45
🏠 North Bay Leisure Park
🚉 Scarborough 2 miles
♿ ☕ 🍴 🅿

Sooty's World

Windhill Manor, Leeds Rd, Shipley,
W Yorks BD18 1BP
☎ 0274 531122

Sooty looks very well for a 42-year-
old bear. He first appeared on TV in
1952, and this is a collection of sets,
props, souvenirs, tapes, even
scripts, although Sooty never says a
word. For very young 40-year-olds.

🕐 All year, Mon–Thu 10.30–4.30,
    Sat/Sun 10–5 (Fri in sch hols)
💷 Ad £2, Chd (to 13) £1.50
🏠 A650
🚉 Shipley 10 min
♿

Stump Cross Caverns

Greenhow, Pateley Bridge,
Harrogate HG3 5JL
☎ 0756 752780

The door to the caves was shut by
the last Ice Age, which sealed in the
twisting passages with towering
stalagmites and cascading stalactites
you now see. Archaeologists have
discovered bones of creatures that
roamed the moors up to 200,000
years ago.

🕐 Mid Mar–beg Nov, daily 10–6;
  last adm 1hr before. Winter/phone
💷 Ad £2.90, Chd £1.45
🅰 B6265
☕ ℗

Walkley Clogs

Canal Wharf Saw Mills, Burnley Rd,
Hebden Bridge HX7 8NH
☎ 0422 842061

Generations of people round here
wore clogs, and they have samples
of styles old and new. There is even
a teddy bear wearing clogs.

🕐 All year, daily 10–5
💷 Adm free
🅰 A646
✳ Hebden Bridge 10 min
♿ 🍽 🛍 ℗

Withernsea Lighthouse Museum

Hull Rd, Withernsea, N Humb HU19 2DY
☎ 0964 614834

Only in England would you find a
museum where the 39m climb to the
top of a lighthouse also offered local
history, Captain Cook relics and the
memorial museum to actress Kay
Kendall. Worth it for the view
alone.

🕐 Jul/Aug, Mon–Fri 11–5;
  Mar–Oct, Sat/Sun/BHM 1–5
💷 Ad £1.50, Chd 75p, SC £1
🅰 A1033
☕

World of the Honey Bee

Hebble End Works, Hebble End,
Hebden Bridge HX7 6HJ
☎ 0422 845557

Close encounters with working
bees. Plus Bugs & Beasties, some of
nature's less attractive creatures like
the tarantula, iguana and gecko.

🕐 All year, Mon–Sat 11–4, Sun 10–5
💷 Ad £1, Chd 50p, f/t
🅰 On canal towpath
✳ Hebden Bridge 10 min

York Castle Museum

The Eye of York, York YO1 1RY
☎ 0904 653611

England's most popular museum of
everyday life. Starting with the
reconstructed Victorian street, you
see complete rooms from the 50s
(Hancock on the primitive TV), and
an Edwardian sweet shop. Look for
Dick Turpin's condemned cell: the
museum was once the castle prison.

🕐 Apr–Oct, Mon–Sat 9.30–5.30,
   Sun 10–5.30; Nov–Mar, 9.30–4,
   Sun 10–4
£ Ad £3.95, Chd/SC £2.85, f/t
🅰 City centre
♯ York 15 min
♿ (res) ☕ 🛍

York Dungeon

12 Clifford St, York YO1 1RD
☎ 0904 632599

Grim deeds of the distant past
brought hauntingly to life in a
series of gruesome tableaux: Dark
Age deaths, Medieval punishments,
the torture of heretics, and the like.
The latest attraction, the Guy
Fawkes Experience, ends with a big
bang - which is more than the real
thing did.

🕐 Daily: Apr–Sep 10–5.30,
   Oct–Mar 10–4.30
£ Ad £3.50, Chd £2.25, f/t
🅰 City centre (nr Clifford's Tower)
♯ York 15 min
♿ 🛍

Index

E

F

W

Wales Aircraft Museum 254

Walkley Clogs 269

Waltzing Waters 182

Warwick Castle 110

Washbrooks Farm Centre 200

Watercress Line: Alresford to Alton 24

Waterfowl Sanctuary 110

Waterfront & Scaplens Court Museum 24

Watertop Open Farm 142

Weald & Downland Open Air Museum 200

Wellbrook Beetling Mill 142

Welney Wildfowl & Wetlands Centre 54

Welsh Folk Museum 254

Welsh Hawking Centre 255

Welsh Miners' Museum 255

Welsh Mountain Zoo 242

Welsh Royal Crystal 229

Welshpool & Llanfair Light Railway 229

Wembley Stadium Tours 70

Wernlas Collection 110

West Midlands Safari & Leisure Park 110

West Stow Country Park &
    Anglo-Saxon Village 54

Westbury White Horse 24

Western Approaches 127

Westminster Abbey 71

Westonbirt Arboretum 111

Wet 'n' Wild 154

Weymouth Sea Life Park 25

Wheal Martyn China Clay
    Heritage Centre 218

Wheelwright & Gypsy Museum 218

Whinlatter Visitor Centre 38

Whipsnade Wild Animal Park 92

Whitbread Hop Farm 200

Whitchurch Silk Mill 25

White Cliffs Experience 201

White Horse & Castle 25

White Post Modern Farm Centre 92

W H Smith Museum 230

Wigan Pier 128

Wildfowl & Wetlands Centre, Arundel 201

Wildfowl & Wetlands Centre, Ormskirk 128

Wildfowl & Wetlands Trust Centre,
    Slimbridge 111

Wildlife Water Trail 55

Willows & Wetlands Centre 219

Wilton House 25

Wimbledon Lawn Tennis Museum 71

Wimpole Hall & Home Farm 55

Windermere Iron Steamboat Co 38

Windermere Steamboat Museum 38

Windsor Castle 26

Winston Churchill's Britain at War
    Museum 71

Withernsea Lighthouse Museum 269

Witton Country Park 128

Woburn Safari Park 93

Wood Green Animal Shelter 55

Woodland Park & Heritage Museum 26

Wookey Hole Caves 219

Working Silk Museum 55

World in Miniature, Oban 182

World in Miniature, Truro 219

World of Beatrix Potter Exhibition 38

World of Butterflies 105

World of Model Railways 219

World of Robin Hood 93

World of the Honey Bee 269

Wylfa Nuclear Power Station 242

Y

Yarner Wood National Reserve 220

Yelverton Paperweight Centre 220

Yew Tree Avenue 93

Ynys-Hir Bird Reserve 230

York Castle Museum 270

York Dungeon 270

Regional Tourist Boards

Cumbria: Ashleigh, Holly Road, Windermere, Cumbria LA23 2AQ ☎ 05394 44444

East Anglia: Toppesfield Hall, Hadleigh, Suffolk IP7 5DN ☎ 0473 822922

London: 26 Grosvenor Gardens, London SW1 0DU ☎ 071 730 3450

Midlands - East: Exchequergate, Lincoln LN2 1PZ ☎ 0522 531521

Midlands - West: Woodside, Larkhill Road, Worcester WR5 2EF ☎ 0905 763436

North West: Swan House, Swan Meadow Road, Wigan Pier, Wigan WN3 5BB
☎ 0942 821222

Northumbria: Aykley Heads, Durham DH1 5UX ☎ 091 384 6905

South: 40 Chamberlayne Road, Eastleigh, Hants SO5 5JH ☎ 0703 620006

South East: The Old Brew House, Warwick Park, Tunbridge Wells, Kent TN2 5TU
☎ 0892 540766

South West: 60 St David's Hill, Exeter EX4 4SY ☎ 0392 76351

Yorkshire & Humberside: 312 Tadcaster Road, York YO2 2HF ☎ 0904 707961

Northern Ireland: St Anne's Court, 59 North Street, Belfast BT1 1NB ☎ 0232 231221

Scotland: 23 Ravelston Terrace, Edinburgh EH4 3EU ☎ 031 332 2433

Wales: Brunel House, 2 Fitzalan Road, Cardiff CF2 1UY ☎ 0222 499909